M000170109

Promoting Healthy
Attachments

A NORTON PROFESSIONAL BOOK

Promoting Healthy Attachments

Hands-On Techniques to Use With Your Clients

Deborah D. Gray

W.W. Norton & Company
Independent Publishers Since 1923
New York • London

Note to Readers: Standards of clinical practice and protocol change over time, and no technique or recommendation is guaranteed to be safe or effective in all circumstances. This volume is intended as a general information resource for professionals practicing in the field of psychotherapy and mental health; it is not a substitute for appropriate training, peer review, and/or clinical supervision. Neither the publisher nor the author(s) can guarantee the complete accuracy, efficacy, or appropriateness of any particular recommendation in every respect.

The privacy of clients has been maintained in this book. All case examples have been altered to protect confidentiality. It is coincidental if examples seem to describe particular individuals or circumstances.

Copyright © 2019 by Deborah D. Gray

All rights reserved
Printed in the United States of America
First Edition

For information about permission to reproduce selections from this book, write to Permissions, W. W. Norton & Company, Inc., 500 Fifth Avenue, New York, NY 10110

For information about special discounts for bulk purchases, please contact W. W. Norton Special Sales at specialsales@wwnorton.com or 800-233-4830

Manufacturing by LSC Communications, Harrisonburg
Production manager: Katelyn MacKenzie

Library of Congress Cataloging-in-Publication Data

Names: Gray, Deborah D., 1951– author.
Title: Promoting healthy attachments : hands-on
techniques to use with your clients / Deborah D. Gray.
Description: First Edition. | New York : W. W. Norton & Company, [2018] |
Series: A norton professional book | Includes bibliographical references and index.
Identifiers: LCCN 2018019200 | ISBN 9780393712599 (hardcover)
Subjects: LCSH: Attachment behavior. | Attachment disorder. | Child psychology.
Classification: LCC BF575.A86 G73 2018 | DDC 155.42/2241—dc23
LC record available at https://lccn.loc.gov/2018019200

W. W. Norton & Company, Inc., 500 Fifth Avenue, New York, N.Y. 10110
www.wwnorton.com

W. W. Norton & Company Ltd., 15 Carlisle Street, London W1D 3BS

1 2 3 4 5 6 7 8 9 0

To my sister, Colleen, who sings the high descant
in my life's song

Contents

Preface

A therapist told me, "I know attachment theory. But my dilemma was, what to *do* with parents and children who come into my office—besides talking about attachment. How do I spend the therapy hour? In your training, I came away with things to do that I used the next day." In the spirit of knowing what to do during therapy hours, I am contributing this practical guide.

Attachment literature is rich. Other authors have covered attachment theory and its history so skillfully that I would not attempt to repeat their successes. This book emphasizes day-to-day processes as therapists coconstruct and carry out treatment plans with their clients, improving the quality of attachments. I include theoretical and research contexts to provide a foundation for techniques and approaches.

While the book is practical, I see therapists as more than mental health mechanics. This book is not a set of instructions. Instead, we clinicians use our skills much as musicians use theirs. Our "music," created with our clients, includes connecting, making sense of life events, and engaging empathically as clients struggle toward integration and regulation. Our skills include graceful phrasing, timing, direction, knowledge application, and technique. (We also may have lousy timing and messy redos—hopefully, with repair.) Beyond the left-brain cognitive skills described in this book, I cheer the use of therapists' right-brain-mediated music as we make connections with our clients and help them to connect with each other.

I have practiced as a therapist at a favorable time. At the beginning of my career, John Bowlby, Mary Ainsworth, and Vera Fahlberg helped me to see patterns of attachment behavior, especially after maltreatment. I remember the excitement of using attachment techniques in a neonatal nursery, and in making connections between parents and their foster children. The parents were thrilled when their children responded. Throughout the 1990s and into this century I was influenced by the work of Mary Main, Mary Dozier, Diane Fosha, Eric Hesse, Daniel Hughes, Michael and Marjorie Rutter, Bruce Perry, Allan Schore, Judith Solomon, Marion Solomon, Daniel Stern, Allen Sroufe, Daniel Siegel, Bessel van der Kolk, and Charles Zeanah. Of course, there are other wonderful authors and theorists not mentioned in this list. These individuals helped me to appreciate the ways that therapists could effect changes in the complex system of parent-child attachments. They helped me to arrange trauma, neglect, loss, and attachment theory into a working model for treatment. Many of the authors in the list above continue to shape our field and my work.

As Allan Schore (2002, 2012) aptly teaches, so much of our therapeutic work is led by our intuitive right brain. This intuitive dimension allows therapists to think well beyond the confines of cognitive-behavioral therapy or other technique-driven skill sets. This book emphasizes that effective therapy with our clients requires a compassionate therapist who also has therapeutic skills. I hope that readers will feel a new appreciation for the dynamic nature of therapy as they express creativity and wisdom with their clients.

Children and families in my practice are my richest sources of information. I have learned from parents as they describe and demonstrate what seems to work best for their children, especially after maltreatment or attachment losses. I have had the opportunity to collect their successful techniques and approaches, passing them on to other families, other therapists. While I have changed identifying information to protect confidentiality of clients, you will hear my clients' voices in the scripts and examples in this book.

The book is organized in parts. In Part I, the first two chapters, I cover parenting from an attachment perspective, describing attachment patterns and factors that alter attachment patterns. We explore the bright lines common to successful attachment-based interventions. In Chapter 2, I summarize some attachment-oriented research projects and ways in which all practitioners can benefit from their lessons

Part II moves into therapy processes, methods, and techniques. I have had an attachment-focused practice for over 25 years; I have worked in child welfare for over 30 years. In Part II, I discuss plans and practical activities that have worked for my clients and me.

Chapter 3 discusses the specifics of forming therapeutic plans, along with a wealth of intervention techniques to use within those plans. I integrate body-based approaches (sensorimotor psychotherapy) in my work. Body-based work is a royal road to changing people's experience of each other—direct in a way that more cognitive approaches cannot be. In Chapter 3 and beyond, I share many physical techniques—with respectful boundaries, of course.

Chapter 4 focuses on children's attachment issues, primarily children with complex trauma or traumatic grief. The chapter provides many practical ways to help families who are attaching to children who have difficulties with trust, regulation, theory of mind, reciprocity, and anger. I have included information on children adopted internationally or through the foster care system.

Chapter 5 concentrates on treatment of adults with attachment issues. The chapter discusses therapist countertransference issues with their clients. When dealing with parenting and children's needs, countertransference issues are particularly vivid. This chapter describes child-parent dyadic work when parents are presenting with insecure attachment patterns.

I incorporated a specific chapter on adolescents. Chapter 6 links the joint tasks of increasing autonomy while improving security in attachment. We look at some practical methods of helping families enjoy the adolescent process of roots and wings. The development of smart technology makes connecting with teens an intentional and sometimes competitive process, as described in this chapter.

Chapter 7 focuses on some specific needs of highly stressed families. I wanted a chapter that provided some accommodations in therapy for these families. Multiple studies point to differences in executive functioning in children after neglect and maltreatment and in parents after chronic high stress (Fisher, Van Ryzin, & Gunnar, 2011; Nikulina, Widom, & Spatz, 2013). This chapter discusses the pragmatics of working with people whose brains were shaped by high levels of stress.

Chapter 8 discusses spirituality and faith. Many people reach out to God as their spiritual attachment figure. I describe working with clients who include their faith in a holistic, attachment-informed, worldview. This brief chapter is meant to provide integration between the spiritual and temporal for people who view God through an attachment lens.

Chapter 9 concludes the book with a discussion on play and attachment. We achieve a light-hearted, but fully alive feeling when playing. It is often an unwrapped gift in attachment relationships. I finish the book with an invitation to enjoy the gift.

This book is a positive one. In spite of my daily work with neglect and trauma, where I am often a witness to suffering, I am compelled by people who create hope and camaraderie, mustering resources to overcome adversity. On a practice level, it is exciting to integrate sensorimotor attachment techniques and to apply the attachment, regulation, and trauma literatures—all while joining with families in a kind manner. The work brings out the truest parts of myself, even as I see and encourage the best in my clients.

Part I

The Development of Attachment: Close Connections, Stress Systems, Sense of Self, and Theory of Mind

CHAPTER 1

Parenting and the Formation
of Attachment Patterns

Attachments are our closest relationships. From infancy, when our social–emotional brains are wired within attachment relationships, throughout adulthood, when we care for and coregulate others, our attachments provide our physiological and emotional roots (Schore, 2003a; Siegel, 1999; Sroufe, 1995). We crave attachments with others, hoping that these people will be caring, resourceful—and long lived. As children, we are the recipients of care from attachment figures. As parents, we are the attachment figures, providing for children. As adults within adult attachment relationships, we engage in mutual caregiving. People learn the responses of caregiving and mutuality through their childhood attachments, replaying the reciprocal role as adults.

Attachment figures are a source of safety when we are in risky situations. They help take care of us when we are sick, stranded, bereft, or broke. We assume the risk of caring deeply, not only because we feel that the benefits are rich, but because we are beings who wither in solitude. Over and over again, in song and story, people value sensitive and loyal attachments among life's transcendent joys. The joy includes the ways our loved ones help us to discover aspects of our own identities.

Our songs and stories are just as full of references to attachment figures who disappoint. One of the most painful experiences for any of us occurs when we care deeply, but attachment figures hurt us or abandon us, especially when we are in need. The way particular attachment figures respond sensitively and reliably, or not, can be classified into attachment patterns.

Classifying Attachment Beliefs and Behaviors

Our basic patterns of attachment are classified in the attachment literature as *secure* or *anxious* (also referred to as *insecure*), with sub-types under headings of *anxious (insecure)*. John Bowlby and Mary Ainsworth, seminal theorists in the field, began describing the patterns over 50 years ago. John Bowlby wrote:

> Three principal patterns of attachment, first described by Ainsworth and her colleagues in 1971, are now reliably identified together with the family conditions that promote them. These are first the pattern of secure attachment in which the individual is confident that his parent (or parent figure) will be available, responsive, and helpful should he encounter adverse or frightening situations. With this assurance, he feels bold in his explorations of the world. This pattern is promoted by a parent, in the early years especially by mother, being readily available, sensitive to her child's signals, and lovingly responsive when he seeks protection and/or comfort.
>
> A second pattern is that of anxious resistant attachment in which the individual is uncertain whether his parents will be available or responsive or helpful when called upon. Because of this uncertainty he is always prone to separation anxiety, tends to be clinging, and is anxious about exploring the world.
>
> A third pattern is that of anxious avoidant attachment in which the individual has no confidence that, when he seeks care, he will be responded to helpfully, but, on the contrary, expects to be rebuffed. When in marked degree such an individual attempts to live his life without the love

and support of others, he tries to become emotionally self-sufficient (1988, pp. 124-125).

Later researchers described disorganized/disoriented attachments, a classification that describes a lapse in an organized pattern. Insecure and disorganized-disoriented attachments are discussed in more detail later in this chapter.

It is important to note that attachments are always between two people. Children with two parents are able to form different patterns of attachment with different caregivers. It is common for a child to have a secure pattern with one parent, and insecure with another.

Secure patterns meet the expectation that the parent figure to whom children are attached will meet their need for loving connection, help them to handle stress, encourage mastery and exploration, care for them physically, stay proximal, and do all of this in a sensitive, attuned manner most of the time. The secure relationship has a sense of flow and rhythm.

In secure relationships, children tend to respond to their attachment figures in a gratifying manner. Their pleasing nonverbals and words weave a positivism into the relationship. When there are relationship mess ups, there is an apology (repair) in which injured feelings are accepted and the injuring person takes responsibility. Then there is a return to a steady emotional balance (regulation). The norm for these relationships tends to be positive and regulated, accompanied by a playful and exploratory quality. Emotional defenses are not typically necessary. This is considered an ideal pattern of attachment. Our attachments are "a secure base," in John Bowlby's (1988) terms, allowing us to explore the world and develop confidence in ourselves. Because of the emphasis on confident exploration, some researchers label the classifications as secure (parent) autonomous (child), with *autonomous* noting children's confidence in exploring their world (Hesse, 2008).

Patterns of attachment are referred to as styles of attachment in the social psychology tradition (Shiller, 2017). These patterns are influenced by environments of parents and children. Insecurity can result from compromised safety, accumulated stresses (poverty, unresolved losses, and hostility in the home), and lack of parenting support during these times of duress.

When people discuss attachments, they generally refer to a secure pattern. For example, medical staff assume this common point of reference when asking new parents, "How is bonding going?" In child-parent attachments, globally and in North America, about two thirds of parent-child dyads are rated as secure (Ainsworth, Salter, Blehar, Waters, & Wall, 1978/2015; van Ijzendoorn, Schuengel, & Bakermans-Kranenburg, 1999). The rate of security falls within groups with low social support and high rates of trauma to about one third in disadvantaged populations (Weinfield, Sroufe, & Egeland, 2000).

The aptly named insecure pattern reflects a reality—people feel insecure or anxious when they cannot receive timely, contingent, or sensitive emotional or physical care from their attachment figures (Bowlby, 1988; Sroufe, 1995). Children in such relationships require defenses to reduce their distress as they try to get their needs met. In adult-to-adult relationships, similar defensive systems operate. (The belief systems of insecure attachments are analyzed in more detail later in the chapter.)

The rate of insecure-ambivalent (also called anxious-resistant) attachments in children is about 8–10%, with the insecure-avoidant rate at 9% (van Ijzendoorrn et al., 1999). The rate of disorganized attachment is about 15–19% of the general population, with a much higher rate, about 80%, in maltreated populations (Cyr, Euser, Bakermans-Kranenburg, & van Ijzendoorn, 2010). However, if a child has a disorganized attachment style with parents, a clinician cannot conclude that the child has been maltreated by the parents (Granqvist, et al., 2017). There are other variables.

Reactions to Changing Attachment Patterns

Insecure attachments are as valued as secure attachments by parents and children. Defenses aside, parents and children are each other's most important people. They have a sense of how their system works. Bowlby (1988) discussed the expectations of parents and children within secure or insecure attachments, referring to them as *internal working models*. These are relational maps that provide predictability. When asked to change a pattern and move to a more secure one, people tend to feel a range of reactions from uneasy to autonomic nervous system–mediated alarm (Schore, 2003a). People will be wary when asked to drop their psychological defenses. A new attachment style reduces predictability and calls for defenses to drop as internal working models change.

Adults and children feel exposed and more vulnerable without the predictability of the old pattern. This is particularly true after trauma and neglect. (The topic is explored in more depth in upcoming sections devoted to specific patterns of attachment.)
The pattern we have with our primary caregivers, whom I will refer to as "parents" throughout the book, creates our template for later attachment relationships (Rutter & Rutter, 1993). The logic behind each attachment pattern helps therapists to understand their clients' points of view. After understanding clients' patterns, we can form a conceptual language with clients for the feelings that they have when they are asked to relate closely or reach out. We can move on to discuss the ways that the old patterns were necessary adaptations at one time but may be altered to more satisfying ones, with therapy.

As clinicians working with attachment know, even if we have the concepts and words, it takes more than a discussion to make changes in the system. Because attachments are formed in the first year of life when there is an available parent, with an attachment pattern recognizable by 7 months of age, much of what people know about attachment is within our implicit memory systems. Attachment behaviors operate below conscious level much of the time. Attachment is largely a limbic system activity, with connections to the viscera and autonomic nervous system (Siegel, 2010; Perry, 2006, 2015, 2016; Buczynski, Porges, 2015). As a result, defenses may be employed without conscious awareness.

When working on insecure attachments, clients may feel a strong gut sense that something worrisome is happening. As one woman said to me, "It is not just my son who is anxious in these sessions working on attachment. I get a knot in my stomach, tears in my eyes, and go home thinking of my tired mother. I feel guilty. I remember that I was always asking for more." As we worked on the push-pull that her son expressed toward her, her childhood attachment to her mother, with visceral sensations, came to her awareness.

Intense, body-based sensations are disconcerting to clients who are working on attachment. Therapists who show empathy are able to help their clients feel better regulated and cared for during this process. As mental schemas about attachment are activated, clients regularly feel gut sensations along with their emotions of sadness, anxiety, or shame.

Our role as clinicians includes providing compassion, a sense of safety, and moment-to-moment help in altering the defensive dance steps of attachment insecurity. Therapeutic support includes nonverbal and verbal compassion as well as psychoeducation. We encourage our clients' desire to change, even though it means that they will temporarily experience discomfort. I have found it helpful to let clients know that it is normal to feel strong emotions and sensations in their bodies, and that those feelings will lessen over time.

A teen told me, "Deborah, I used to be so afraid of you for the first year. I don't know why. That's why I was so mean to you. You have helped me a lot with my parents. But back then I kept feeling that something bad was going to happen—that you were going to hurt me."

In fact, she had been neglected and physically injured in her toddler years. My therapeutic approach looked past her off-putting behaviors to the wounding of her core self. I showed compassion, concentrating on coregulation, as I helped her to reduce her fears. Her aggressive behaviors at home and school resulted in consequences but were a side issue in our therapy. Her successful outcome in therapy, with increases in emotional regulation and self-acceptance, was due to improvement in attachment security with her parents. As she was able to connect to better-regulated minds, her parents' and mine, she was able to better regulate herself.

In attachment-focused therapy it is critical to form an empathic connection in spite of clients' avoidance, provocation, or anxiety.

Key Areas That Improve Security in Attachment

I think of four key areas when analyzing and preparing to alter attachment patterns:

1. states of mind toward attachment,
2. effectiveness in recognizing and meeting the needs of the other in attachment relationships,
3. high stress (including traumas), and
4. emotional state regulation.

The *state of mind toward attachment* refers to people's perceptions and beliefs about meeting emotional and physical needs within an attachment relationship (Hesse, 2008). What value do they place on attachment relationships? Do they believe that it is best to respond in a sensitive, timely, and attuned manner? Or is the need dismissed, exaggerated, or met with a confusing or angry response? The differences in state of mind show in the following example. One mother said, "I became more open and loving with my third child. Before that, I thought that it was a tough world. Children shouldn't be coddled. I parented like my mother parented me. But by the third child, I changed. I used the word *love* and cuddled her. That's when I changed into a tender mother. She was such a loving child, smiling and telling me that she loved me. My husband and I were closer by that time, which helped me to change our family to be a loving one."

State of mind also influences how worthy people feel in asking for their own needs to be met in the relationship. Do they expect to be treated with sensitivity and respect? Or do they feel shame or fear? Do they anticipate losing the attachment figure's attention, resisting even before this happens?

The concept of state of mind includes learning from life experiences and the conclusions that people make about the way they want to approach others. Are close, warm relationships the ideal, or do people select cool distance? Are relationships a priority as they assign time? Is it essential to work on problems that emerge? Or do they think it is better to ignore them and avoid problems? Is there a likelihood of success if they do address problems, or is avoidance the best strategy? Will they be able to withstand the emotions that are part of resolving a disagreement without inflicting damage or being damaged? As we move into the section on patterns of attachment, we will look at beliefs about state of mind.

A second major area of attachment focus is sensitivity and effectiveness in meeting expressed needs. Attachment's role includes meeting basic needs. In infants' development, parents must have a mental construct of what their babies need—food, clean diapers, touch, proximity, or stimulation level. The ability to meet needs, and the timeliness with which the needs are met, can be classified into patterns of attachment. For example, does the parent feed the baby when the baby first cries, holding the baby tenderly during feeding? Or does the parent ignore early signs of distress, responding later, while staring at a cell phone during feeding? Or does the parent dissociate when the child is crying? For therapists, this is an area of both analysis and intervention.

A third major area of focus is stress. When people are forming attachment relationships, high stress alters their emotional availability to others. Stressors can be environmental, such as food insecurity, unsafe housing, and illness. The stressors include trauma. When parents have been traumatized or are in acute grief, particular parts of the brain associated with trauma and grief are activated (Fonagy, 2002). In attachment relationships, when infants and children make a brain-to-brain connection with their parents' grief and trauma brain patterns, they are overwhelmed. Young minds have not yet developed the capacity to endure connection to the dysregulated brain states of trauma or unresolved grief. Parents' grief and trauma states interrupt the continuity of connection and regulation with their infants and children.

The fourth area, which overlaps with stress, is emotional state regulation. I have separated it from traumatic stress states even though they overlap. Some parents have never developed basic emotional regulation. Even mild stresses cause significant dysregulation. Helping dysregulated parents to become better regulated in everyday life will improve the security of attachment in dyads.

Developing Stress Systems and Attachment Patterns

A major process in parenting is assisting children's development of emotional regulation, optimally with parents' soothing, buffering, distracting, and stretching positive moods (Sroufe, 1995). Parents who are in chronic dysregulation tend to reproduce chronic dysregulation in their children unless there are alternate attachment figures.

The brain patterns of security and stress regulation are laid down in infancy and early childhood (Sroufe, 1995). These become the emotional regulation templates used in daily life. It is much easier for adults to form secure attachments, with coregulating qualities, when building on templates of security and regulation as developed in the first two years of life.

Parents who struggle with state regulation often seek help in attaching to their children. Therapists respond by providing a reparative, brain-to-brain connection for these clients. This process will require therapists to coregulate parents and their children. The building of emotional state regulation between a parent and therapist may be an unconscious process that the conscious brain comes to recognize. A client with childhood loss and trauma expressed it to me in these words: "After therapy I feel like I have had a massage. I relax." The brain-to-brain connection with this client was felt physically as reduced stress.

In situations in which parents are struggling with emotional regulation and their children are showing the effects, I have found it helpful to regulate parents and their children in sessions together. I provide extra help with parent regulation through extra parent sessions or 10 minutes alone with parents at the beginning of parent-child sessions. Eventually the goal is that parents are able to regulate themselves, regulating their children, in turn.

Adult Attachment Interview and Strange Situation

In there are two major assessment tools that have been used to classify attachments. The Adult Attachment Interview is a structured 50-minute interview. It can be analyzed by skilled coders to categorize the parent's state of mind toward attachment (Hesse, 2008). It has strong predictive value for the parent-child pattern of attachment. The Strange Situation, designed by Mary Ainsworth, requires a child to separate from the parent for a short period of time. The attachment patterns of children and their parents can be assessed through children's reactions to the separation and their reunion with their parents (Ainsworth et al., 1978/2015). These are reliable and valid research tools useful in assessing attachment categories.

The adult categories described by Mary Main and Eric Hesse are secure, insecure-dismissing, or insecure-preoccupied (Hesse, 2016). They correspond to the children's patterns of secure, avoidant, and resistant. L. Alan Sroufe, Byron Egeland, Elizabeth Carlson, and W. Andres Collins use the terms *anxious avoidant*, *anxious resistant*, and *anxious ambivalent* to describe children's patterns of response to the dismissing parent, preoccupied parent, or ambivalent parent, respectively (2005a, 2005b).

In addition to the categories listed above, there is a major category called disorganized/disoriented. Charles Zeanah (1996) used the term "beyond insecurity" in his landmark article describing the disorganized/disoriented category. The disorganized/disoriented child shows an inability to use a consistent strategy. This has been termed a "collapse of strategies." This is seen when children are in overwhelming situation (Lyons-Ruth, Jacobvitz (2008, 2016); Hesse, Main, (2006). When describing the disorganized style, there is still a preference for one particular pattern, which may be labeled disorganized-secure, disorganized-avoidant, and so forth.

Secure Attachments, Repair, and Stress Regulation

A summary of the secure attachment pattern was provided earlier in this chapter. In this section, I explore the secure pattern's potential in regulation, empathy, integration, and repair in preparation for the techniques in Part II. Readers will find that some secure attachments may be noted as *secure* (parent) *autonomous* (child) or secure/secure (Main, Hesse, & Kaplan, 2005).

Through secure attachments, parents help their children to develop the brain wiring and skills for emotional regulation and socioemotional connections. Secure attachments provide feelings of safety and acceptance. On this secure foundation, people risk venturing further. After all, they have a recharging station and cheering section. People believe in them and help them to regroup and try again when they have setbacks.

The secure attachment state of mind has a foundational belief that relationships are important—well worth the time and focus required to create and sustain them. This is an advanced, emotionally complex appraisal that is informed by the right brain (Schore, 2012). Rather than a dry and considered pro-versus-con, it is intuitively known.

Security in attachment does not mean that children and parents never have doubts about their worth to each other. But feeling secure in the relationship is the norm, not the exception. People in the relationship have ways to reassure and accept reassurance when there are doubts. When there are emotional upsets, families work on repairing or soothing hurts, accepting responsibility for breeches, and reassuring each other about their worth. This repair is done not just with words, but with body-based affirmation—a hand on the knee, a hug, kind eyes, soothing touch, matched body postures, and melodic voice tones.

People who are in family relationships characterized by secure attachments seem to have an intuitive north star guiding them to construct and guard loving contexts (Gray, 2014). They select activities and environments that promote family connections, moving into an activated problem-solving mode when these connections are suffering. They sense threat through their rapid, intuitive right-brain functioning (Schore, 2012). What does this look like?

An example can be drawn from my own life. Early in my career, a trainer approached me with an invitation to attend a 2-week, on-site attachment educational program. He wanted participants to spend their evenings and weekends with the other class members, leaving their families home. I had very young children. I intuitively knew that the program would stress my children. Even if I did not know the time frames that cause separation loss, as accessed by my left brain, my right-brain emotional responses would still have been spot on. Most people with secure attachments have this quick leap of right-brain decision making that guides them to protect attachment relationships.

Parenting That Forms Secure Attachments

Parents who form secure attachments have major factors noted above and summarized here:

- state of mind that values attachment;
- ability to meet attachment needs in a timely, sensitive, and consistent way;
- stress regulation and coregulation capacity; and
- ability to repair.

Mary Ainsworth, who did seminal work on attachment patterns, described the mothers with secure attachments as ones who were sensitive, accepted parenting roles, cooperated with their children's moods rather than trying to control them, and were accessible to their children rather than ignoring them (Shiller, 2017).

Support for Both Dependency and Autonomy Needs of Children

Secure attachments encourage children's independence, mastery, and individuality. Parents who are anxious that their toddler, and later teen, will abandon them as they become independent can quickly temper those feelings by trusting in the quality of their relationship. Parents enjoy getting to know their children and teens as they develop and have outside interests.

A parent who shows secure attachment qualities meets needs sensitively, helping to soothe infants and children who are upset. They possess a sense of good timing, or synchrony, as they decide whether to move in closer to help or give their children a moment to practice self-skills like calming or trying something challenging again. These parents maintain their own regulation and sense of themselves as separate individuals. Parents encourage children's mastery and autonomy, celebrating achievements. Children and I discuss this as having, "mom or dad in your head and heart." The parents' voice tones and soothing become internalized templates. Past infancy, children and parents have a continuing awareness of each other, without having to constantly monitor or cling to each other. Some parents complain of their children being overattached (their term) which I see with children's anxious clinging. However, this is actually based on insecurity, with too little confidence in the relationship.

Attachment is a basic system for survival. A parent can have a secure state of mind toward attachment, but if the home lacks food or is unsafe, or if the parent cannot provide basic care, the attachment is not secure. Many adopted children, who were chronically hungry, have shared with me their mistrust toward biological parents. These children could not depend on their parents for the basic survival need of food.

Secure Attachment, Emotional Awareness, and Social Competence

Emotional intelligence is woven into sensitive attachment relationships. As parents relate to infants, children, and teens, they respond to the facial and body cues of their children. In early development, parents will exaggerate their children's expressions, amplifying their words and gestures, thereby helping children to connect their body sensations with words. Children are able to develop an integrated self-awareness, initially expecting others to alleviate distress but later acting with more self-agency. Children develop integration between body-based feelings, the meaning and name of feelings, and an expectation that their feelings are valid.

Because of reciprocity in attachments, children also become aware of the thoughts and feelings of others. By the age of 6 or 7, they are able to hold on to their own thoughts and feelings and those of another person, which is a key quality in social situations. They are also able to read expressions on the faces of others and relate empathically to others. In a rapid mental appraisal, they know how they might feel in a social situation and respond in an appropriate manner.

This rapid and empathic response undergirds cooperation in social groups and in friendships. It allows for conscience development to progress beyond the initial level of getting caught and having negative consequences.

Secure attachments benefit children as they enter elementary school. Kathryn Kerns and Laura Brumariu conclude, "similar to what has been found at younger ages, secure attachment in middle childhood is associated with greater social, emotional, and cognitive competence, and less clinical symptomatology" (2016, p. 359).

The Minnesota Longitudinal Study followed a moderate-risk sample of mothers and their infants for 20 years. This group described attachments as "the ultimate organizational construct, drawing upon all facets of development (cognitive, emotional, social) and being manifest in the balance between exploration and comfort seeking" (Sroufe, et al., 2005a, p. 49). They describe the role of attachment in supporting peer relations and providing "(1) a motivational base, involving expectations of connectedness; (2) an attitudinal base, involving expectations of responsiveness; (3) an instrumental base centered on exploratory and play capacities; (4) an emotional base, including entrained capacities for arousal and emotional regulation; and (5) a relational base, involving empathy and expectations of mutuality" (Sroufe, 2005b, p. 57). Even if children do not start life with secure attachments, as we promote security we help children with the substrate of positive peer relationships.

Repair in Secure Attachments

Security in attachment includes missed signals and bad moments. Significantly, in secure attachments parents tend to try to regain a sense of connection and regulation, or repair. Repair can be an apology, hug, or snuggle. In moderation, these bolster security in attachment. They teach children that they can tolerate some stress in a relationship. Children learn the process of getting back in sync (Schore, 2003b).

People who have secure attachments attempt to repair, mustering their regulation abilities even when it is challenging, as when parenting teens or toddlers. They show confidence in their abilities to respect and hear their children's or teens' feelings and views, rather than dismissing or avoiding upsetting situations.

Parents who show security in attachment are open to the possibility that they might have misread a situation or acted in error. Parents have a standard that they should use empathy and insight concerning their children and themselves. Parents who are accustomed to repair will try to use their empathy and soothing to move children to a better emotional place, reestablishing connection and coregulation. Especially for older children, this moves into a discussion of each person's perspective, which builds reflective ability and theory of mind in both children/teens and adults. They improve their understanding of the other's thoughts and feelings, even when they disagree.

Secure Attachments and Gratifying Relationships

Secure attachments have a quality of joy. Parents look at their children and delight in them. Children look back, sharing the delight. This delight has nonverbal expressions with meaning: voice tones, body language, positive gestures, and smiles. An exuberant, playful quality streams through the relationship. People in secure attachments find pleasure in spending time together. The anticipation of this pleasure causes children to reach out with expectation of positive attention or help. Stress and arguments may interfere for periods of time, but the positive qualities tend to reemerge as stress diminishes. As clinicians work with families, they can encourage joy by modeling playfulness and asking families to create times to play.

Some interventions to help with attachment security are described in Chapter 2. Parents who have received intervention services often describe parenting as more enjoyable. The children are gratifying, which then causes parents to continue to give positive attention to them (Berlin, Zeanah, & Lieberman,2016). While I have discussed parent qualities common to secure attachments, I am also interested in helping children to have gratifying responses. Without moving into a role reversal, it is important for children, especially after adversity, to learn to respond to the emotional needs and positive signals from their parents.

Intergenerational Parent-Child Attachment Patterns

Attachment patterns are commonly passed to the next generation. Children can have a different pattern of attachment with each parent. They may have a secure attachment with a grandparent with whom they spend ample time, and insecure attachments with their parents. People who had secure attachments as children will tend to form those attachment patterns as adults (Sroufe, 2002). It is common for people to move into a secure pattern from an insecure one when they have positive influences—like a loving new attachment figure, relief from high stress, or therapy. People who grew up with insecure attachments, and who became secure as adults, are referred to as *earned secures* (Hesse, 2016).

In therapy, as clients discuss their patterns of attachment, they tend to reference their life narratives and their feelings. One client said, "My father distanced when I hit puberty. I was confused and hurt, although I acted like I didn't care. In therapy, I thought about my teen years and how I was treating my teen daughter. I began to distance when we'd argue. I stopped spending as much time with her. I think that my daughter was reacting, yelling, 'You don't even care! When's the last time you really talked to me?' I felt like pushing away further. When we were working in therapy last week, I thought, I want a good relationship like my mother had with me as a teen. We shared so much fun with my friends and sports. This week I made an effort to stay connected to my daughter. We are not arguing as much, and I've stayed off my phone when we are together." In the example above, this client took lessons from his secure parent, as he changed his approach. Even when parents have only had insecure parenting, they often model themselves after people in their lives who related to them in a sensitive and attuned manner. In fact, many people who have insecure attachments as children will go on to form secure attachments. The term *transmission gap* describes the move from one attachment pattern to another between childhood and adult years (Belsky, 2016).

One of the salient issues that arises in the discussion of the transmission gap involves individual vulnerability or resilience (Belsky, 2016). Some more resilient individuals with insecure attachments develop secure attachments, presumably through other role models or routes not well understood by researchers (Feeney, & Woodhouse, 2016).

Since security in attachment confers significant resiliency factors, this is particularly important for vulnerable children. Some researchers suggest that "infant negativity should not be considered a risk factor, but rather an endophenotypic marker of susceptibility to the environment" (Feeney, & Woodhouse, 2016, p. 831). There is an emerging research literature that describes genetics as conferring more or less sensitivity to the environment. It is postulated that there is a marker on the 7th allele that makes children more sensitive to their environments, negative and positive (Fearon, Belsky, 2016). The child has the potential to react more positively to supports and interventions, although more negatively when there is a lack of support. As described by Jay Belsky (2015), support given to fussy babies and more sensitive children seems to yield great benefits. When we are treating families whose children struggle with their moods and positivism, it helps to think that our efforts could create a positive trajectory for these children's development.

Insecure-Dismissing (Parent)/Avoidant (Child)

Parents who dismiss their children's needs by ignoring or shaming them when they have needs tend to form the insecure-dismissing pattern with their children. The child, as a result, tends to avoid the parent. Because these parents exact a price for giving help, their children tend avoid parents and issues rather than reaching out for help. Children are met with parental disapproval or rejection when they are upset. They learn to self-regulate, although largely by trying to shut themselves off from their emotions. The parents are not easily accessible, sensitive, or positive. They show irritation at many of the tasks of parenting, with reduced enjoyment of parenting.

These are parents who love their children and are committed to them. Children know that they can go to their parents in an emergency. Parents tend to describe wanting their children to be self-reliant. They do not want to raise weak children. There is a stiff-upper-lip quality to these parents. A parent said to me, "My parents and I always looked down on anxious or needy people. I would rather that my kids handle things themselves. When I realized that my child had been sexually abused, and I had missed it for 3 years, it shook me. Where was I? I had to face that my daughter did not feel that she could come to me." Avoidant children do come to their parents for help, but are leery about the price tag.

When meeting with therapists, these parents are often surprised to hear about their children's hurt. If their defensive systems are not overly activated, parents may respond with kindness and attempt repair. These parents may want to take some therapy suggestions and then scoot out of the therapy room, relieved that they could get help without dire consequences. With positive experiences, they will come back for more help as needed.

These parents are less likely to give physical affection to their children. Detailed and specific behavioral indicators of this style are included in Chapter 3. The children tend to keep their distance. If their avoidance strategy does not work, they may become highly anxious (Sroufe et al., 2005a). Future chapters describe working with these children and their parents.

Insecure-Preoccupied (Parent)/ Insecure-Ambivalent (Child), Also Called Anxious Resistant (Child)

Parents who are preoccupied with events in their own lives are with their children, but not really mentally available. Babies and toddlers find their inability to hold their parents' attention anxiety provoking. Over time, children tend to become resistant to their parents when they are given attention. It seems that children are anticipating the loss of parental attention, so begin to protest even when sitting on their parents' laps.

Often these parents describe an idealized attachment with their own parents, but have no facts to back it up (Hesse, 2008). Parenting requires that people respond out of their own life narrative. Preoccupied parents have hurt and stuck places in their own life story. Rather than a smooth response from an integrated life narrative—with empathy and soothing of children or delighting in children—parents ruminate about their pasts. For example, if I model looking at a child's face in therapy, enjoying his expression, a parent's first reaction may be, "Why didn't my parents delight in me?"

When these parents come into the therapist's office to speak about their child, they tend to become involved in the hurts of their life narrative. It can be confusing to therapists who heard how wonderful the adult clients' parents were during an intake session, and then to hear the painful reality. A parent who described her parents as "fabulous" at intake described a few months later the way her mother and father ignored steady and brutal bullying by a sibling. "They really were not there for me. I felt like I wasn't worth much since they ignored the situation." She went on, "When they told me that they had done a great job raising us, but now they were done and were planning to divorce and downsize, I didn't know what to say."

At times this parent would look blank when asked to respond to her daughter. Her daughter struggled to keep her mother's attention and would repeat, "Mom! Mom!" Parents with this pattern will need help in processing the past so that they can show up in the present, mindfully. Part II gives practical interventions.

Insecure–Disorganized (Parent)/Disorganized–Disoriented (Child) and Disorganized (Parent)/Disorganized–Controlling (Child)

This category is not an organized, logical pattern. Instead it shows fragmentation. When children are in this category in research studies, it is predictive of high rates of later psychopathology. Parents in this category tend to be frightened of or frightening to their children and infants. The infants or children show a collapse of response strategies, often with early indicators of dissociation, like "still face" (staring with a frozen expression) and dissociation. The parents may employ a role reversal in parenting. Or they may be abusive. Parents who have unresolved grief and trauma may show disorganized behavior with their child. This is also called unresolved (parent)/disorganized (child) (Hesse, Main, Abrams, & Rifkin, 2003; Hesse, 2016; Solomon, George, 1999, 2016).

These children appear for therapy with high rates of hostility, anxiety, and/or aggression. Some parents come in for therapy, appearing beseeching, helpless, and needy, eliciting care. Other parents are emotionally or physically abusive. Children correspondingly respond with disorientation, hostility, control, or exaggerated caregiving. Children are just as controlling and hostile to the needy parents as to the harsh parents, although therapists seem to regard the needy parents with greater sympathy (Lyons-Ruth & Jacobvitz, 2008).

The children and parents in this category regularly elicit community concern. They tend to enter therapy referred by schools, medical professionals, and child welfare agencies. Children with disorganized attachment styles do not usually have a basis of trust in adults. They are often wary of therapy and afraid to believe that the therapist will provide relief from overwhelming feelings, especially fear and shame. Researchers have found them to be avoidant of tasks of therapy, either playing chaotically or choosing to ignore themes of therapy (Lyons-Ruth, & Jacobvitz, 2008). Because of this, adaptations have to be made in the way that therapists approach children and families. (These adaptations are described further in Chapters 3 and 4.)

Because this is a disorganized style, a quick appraisal of children may provide a misleading opinion. Children may be demonstrating security, avoidance, or caregiving of a parent at a particular session. They may be quite different at another time, because of the very nature of the disorganized pattern. Some children will have a dazed smile on their faces, which is evidence of being overwhelmed rather than joyful. After trauma and traumatic loss, many children show this pattern. The rate of disorganization in attachment is about 80% for foster children who come into care (Dozier, Stovall, Albus, & Bates, 2001). Interestingly, infants and toddlers begin to attach, moving to a secure pattern within weeks if foster mothers demonstrate secure qualities (Dozier et al., 2001; Dozier, Rutter, 2016). Disorganized styles are described as disorganized along with aspects of the organized pattern that best describe the child, such as disorganized/secure.

Disorganized Category and Stress, Coping, and Resilience

Children with a disorganized style tend to be controlling. Their stress is high, living in a world in which adults do not provide security. Most have had scant encouragement to develop ways to cope. Many become angry or dissociative if control is not possible. The children have stress systems that have been influenced by unrelenting high stress, either through their exposure to highly stressful events like domestic violence or abuse, or through exposure to parents' dysregulated emotional states like trauma and traumatic grief.

These children may have had emotional or physical neglect, left alone with emotional or physical needs unmet. The response to extreme neglect is a biological bias toward hypoarousal, with its slowed heart rate, respiration, and shut-down feelings. Hypoarousal makes children less available for therapeutic interventions. The children also tend to show hyperarousal, causing therapists to struggle to maintain therapeutic pacing in the sessions. Hyperarousal and hypoarousal in children informs their need for such high control. These children tend to have mood states that are brittle and underdeveloped. Anger is high in children exposed to violence (Schore, 2003c).

Therapists often look for a specific event to treat, as in a one-time trauma or life event. But chronic or toxic stress, which is typical for these children, causes an early shaping of specific brain systems (Schore, 2003c). The work with children and parents will concentrate on assisting the development of secure attachment, with its potential for stress regulation. Specific work on trauma is almost always indicated. Therapists should approach trauma differently than they would a one-time traumatic event. The therapeutic interventions are only successful if they address their client's complex and interwoven responses to long-term trauma (Levine, 2015). When therapists are working with attachment and complex trauma, clients will tap into the therapists' own attachment qualities, chiefly regulation and empathy, to work successfully. There is more detail in upcoming chapters.

When therapists are working with children and parents with disorganized attachment patterns, anger and aggression will be prevalent problems. Yet the promise for change lies within empathy and connection. It is important to have plans for behavioral control; it is paramount to have experiences of warmth and engagement.

Attachment Terms

While researchers are in agreement about the major attachment categories (patterns), they may use additional select terms.

- Secure (parent) is sometimes called "confident."
- Secure (child) is also called "autonomous" and "secure balanced."
- Insecure is also called "anxious."
- An insecure-ambivalent (parent) may be dismissive and preoccupied in turn, but not disorganized.

- An anxious-ambivalent (child) may have an approach and avoidance mixture, or push-pull.
- Disorganized/disoriented, frozen/fearful children may be fearful, frozen, and disoriented some of the time when with parents.
- Disorganized/unresolved parents show unresolved grief or losses that influence attachment.
- A disorganized child is called "disorganized/controlling."
- An avoidant (parent) has been called "casual or detached."
- A disorganized (parent) may also be called "hostile/helpless" or "frightening/frightened."
- Other terms include insecure/other or unclassifiable for mixtures of insecure indicators including disorganization (Solomon, & George, 2016).

Attachment Disorders

I find it helpful in clinical work to think of patterns rather than categories. On balance, the *DSM-V* categories of attachment disorders are necessary in order to have commonality in referencing. They are also important in helping to understand pertinent research information. I have included the attachment descriptions from the *DSM-V* below (American Psychiatric Association, 2013).

Reactive Attachment Disorder 313.89
Diagnostic Criteria

A. A consistent pattern of inhibited, emotionally withdrawn behavior toward adult caregivers, manifested by both of the following:
   1. The child rarely or minimally seeks comfort when distressed.
   2. The child rarely or minimally responds to comfort when distressed.
B. A persistent social and emotional disturbance characterized by at least two of the following:
   1. Minimal social and emotional responsiveness to others.

2. Limited positive affect.
3. Episodes of unexplained irritability, sadness, or fearfulness that are evident even during nonthreatening interactions with adult caregivers.

C. The child has experienced a pattern of extremes of insufficient care as evidenced by at least one of the following:
   1. Social neglect or deprivation in the form of persistent lack of having basic emotional needs for comfort, stimulation, and affection met by caregiving adults.
   2. Repeated changes of primary caregivers that limit opportunities to form stable attachment (e.g., frequent changes in foster care).
   3. Rearing in unusual settings that severely limit opportunities to form selective attachments (e.g., institutions with high child-to-caregiver ratios).

D. The care in Criterion C is presumed to be responsible for the disturbed behavior in Criterion A (e.g., the disturbances in Criterion A began following the lack of adequate care in Criterion C).

E. The criteria are not met for autism spectrum disorder.

F. The disturbance is evident before age 5 years.

G. The child has a developmental age of at least 9 months.

Specify if:
Persistent: The disorder has been present for more than 12 months.

Specify current severity:
Reactive attachment disorder is specified as severe when a child exhibits all symptoms of the disorder, with each symptom manifesting at relatively high levels.

Disinhibited Social Engagement Disorder 313.89
Diagnostic Criteria

A. A pattern of behavior in which a child actively approaches and interacts with unfamiliar adults and exhibits at least two of the following:

1. Reduced or absent reticence in approaching and inter-acting with unfamiliar adults.
2. Overly familiar verbal or physical behavior (that is not consistent with culturally sanctioned and with age-appropriate social boundaries).
3. Diminished or absent checking back with adult care-giver after venturing away, even in unfamiliar settings.
4. Willingness to go off with an unfamiliar adult with minimal or no hesitation.

B. The behaviors in Criterion A are not limited to impulsivity (as in attention-deficit/hyperactivity disorder) but include socially disinhibited behavior.
C. The child has experienced a pattern of extremes of insufficient care as evidenced by at least one of the following:
    1. Social neglect or deprivation in the form of persistent lack of having basic emotional needs for comfort, stim-ulation, and affection met by caregiving adults.
    2. Repeated changes of primary caregivers that limit opportunities to form stable attachment (e.g., frequent changes in foster care).
    3. Rearing in unusual settings that severely limit oppor-tunities to form selective attachments (e.g., institutions with high child-to-caregiver ratios).
D. The care in Criterion C is presumed to be responsible for the disturbed behavior in Criterion A (e.g., the disturbances in Cri-terion A began following the pathogenic care in Criterion C).
E. The child has a developmental age of at least 9 months.

Specify if:
Persistent: The disorder has been present for more than 12 months.
Specify current severity:
Disinhibited social engagement disorder is specified as severe when the child exhibits all symptoms of the disorder, with each symptom manifesting at relatively high levels (American Psychiatric Association, 2013).

Similar to the rates reported by others, Zeanah describes toddlers in foster care as having an attachment disorder rate of 38–40% (DeKlyen & Greenberg, 2016). These children can be moved into more security and prosocial patterns when foster care moves are minimized and when children are living with parents who are nurturing. I regret that the term *attachment disorder* has a dramatic connotation. Public perception, shared by a few clinicians, seems to be that the children are "other" when they have been categorized as having attachment disorders. Since they are viewed as other, it opens the way to treat children harshly. Obviously, this does not promote security in attachment.

Approaches that overwhelm children, like holding, which is the forced containment of a child followed by connection between a child and parent, are not acceptable practices. I have met children, now adults, who described that it helped them. But I have met children who have been emotionally harmed. I have had to apologize to children, on behalf of the field of therapy, to children who experienced such an awful event. When treating children who were terrified by holding, I have met nearly insurmountable obstacles of mistrust. Before proceeding into our therapy, I have had to promise these children that I will never terrify them in this way. While practitioners who used holding were trying to help, coercive methods do not promote healthy attachments. Cradling a child for comfort is quite appropriate and is not forced on an unwilling child.

Theory of Mind Distortions

Standing up for ourselves and connecting with other people require the ability to know the thoughts and feelings of others with a continuing awareness of our own thoughts and feelings. Parents with attachment issues tend to struggle to understand what their babies or children want from them. Parents may think that their little ones are mad at them, spoiled, selfish, too demanding, and so forth. They do not have an accurate theory of mind about their children.

As a result, their children grow up without the day-to-day guidance necessary to develop a continuous awareness of their own feelings and thoughts or the motivations or feelings of others. Their sense of self lacks integration. Their theory of mind about others remains underdeveloped. This makes it difficult for them to connect with others while maintaining a sense of themselves. They tend to show rigidity instead of cooperation, or else they capitulate, giving up what is in their own interest. Children who are in a role reversal, taking care of the needs of the parents, may appear to have a pseudomaturity. But they struggle with competence in social situations.

When working with families, I recommend spending ample time with clients helping them to develop an understanding of the thoughts and feelings of others—while remaining aware of their own thoughts and feelings. When children have had role reversals, they may be good at recognizing the needs of others, but may lose their self-interest in the meantime. Real-time experiences in therapy that include being aware of their thoughts and feelings as well as their parents' is an important step in developing competence. Often I turn to fun games and experiential exercises, as detailed in upcoming chapters.

CHAPTER 2

Changing Attachment Patterns

Attachment security includes valuing relationships, and especially the qualities of sensitivity, trust, and repair. Through secure attachments, we develop an awareness of our feelings, such as love, fear, or shame. We note and make some sense of our internal physical states and signals such as heart rate, dry mouth, visceral upset, happy belly, face flushing, pleasure, or desire to flee.

Many adults notice the ease and joy with which others connect, and decide they want that for themselves. They value relationships even if they did not have security in their early lives. As children they may have had a relationship with a grandparent, teacher, or neighbor who provided an alternative secure base model.

Some individuals will come into therapy looking for help in their parenting relationship. In the first session, they will mention someone who helped them to believe that there was a better way of connecting than the one they had with their parents. I encourage eliciting more information, while noting their wisdom in forming their earlier, positive relationship. This beginning reflection helps clients to believe in their potential to have healthy attachments.

Adult Relationships That Develop Security

After formerly abused people have participated in therapy, developed loving marital relationships, or received nurturing support from an adult, they can show a change in their attachment style, as discussed in Chapter 1. L. Alan Sroufe (2002) has remarked on the positive changes in parent-child security that some of his moderate-risk, single mothers showed after developing supportive partner relationships. Changes reflect increased emotional support and decreased daily life stress as someone helped to carry the load of the household.

When working with families, I enjoy thinking of ways that parents can coregulate each other better as well as reduce stress. These changes are early wins in therapy that benefit families. For example, one parent could volunteer to take care of dinner and the children while the other parent has a weekly evening to spend with a friend. Or, for two weeks, at least 10 times daily, one parent could notice and speak about the kind, positive things that the other parent does for the family. Many ideas are mentioned throughout Part II.

At this point, I want to emphasize that attachments are patterns that are usually mutable with supportive coregulating adults and decreased stress. Therapists are in ideal positions to help with suggestions in these areas. Individual therapy is a classic avenue to create secure attachment patterns. As clients form attachments to their attuned and empathetic therapists, with therapists bonding in return, clients form abilities to connect and regulate (Siegel, 2015). Therapeutic interventions have included a number of model research-based programs, some of which are briefly described here. For a more thorough discussion, I recommend Chapter 32 in *The Handbook of Attachment* (Berlin et al., 2016).

Child-Parent Psychotherapy or Preschool Parent Psychotherapy

This dyadic model's "principal goals are to help the parent (1) reconnect with the pain, fear, anger and helplessness evoked by frightening childhood experiences and (2) understand his or her current negative feelings toward his or her infant as a reenactment of unresolved conflicts about his or her own parents or other important childhood figures resulting from these frightening experiences. The therapist's empathic guidance is considered the essential ingredient for helping the parents explore their past, practice new parenting behaviors, and free their child from engulfment in the parents' conflicted childhood experiences" (Berlin et al., 2016, pp. 741). A manual for Child-Parent Psychotherapy (CPP), titled *Don't Hit My Mommy!*, explains the program for those interested in reading further (Lieberman, Ghosh Ippen, & van Horn, 2015).

A number of research projects show CPP and Preschool Parent Psychotherapy (PPP) programs' effectiveness in changing parents' working models of attachment. These studies show decreases in children's behavior problems and increases in maternal empathy, maternal interaction and involvement, dyadic goal-directed partnerships, and lower avoidance (Berlin et al., 2016). CPP and PPP are effective interventions for children who have been exposed to trauma. Other study findings have shown a decrease in maternal trauma symptomatology, an increase in language development in children, and positive effects on cortisol regulation in children (Berlin et al., 2016).

In describing the intervention, Berlin and colleagues write:

> The CPP therapist uses play and unstructured interactions as vehicles to promote a goal-corrected partnership, translate the motivations and feelings of the child and the parent toward each other, address trauma reminders, and reframe mutual negative attributions. When this therapeutic focus on the present is not sufficient to promote improvement, the CPP therapist guides the parent into an exploration of her or his childhood experiences that are being reenacted in relation to the child. CPP therapists also provide case management and connect the family to relevant community service when concrete problems of living interfere with the parent's ability to create a safe family environment (2016, p. 741).

The success of this intervention is based on the formation of a relationship between parents and their therapist, followed by the therapist introducing changes in the dyadic relationship. This year-long manualized program has noteworthy research outcomes. Interestingly, this is about the length of time that many private practice clients spend in therapy on parent-child attachment issues. I included the key tasks in the descriptive paragraph above, since many therapists will be undertaking these activities in their practices, even if they are not part of a CPP or PPP program. They may perform more casework tasks than they would do with other types of families, as occurs in CPP cases. The therapists are encouraged to develop a trusting relationship with the parent first, followed later by changes in the parent-child relationship (Berlin et al., 2016).

Circle of Security

Circle of Security (COS) assists at-risk mothers with a developmentally appropriate understanding of their infants' and children's needs. This program uses videotapes of infants and toddlers, helping parents to identify infant cues and miscues. It provides information on attachment and autonomy through instruction and clear graphic illustrations. The facilitators help parents develop sensitivity to children and infants, realizing how much infants and toddlers want their mother's love and attention. They also work on children's exploration and mastery, helping parents to appreciate their roles as a secure base. A group-based version of the program meets in 75-minute sessions for 20 weeks. The program shows effectiveness in increasing security of attachment and decreasing the rate of disorganized attachment, even though it does not directly treat children with their parents (Berlin et al., 2016; Hoffman, Marvin, Cooper, & Powell, 2006).

Attachment and Biobehavioral Catch-Up

Attachment and Biobehavioral Catch-Up (ABC) supports sensitive parenting of infants and young children in foster care. Knowing that the infants and children often give contradictory or muted cues, the 10-week program helps foster parents understand the needs of abused infants and children. It encourages foster parents to respond in a nurturing and contingent manner. The parents in the intervention complete an attachment diary. The diary entries demonstrate the foster parents' growth in understanding the needs of young children, how those needs are expressed, and the parents' sensitivity in meeting the expressed needs. Infants show a remarkable rate of movement into secure attachments if their foster parents also have secure attachment states of mind (Dozier et al., 2009).

A research project using the ABC model followed 115 children with a history of Child Protective Services involvement in infancy. All children were living with a biological parent who was a voluntary participant in the program. Assignment to ABC or control was random. All infants were under 2 years of age. The goals were threefold: increase nurturing during times of distress, decrease frightening parental behavior, and increase synchronous interactions. Sessions 1–2 focused on nurturance, 3–4 on "following the lead," 5–6 on reducing intrusive and frightening behavior, and 7–10 on parents' histories of care and how that influenced their care. The program gave live coaching. The authors described a major success factor as "in-the-moment feedback, with moment-to-moment alterations in parent-child interaction" (Bernard, Hostinar, & Dozier, 2015, p. 115). The parents had opportunities to practice new parenting approaches in real time with their children. Therapists introduced the changes and supported parents as they made those changes.

The control intervention was Developmental Education for Families, a home visitation program focusing on parent education about children's motor, cognitive, and language development. They followed up in preschool, when children were between 46 and 67 months. They found that the children in the ABC group showed:

> a movement toward typical cortisol production, with higher morning levels and a steep decline across the day, whereas children in the control condition exhibited blunted morning levels and flattened diurnal cortisol slopes that are typical in pediatric samples experiencing neglect and more generally

in groups experiencing ongoing stress. The results suggest that the intervention was successful in having persistent, long-term effects on the functioning of the HPA stress system. This may have beneficial implications for preventing child psychological and physical health problems, given previous reports linking cortisol disruption to those deleterious child outcomes. (Bernard et al., 2015, p. 114)

Yet another study using ABC showed better receptive language in children who received the ABC intervention versus control. They noted the responsiveness of parents as the critical factor in the improved language development of children (Bernard, Lee, & Dozier, 2017).

I have included these model research programs because they help us to focus on what seems to work best when improving attachment outcomes in children. ABC gives parents many opportunities to practice interactions with their children, with support. The work with ABC, COS, and CPP all emphasizes parents' developing theory of mind for their children or infants. Parents are provided with someone who cares for them as they care for their children in the ABC and CPP models. The CPP and PPP programs include the practicalities of help for parents with stressors. The models decrease parental stress and increase attachment capacity. Those are bright lines that link successful programs.

Attachment Patterns Improved Through Reduced Stress and Increased Support

Other notable programs that specifically target attachment security in traumatized or highly stressed children include: Attachment Regulation Competency (ARC) with researchers Margaret Blaustein, Kristine Kinniburgh (2007, 2010), and Multidimensional Treatment Foster Care (MDTFC) with Phillip Fisher and collaborating researchers (Kinniburgh, Blaustein, & Spinazzola, 2005; Fisher, Van Ryzin, & Gunnar, 2011). Both of these programs have a goal of improving attachment security in the vulnerable population of foster children. The programs include psychosocial competencies and behavioral contingencies. Descriptions of ARC include both attachment and trauma approaches, with a strong emphasis on children's agency and mastery.

I have included MDTFC's program as an example of using direct psychosocial support along with extra help for foster parents and their use of behavioral contingencies. It has been extremely effective in improving hormonal (cortisol) levels in children, preparing for school success, and reducing foster care disruptions sharply (Fisher, Chamberlain, 2000; Tinienko, Fisher, Bruce, & Pears, 2010; Fisher, Kim, 2008; Fisher, Stoolmiller, 2008).

When I am working with the highest-risk children, I look at the supports of MDTFC, attempting to replicate many of them through existing community programs and my own efforts. Their model includes:

1.   12 hours of specialized instruction for foster parents that includes sensitivity to children, discipline, and home structure;
2.   24-hour phone access for foster parents;
3.   weekly parenting group meetings;
4.   daily telephone contact;
5.   weekly skills group for pre-K children for school readiness;
6.   transition help to a permanent home that is prepared to use the structure and sensitivity that parents have provided and skills that children have learned; and
7.   treatment with a child therapist whose focus is to improve functioning and prosocial skills in preschool or day care and home settings (Tinienko et al., 2010).

This model has had success with older children and teens as well, using treatment in foster care as an alternative to residential placement (Fisher & Gilliam, 2012).

In the MDTFC model, foster parents' cortisol levels were measured. They were strongly correlated to children's externalizing

behavior, as seems only logical. After caseworkers provided support for foster parents, they measured cortisol levels again, which
dropped. Interestingly, externalizing behaviors in children declined
as well, even though the parent support did not include children
(Fisher & Stoolmiller, 2008).

The two programs, ARC and MDTFC, demonstrate effective
use of two factors: including therapists as coregulating helpers for
parents, and targeting psychosocial factors to increase competency
and decrease stress. The authors of ARC explain:

> ARC is a strengths-based model, which emphasizes the
> importance of building or re-building safe relational sys-
> tems. In the context of that safe system, the model focuses
> on skill-building, stabilizing internal distress and enhancing
> regulatory capacity in order to provide children with gen-
> eralisable skills which enhance resilient outcomes. In many
> ways, the model of ARC mirrors the healthy development
> that takes place within the normative secure attachment sys-
> tem, in which the safe relationship provides the foundation
> for healthy outcomes. (Blaustein & Kinniburgh, 2007, p. 49)

These projects use cognitive-behavioral approaches in tandem
with relationship approaches out of the psychodynamic tradition.
Readers will note that they coexist in the case approaches in Part
II. I have found value in both, with benefits for my clients as I
use them in a strategic manner. This chapter has described some
important research-based interventions from both psychoanalytic
and cognitive-behavioral therapy, along with the salient features
of these approaches. When clients move into extreme hyperarousal
or hypoarousal, it can be beneficial to shift away from cognitive-
behavioral approaches to other therapeutic processes. Being able to
move between cognitive and psychodynamic approaches helps therapists to move with their clients' needs. I discuss when and how to
make this shift in the upcoming chapters.

Part II

Therapy Processes, Methods, and Techniques in Treating Attachment Issues

CHAPTER 3

Attachment-Promoting Methods,
Plans, and Techniques

This chapter discusses attachment-focused therapy: therapy approaches with applicable techniques, life narrative work that is attachment-enhancing, and treatment plans.

Combinations of Therapy Experiences

Daniel Stern (1995) used the metaphor of "port of entry" in describing how we approach changes with our clients. I like the flexibility inherent in his concept. What port is open and available? In therapy we can work to change

- the representational view our clients have of themselves, which may help them change the way that they relate to others;
- their representational view of each other;
- their way of relating within their dyadic relationship, which may change their representational view over time;
- their part in family dynamics.

In social contexts, we

- help our clients to develop relationships with people who will coregulate them, which, in turn makes our clients more emotionally accessible to their children;

- reduce stress on people, assisting with psychosocial stressors.

The most effective way to achieve change in almost all cases is through direct work between dyads or within families. As something positive and different happens in therapy, it requires parents and children to alter their representational views of themselves and each other.

Direct approaches when working on attachment are emotional, warm approaches. We also have cool approaches, including written information like pamphlets and websites, as well as psychoeducation about attachment.

Direct Therapy Experiences

Direct therapy experiences have a profound influence on both children's and parents' representational views of themselves and others. With the help of a therapist who assists with changes in body position, eye contact, comforting voice tones, regulation, emotional sensitivity, and emotional availability, people's experiences alter their patterns of connection. As direct methods change how people feel, they drop defenses. For example, when a parent uses a gentle voice, a child perceives himself as valuable and his parents as caring. An important aspect of the change occurs as therapists reflect on and notice changes. Mirroring by therapists helps clients to incorporate changes into their schemas of themselves and others (Fosha, Siegel, & Solomon, 2009).

In therapy this concept can be illustrated through the following example. I asked a father to lay a hand on his daughter's back as she struggled with tears. As she responded, leaning into him for comfort, I reflected quietly, "Ahhh. Good to know that he cares." Without getting chatty, I noted the degree of tenderness in her father, commenting in low, warm tones about the way that they related. In this way, I was able to enhance the caregiving within the session as well as help the father and daughter to retain the changes in their attachment schema as I reflected what I saw. In a later session, I mentioned their shared courage in his reaching out to care and her accepting care. I allowed their experience to be a true one, although I amplified the positive tone slightly, without making the tone so bright as to feel disingenuous. I shared their interaction without turning it into my moment My nonverbal expressions created an atmosphere that felt emotionally safer. My noting allowed the dyad to see themselves reflected in my mind. They allowed their mirrored relationship changes to become integrated into their self-other representations.

The attachment-producing experiences sought in session tend to center on

- expressing needs with the meeting of needs,
- autonomy/mastery that is met with connection and affirmation, and
- support from parents that helps with children's regulation and self-worth.

Healthy attachments connect people but also give space for individual perspectives of family members. So, while meeting dependency needs, there is a balancing value on respecting boundaries and differences. Dan Siegel referred to the concept of sovereignty of mind as a characteristic of healthy family relationships (Siegel & Hartzell, 2003). This respects a person's ability to make up his or her mind and to be unique. It addresses, "Can you love who I really am? Am I seen authentically?"

In the sessions, a theme of respect for people flows through our interactions. People are not using connections in a generic way. Instead there is encouragement of people's individuality while they are working in session. I look for opportunities for children to make choices in the order that we work on issues and the materials used. I encourage parents to find places where children have normal control.

Starting from the waiting room, clients often demonstrate where to approach the direct work. For example, a teen's elbow may jut into a parent who attempts contact; a parent may reach toward and then freeze before touching a child; a parent may distract herself as her child or teen describes frustration—or vice versa.

All these relational misses are opportunities for intervention. For example, an 11-year-old child was in my waiting room, angry and resisting physical contact with her parent. I started our session by inquiring about the meaning of her behavior. "Can you tell me why you put your elbow out to keep your mother away from you? I am not criticizing you. I'm not mad at you. I'm trying to understand."

She twisted her body away from her mother, and spit out, "She yelled at me the entire way to your office. Now she's trying to be nice. She never apologizes!" That opening led me to work on regulation and repair. I kept the mother regulated, with nonverbals as well as words. I helped her to script a response and then helped her to use the wording.

Her mother said, "I am sorry that I yelled at you and did not fix that. Please forgive me."

But the girl was angry from issues in the past. I responded by helping her mother not to react and to wait, indicating this with a reassuring nod and a hand gesture. I told the girl that I was curious, and cared enough to hear her thoughts and feelings. As she started to talk, I gave a verbal prompt so the mother did not talk over her daughter, following the prompt by a couple of suggestive deep breaths.

The girl said, "I start to trust her. We are really getting along, and then she goes off on me. I feel like I want to jump out of the car when she screeches at me. She treats me like a piece of garbage any time I make a mistake. She has to go through all of my failures, all the ways that I don't meet her expectations as a daughter. I don't trust her anymore. She always lets me down when I let her get close to me."

I nodded and added, "It sounds like you must feel so alone under all that anger and frustration."

"Sometimes I feel like giving up," she replied in a broken voice. The girl bowed her head and dripped tears onto her jeans, showing desolation and shame. After about 90 seconds, I said to the mother, "As you look at your daughter, are you able to see how lonely and sad she is? What does that make you feel like you want to do?" I wanted the mother to experience her daughter's pain, with an increase of empathy.

Her mother said, "I just want to hold her. I didn't know that she felt like that."

I said, "Are you able to tell your daughter that you feel sad that she is lonely?"

She leaned toward her daughter, saying, "I am sad that you feel so alone." I asked if the child would accept her mother's touch. When she did, her mother moved to sit next to her daughter, giving her a hug, then spontaneously said, "I'm sorry. I'm here to work on making things better. Do you forgive me?"

When the daughter accepted the repair, they sat together for a few minutes, as we talked back and forth about building connection and trust.

If we alter the example, there is a different process. The mother might find a point of contention, attempting to distance from despair. If she argues, I could say, "Does it feel better to argue than to connect with your daughter, feeling her loneliness?"

Or I could ask the mother what it is like to find herself unable to touch, comfort, or connect with her lonely and sad child. The mother might say, "I'm not sure that I can help her. I feel horrible and don't know what to do."

I could ask, "Will you allow me to help you help your daughter?"

If she assents, I could ask her to sit next to her daughter, taking her daughter's hand. During this time, I would reduce the mother's confusion with my nonverbals. I could point to a place to sit on the sofa and cue the mother with eye contact. As the mother responds, her daughter could feel her empathy and desire to care.

If the girl did not accept the apology, I might ask what would need to happen for her to accept repair. If children cannot generate choices, I make some suggestions. I expect some opportunistic choices, so, laughing a little, I could say, "Aside from tickets to a concert or a gift card . . . although that would be great, wouldn't it?" Then the girl, after some struggle, could try an option, assisted if needed. The girl might say, "She could watch a program with me instead of being on her phone all night." Or "She could stop yelling at me when I put my clean clothes in the laundry. Just tell me that I have to sort it out or wash it myself instead of making it such a big deal." Or "Don't threaten to make me move to my dad's house and away from my friends when we are having trouble."

As we make progress, the sessions allow the mother and daughter to experience better patterns, working on the ambivalence between them.

Observational Checklist for Attachment-Related Behaviors

Children and their parents routinely display their attachment pattern through their behaviors. Below I list common behaviors by attachment pattern (Gray, 2014). Because children or parents have attachment experiences with others, or because traumas or losses influence patterns, I constructed it to show instances when parents or children are displaying noncorresponding patterns. In direct work, these indicators provide a rich source for minute-to-minute changes within the session. Most of these behaviors can be seen during playtime or when eating a meal, and could be assessed in the therapist's office or in the home.

Secure/Autonomous Indicators

Secure Child
- ☐ Child clings to parent when uncertain.
- ☐ Child references parent's face for cues about the therapist and/or setting. She is reassured.
- ☐ Child follows parent around room with eyes, without being wary.
- ☐ Child smiles back at parent.
- ☐ Child initiates smile at parent.

☐ Child initiates or responds to little games, playful interactions with parent.

☐ Child prefers being within 3 feet of parent rather than alone, while getting used to the therapist or space.

☐ Child brings parent into proximity when playing.

☐ Child shows enhanced enjoyment when getting parent's attention.

☐ Child reaches toward parent, and then moves toward parent.

☐ Child anticipates that the parent will help when child is distressed or frustrated.

☐ Child references the parent with a look, anticipating parental involvement.

☐ Child looks to parent to share positive affects.

☐ Child leans against parent and relaxes.

☐ Child looks to parent when confused and then looks reassured.

☐ Child climbs onto parent's lap or allows their body to drape comfortably on the parent's body when needing a break from stimulation.

☐ At a misstep in play or a tough transition, parent attempts a repair. The child accepts the repair.

☐ Child protests and becomes mildly upset if the parent leaves room. Child calms quickly when parent comes back.

Secure Parent

☐ Parent calms the overexcited child with voice tones, distraction, or touch.

☐ Parent organizes the child's time just enough, providing structure in a calming voice.

☐ Parent touches child to guide, reassure, or connect.

☐ Parent uses gaze to share delight.

☐ Parent's talk allows for pauses that the child can fill.

☐ Parent allows the child to introduce items into the play—then follows lead.

☐ Parent matches or verbally notes the child's facial or body expressions.

☐ Parent interprets child's expressions, indicating awareness of the child's point of view.

☐ Parent distracts when child is frustrated.

☐ Parent prepares child for transitions.

☐ Parent's body and voice tones are responsive, steady, and empathetic, when child is dysregulated.

☐ At a misstep in play or during a transition, parent attempts a repair. The child does not accept it. The parent stays regulated.

☐ Parent guides child through transition, speaking to the child's feelings if the child is upset.

☐ Parent sets limits if play gets too unruly. Puts items away and introduces something else.

Insecure Attachment Indicators: Preoccupied Parent

☐ Parent talks over child.

☐ Parent talks more to the therapist than to the child during playtime.

☐ Parent begins to play and then talks about self.

☐ Parents makes statements like, "I don't know what you want. I don't know what to do."

☐ Parent references the child's facial expressions but does not sustain interest in them.

☐ Parent talks about self and own point of view during play or transitions without trying to include the child's point of view.

☐ Child looks at the parent for play cues but finds that the parent is thinking about something else.

☐ Parent conveys anxiety to child with nonverbal cues and facial expressions. Sees anxiety in child and amplifies the anxiety.

☐ Parent announces a transition with too much advance warning and conveys tension before and after the transition.

☐ Parent apologizes to the child for the structure rather than supporting structure.

☐ Child asks repeatedly for needs or items, needing repetitions to get parent's attention.

☐ Parent asks for reassurance from child. Example, "Am I doing this right?"

Insecure Attachment Indicators: Dismissive Parent

☐ Parent moves out of postures that allow child to nestle.

☐ Parent discontinues the play without signaling a transition.

☐ Parent spends a lot of time in silence.

☐ Parent complains about length of time spent playing with the child.

☐ Parent's face shows irritation when child asks for help.

☐ Parent sighs in resigned manner when child asks for help.

☐ Parent sits or stands so that child cannot easily scan facial expressions or have body contact.

☐ Parent argues with child over the play activity.

☐ Parent is impatient with child's anxiety when parent needs to leave the room and when returning to the room.

☐ Parent threatens the child rather than giving limits: "You do that and you'll be sorry."

☐ Parent makes negative comments about the therapist's interpretation of the quality of the parent's time with child.

☐ Parent does not share time or activity with child. Example: competes with child during playtime by building his or her own structure.

☐ Parent is critical or sarcastic with child.

☐ Parent shrugs when child ignores, excludes, or resists parental interaction.

Insecure Child: Anxious Resistant, Ambivalent

☐ Child looks at parent quickly, and then looks away, carrying some of parent's anxious expression.

☐ Child gets frustrated with a problem in play, but does not reach out to parent confidently. May say, "You probably won't help me with this." Complains after parent helps.

☐ Child clings to parent but does not settle or regulate better with body contact.

☐ Child climbs parent's body roughly, with parent wincing, and with no change in child's expression in relationship to parent's nonverbal cues.

☐ Child drums feet against parent when being held.

☐ Child asks for items but then abandons them.

☐ Child discontinues gaze with parent in order to better regulate herself.

☐ Child continues to signal distress long after a transition (whines, complains, bats at parent).

Insecure Child: Avoidant

☐ Child sits outside of social distance from parent throughout playtime.

☐ Child sits with back to parent.

☐ Child stiffens when touched by parent.

☐ Child gets frustrated with a problem in play but does not reach out to parent confidently. May say, "You won't help."

☐ Child grabs toys away from parent during play.

☐ Child leaves the toy when parent comes to join.

☐ Child looks at parent quickly, and then looks away.

☐ Parent does not hold child's attention, with child moving on before parent can respond.

☐ Child persists with negative behaviors that are not allowed until parent gets angry.

Disorganized/Disoriented or Unresolved Pattern: Parent

☐ Parent gives up on limits and begins to ignore behaviors. Examples: lets child use markers when sitting on floor when asked to move to table, or stand on sofa when parent requests that child sit, or go through therapist's briefcase when parent says no.

☐ Parent begins to use avoidance and helpless, beseeching manner with therapist.

☐ Parent comments positively about child's misbehavior.

☐ Parent becomes tearful and overwhelmed.

☐ Parent comments in defeated manner about failure in limit setting with the child.

☐ Parent makes negative attributions to the child in regard to limit setting. Example: "She does what she wants, just like my sister the drug addict."

☐ Parent asks the therapist for help in overall care of child.

☐ Parent describes psychologically painful losses or traumas during playtime with child.

☐ Parent does not reference the effect that above discussion has on child.

☐ Parent has the child take charge. Parent moves to play the part of the child rather than just allowing child to lead. Asks child for reassurance or support.

☐ Parent does not successfully move the child through transitions and abandons the goals. Examples: does not follow through on putting coat on, putting toys away, or doing tasks that will cause frustration.

☐ Parent describes therapist as cause of frustration. Example: "The therapist will get mad if we don't put her toys away."

☐ Parent describes child as, "Just like that. He was always that way." Does not have a theory of mind.

☐ Parent scares child. Child looks scared. Parent laughs.

☐ Parent does the same behavior as above, repeating the overwhelming interaction.

☐ Parent gets bored and describes playtime with child as onerous.

☐ Parent gets tense and angry if therapist will not watch child while parent takes a break.

☐ Parent repeatedly moves out of social distance from the child.

☐ Parent attempts to bring up adult subjects of interest—does not moderate content to suit a child. Asks child for permission to do so.

☐ Parent does the above and encourages the child's support.

☐ Parent makes negative attributions about the child.

☐ At a misstep in play, parent attempts a repair. The child does not accept the repair. Parent responds in a peer manner, "Be like that."

☐ Parent repeatedly overstimulates child, even positively.

☐ Parent uses stalking movements that frighten child.

☐ Parent uses too frightening a voice in play, notes that the child is frightened, but then does not self-correct.

☐ Parent brings up trauma themes in play.

☐ Parent dissociates during playtime.

☐ Parent lifts lips and shows teeth in play. Child is frightened. Parent laughs.

☐ Parent and child play babies. Parent is baby repeatedly.

☐ Parent asks the child to come close, and then moves further away.

☐ Parent does not attempt to attribute a meaning to child's fears.

Disorganized/Disoriented Child

☐ Child uses avoidance strategies (covering ears, shouting, etc.) if parent describes psychologically stressful life events.

☐ Child gets angry at parent as parent describes psychologically stressful life events. (Note whether child hits or throws things at parent.)

☐ Child comforts parent when parent describes psychologically stressful life events. Note how the child's comfort is reinforced by parent.

☐ Child asks for the parent and then lies on floor, face averted from parent or face down.

☐ Child watches parent warily.

☐ Child makes punitively controlling comments to parent.

☐ Child makes controlling comments to parent as in taking care of parent.

☐ Child warns therapist not to hurt or upset parent.

☐ Child freezes when parent comes close.

☐ Child becomes still-faced when parent holds or snuggles child.

☐ Child rubs parent's breasts or genitals. Parent laughs and responds with a sexualized connotation. Examples: "These belong to Daddy." "You are too young for that."

☐ Child covers genitals when parent comes close.

☐ Child covers face when parent comes close.

☐ Child wails and becomes disorganized when parent leaves room. Child is aggressive to parent when parent comes back.

☐ Child runs around room in a frenzied manner. Gets less organized when closest to parent.

☐ Child hits parent, throws things at parent, slams items on parent's hands. Child follows up with a look of triumph or panic.

☐ Child runs to parent, veers away, and then cries.

☐ Child appeals to therapist when needing help with aspects of play. Examples: attach toy parts together or take them apart, reach for something. Continues to do this even when directed back to parent.

☐ Child avoids parent gaze, looking at parent covertly. (This should be culturally interpreted for Asian or Native American families.)

☐ Child looks dazed, moves in slow motion.

☐ Child freezes when approaching parent.

☐ Child expresses anger in observation much more than typical of age.

☐ Child makes large motor movement to scatter parent away.

The value of using this type of checklist is that it provides both clarity and intervention targets. Most of the information is collected through observation, which provides the minute bits that can be used in minute-to-minute interventions.

When I use this checklist to mark behaviors, I will have a flurry of marks in one child or parent pattern, with very few marks in others. The observational checklist is especially helpful when children transition from one family to another through custody changes or foster care placement. It is easier to see what parents are doing versus what children are doing. Sometimes parents are working very hard to create security, but children are still relating in ways more adapted to their past parent figure. Or children might be in such grief from a move that they are closed to a new parent. This is explored in more depth in Chapter 4.

The information in the checklists above gives the practitioner many specific ways to physically intervene and provide new experiences. For example, the therapist could say, "Would you move one foot closer to your child as you play?" Or "Will you please sit further back in the sofa so that your child can sit on your lap?" This is a checklist that can help therapists with specific things to do in therapy sessions. It is an effective port of entry since it directly influences people's representational models.

Direct Work's Emphasis on Repair and Hope

Guiding families as they experiment with repair changes their attachment dance. They experience some hope and success instead of despair and disconnection. The focus is on minute-to-minute interventions, led by the therapist, causing them to change how they experience each other. We create new experiences of connection, improving theory of mind for parent and child alike, with warm support and feedback. The in-session parenting practice, along with in-the-moment feedback, changes children's and parents' perceptions of each other and themselves. In a particular session, alterations in the parenting pattern will occur at least 15 times and as often as 45–50 times. This frequency is similar to the results seen in the ABC model, with alterations in the dyadic relationship occurring about once per minute, with moment-to-moment feedback (Bernard et al., 2015).

It can be a struggle for some parents to think of events from their child or teen's point of view. I sometimes include an example from my life, from a client composite, or a movie. Examples have themes, or flows of emotions, similar to the ones that the parents and children are facing. The examples help people understand emotions or points of view, while sidestepping some of the parents' defensive systems. Therapist examples can be useful as examples of feeling and regulating shame. (When using personal examples, take care not to give unwarranted personal information, or to meet therapists' needs rather than clients'.)

The therapist's skills are employed to change the dyadic nonverbal communication. I can ask clients to sit closer to their children as they look at each other and describe what they feel when they see the expression on the other's face. I can guide discussions around dependency or autonomy, investigate attachment mishaps and associated feelings, and teach the power of repair. We can talk about how people show avoidance or anxiety and what causes those reactions. I can model and teach deeper breathing or notice the meaning of body postures and perhaps ask for changes in posture. This is a partial list, of course. I can also draw on healthy ways to decrease intensity—blowing bubbles with bubble gum, playing games, or telling jokes.

Direct Work and Executive Functioning

Direct experiential work has clear advantages when working with people with executive dysfunction. Executive dysfunction is prevalent in people who have had chronic stress and trauma (Anda & Brown, 2010). Children who have multiple placements in foster care show similarly high rates of executive dysfunction, particularly after prenatal exposure (Tinienko et al., 2010; Bledsoe, 2016; Lewis-Morrarty, et al., 2012). They tend to

- have reduced working memory—especially auditory working memory,
- focus on details rather than the big picture,
- have difficulty generalizing information from one situation to another,
- react impulsively, rather than inhibiting behaviors or comments,
- need help in categorizing or classifying related information unless the information is familiar or especially meaningful,
- have difficulty with effortful attention (Cox, 2008; Gray, 2012b).

If the therapist is working to provide verbal information in one session, and then asks for application in a dyadic situation a week later, then the odds of success are slim for people from high-stress backgrounds. Working in real time, with activation of emotions, helps the brain store the information and find it more efficiently in similar situations. If therapists can summarize sessions with clients, helping them to bridge to other contexts in which a learned approach can be used, therapists can assist clients in generalizing skills to new situations.

People with prenatal exposure to alcohol and drugs are overrepresented in having executive dysfunction. Many have difficulty moving information across brain networks from one sensory modality to another. Most therapists assume clients have brain networks that integrate one sense with another, such as hearing (auditory) and actions (motor skills), or visual and motor. If therapists want people to do something (motor skill), then practicing within that motor area is quite useful. Role-plays and visuals tend to be the best methods for working with people who have been prenatally exposed to substances.

Auditory memory is often compromised by exposure to high stress during development. One particular example stands out. I had a child and mother who escalated into violence over food. Eating together is an attachment-related activity, so it was a potent issue. The boy had food scarcity issues, the mother heavy control needs with food. As we verbally summarized their plan for the week, they left with the direction to sidestep any food-related issues. A crisis team called me within 90 minutes after they left my office. The parent had called the team in due to escalation over food. The parent told me that she only remembered about the food directive after the fight. Both parent and son were impacted by poor auditory memory, although they were willing conversationalists. The next session, I learned from experience. I drew their visual plan with a few words and three pictures. It included one idea each for de-escalation and a compromise food choice if they had conflict. Their plan was taped on the refrigerator. Attachment improved and food symptoms decreased.

Working with direct experiences and accommodations can avoid impediments to success for clients whose brains have been shaped by adverse experiences. Visual forms of information are provided. Certainly therapists can speak, but I recommend shorter sentences and slower speech speed until the subject matter is well understood by clients. I also recommend asking clients how much they understand of what I say. I can show amounts, stretching my hands to indicate all of it, almost all, some of it, or a little. I ask, "What is the part that you got?" That way, I don't start from the beginning, boring them and losing them again.

After clients integrate the subject matter better, and find it meaningful, then it is common to move into a more verbal mode. By that time, clients are better able to access the information during stressful times.

This means that when working with children and teens, I am often drawing or making short lists that they can refer to. Many of my clients surpass my artistic talents. They help me out as we sit side by side working on an oversized art pad together. I have an easel if we need more physical space between us. I can work with a pillow between us and a small table in front of us when children need more space. Just helping children to think of options for their comfort helps them to downregulate. Because of auditory memory weakness, I might point to one hand's palm and say, "You could sit on the therapy ball," or, pointing to the other palm, "We could use a pillow." Then they point. I might have to state that I really don't have a preference before they choose. Then I say, "I like how you know what's best for you. I want you to feel," (here I exhale) "comfortable."

I often use small, self-laminating sheets from the dollar store, creating prompts that children and teens take with them. They range from a picture of a child with a parent with a prompt saying, "Breathe out. Your mom and dad love you. You are safe," to two pictures of a child using a relaxation/de-escalation skill like a seat push-up at school or a shoulder roll. We sketch these quickly, with kids taking over the drawing much of the time.

Life Narrative Work

Narrative work helps people to create a life story, integrating their thoughts and emotions around attachment. It allows for different responses in improved circumstances. Therapy creates an affirming narrative, including clients' right to expect sensitive and timely care, normal reactions of shame and anger at not receiving it, and their view of themselves as worthy of love and care. It includes an understanding of why parents acted as they did.

During intake sessions with clients, I describe the need for direct work, but also the need to understand what will work in the present versus the past. The goal is to help clients access a life narrative that integrates thoughts and feelings in a way that makes sense for them. When responding to emotion-evoking daily events, people quickly access their life story line, responding out of that narrative. This rapid referencing typically occurs on an implicit level. Lessons from the Adult Attachment Interview show that slow-motion responses, confusion, or areas of incoherence occur when there are unresolved issues in our lives. It is helpful to explore the attachment experiences of people as carefully as trauma and loss experiences. One of the achievements of the Adult Attachment Interview is capturing some of these unconscious responses and the consistencies or inconsistencies in what people say they believe about attachment relationships (Hesse, 2016).

When people are asked to change, trying behaviors and beliefs indicative of secure patterns of attachment, they do best if they recognize why something happened and what's different now. It is frightening at worst, and unsettling at best, to be asked to change attachment patterns when there is possible exposure to rejection, or even trauma. Thinking about what's different now allows people to recognize changes in circumstances.

Simply drawing a time line for people helps them to see what made sense in one situation, and what might be more adaptive and satisfying now. I suggest using faces with expressions on the time line so that people connect to the emotions of that earlier time in their lives. (If adults are competent in maintaining a mental time line, omit the paper and pencil and use a more typical linguistic mode.)

The life narrative work is typically integrated into an overall treatment plan. Using a visual time line, with pictures of children or people at various stages of life, is effective as a discussion or memory aid for clients. I can briefly sketch these, or pictures can also be brought in. These can be simple, as saying, "When you were a baby, your mother was clinically depressed," with a picture of a baby in a crib and a mother looking away. "What would a baby learn from that?" The therapist could write the word, "depressed" by the picture of the mother. She would write the child's response. For example, "Her mother won't come." Or, "I am left alone." What makes sense for a baby to expect?" Other major experiences can be put on the time line, along with the reality of their current situations.

The narrative approach can move from more visual to verbal after people have integrated information. Verbal may be helpful in slowing down the pacing and emotional arousal in the session. Pictures or the use of role-play tend to heighten emotion, eliciting more attachment-relevant material. Attachment is a hot system, meaning that the processing of attachment schemas must include emotional activation. Schemas around attachment are best elicited through sensory approaches and right-brain-led nonverbals. Visuals tend to be right brain and emotion evoking.

Shame can be debilitating in attachment narratives. People may behave defensively when shame is evoked in an attachment context. The messages that infiltrate a person's core are on the order of, "I was not worth loving. I don't know how to care." Or, "I feel overwhelming shame about myself."

During this work, often children or teens who had poor early care need to be coached to recognize that things are different now. They can reach out for connection with a different outcome than before. They do not have to stay frozen within emotional frames. A teen who had been neglected in an orphanage for the first 15 months of her life said, "I feel this awful *whoosh* in my chest and gut. I am alone. No one cares. It's awful. I have that feeling some of the time every day. I now have a plan to reach out, even though I still have the urge to hide in my room. I see that time line and fast forward to the present." The fast forward was a technique that I used in which I gave her an imaginary remote, leaving the orphanage and forwarding to each birthday party from age 3 to the present (Gray, 2012b)

Using simple time lines helps people to understand that they actually did the best that they could in earlier situations. They adjusted to fit their circumstances. It is important to emphasize that things have changed, and that they have the support and opportunity to change, grow, and risk being happier. While I am working with time lines, my voice tone of acceptance, gaze with warmth, and intonations of inclusion help with regulation. As Allan Schore points out in his book *The Science and Art of Psychotherapy,*

> There is now agreement that verbal, conscious, rational, and serial information processing takes place in the left hemisphere, whereas nonverbal, unconscious, holistic, and subjective emotional information processing takes place in the right . . . Much of the therapist's knowledge that accumulates with clinical experience is implicit, operates at rapid, unconscious levels beneath levels of awareness, and is spontaneously expressed as clinical intuition. On the other side of the right brain–to–right brain communications within the therapeutic alliance, I see the change mechanism of long-term psychotherapy as being located primarily in the connections between the patient's prefrontal, cortical and subcortical areas of the right brain (2012, p. 7).

As therapists are working on the left-brain narrative, they are also assisting this fluid, empathic development associated with the right brain. Therapists describe a felt sense of having our minds and bodies well integrated as we reach out and connect with clients. When working with children, therapists can turn to parents, inviting them to participate in this flow of information and meaning.

Narratives that include photos or pictures help people to understand their limited options when attachment-related events happened in childhood. Often clients retain their preschool-level grandiose sense of their early selves. At those ages it is developmentally normal to believe that are central or causative to events. When looking at a photo of themselves at early ages, clients have a reality check. They were so young and so obviously not in charge of events. The photos may elicit a desire for them to care for their earlier selves. Clients may say things like, "I was just a stupid little kid," describing their self-contempt at their helplessness. A parent in the room will often remark compassionately about the young child's vulnerability. If parents' compassionate feelings do not emerge, I add my compassion to the session, helping children to develop self-empathy with parents seeing empathy modeled. A follow-up later with a parent often includes stories of when their parents lacked empathy.

Narrative work can be done in a simplistic manner for children as young as 3. One of the advantages of narrative work with young children is in reducing their shame-based beliefs and defenses as early as possible. When children have parents in the room during this work with the therapist, the parents can be guided to respond to children's signals. As children hide their faces or start to spin around the room, I can intervene by pointing out the children's overwhelmed stress systems, guiding parents to soothe and comfort children. Parents become aware of the stress patterns in their children. They move beyond a concern with behavior problems to become more psychologically minded. Parents' own schemas around care and shame may be activated, with the parents accessing their own narratives and becoming empathetic to children's despair and shame, as I am empathic to parents' narratives.

Adults who understand their narratives, and those of their family members, can create mental maps of where they or others are vulnerable, thus creating strategies for support when these issues are likely to come up. For example, a parent knew that starting school might cause fear in her child, who was moved into foster care from her day care center. She made a plan with me. Before the start of school, the child met with the kindergarten teacher, who was playful and reassuring. A photo was taken with this nurturing teacher. She referred to this picture at home, remembering that the teacher liked her, which calmed her. Special permission was given to this girl to call home if she needed to check in with her mother. She carried a pocket-sized laminated picture of herself with her mother, which was kept in her backpack.

In working on highly charged areas, therapists keep track of the stress tolerance of clients, taking responsibility for not overwhelming people. Parents may bring up more than a child can handle in the sessions. Or they might try to prevent certain themes from emerging. While it is important to include parents in attachment-focused therapy, therapists carry the responsibility for pacing.

In narrative work, it can be obvious that adults need some extra help before they are able to hear children's stories with empathy. Therapists cannot promote the concept of security when family members feel unsafe. Sometimes defensive patterns are well warranted in the here and now. When teens have attachment figures who are unsafe, their narratives include the reality of the grief of living without attachment security, ways to maintain a state of mind that values security in attachment, while finding role models for attachment within community and therapy settings.

Treatment for Attachment, Traumas, and Loss

Secure attachments improve people's capacities in trauma therapy and when processing losses, especially traumatic losses. Problematically, losses and trauma tend to compromise attachment security. Children who are moved between attachment figures after trauma and loss have trouble forming new attachments (Gray, 2012a, 2012b). Because neurobiological systems are just developing, children are especially vulnerable to the corrosive effects of trauma and traumatic loss on their attachments, even without moves between attachment figures (Cook, Blaustein, Spinazzola, & van der Kolk, 2005).

People who have unprocessed trauma tend to form disorganized or disoriented attachment patterns, as evidenced by multiple researchers. Mental imagery and physical reactions due to trauma reprocessing interrupt day-to-day connection. The degree of discontinuity depends on the extent of the impact of the trauma on the person. Parents with trauma backgrounds are often motived to get help for their traumas as they become parents, since they see the effect on their children.

Relational trauma, trauma within intimate relationships, is especially deleterious to attachment formation. When people have been in situations in which they have been abused or threatened by attachment figures, they have a competing desire for proximity and distance. Neither works. This causes tremendous stress on body systems. There are surges into hyperarousal or decelerations into hypoarousal. Clients are prone to panic or dissociation. Whether working with adults or children with early relational trauma, therapists will be particularly attentive as they help these clients coregulate and use regulation skills.

Promoting attachments in traumatized people includes the therapist's working expertise in attachment, loss, and trauma. This book's focus is attachment. But the treatment of attachment issues, trauma, and loss is intertwined.

Intake assessments should include an understanding of traumas that people have experienced and the day-to-day impact of those traumas. For that reason, I typically meet with parents first, without their children. If a traumatized parent is seeking immediate attachment-specific work for themselves, I refer the parent to another therapist for trauma work after explaining the connection between attachment and trauma. In collaboration with the parent's therapist, I will provide some trauma help within the context of our attachment work. If a parent's situation does not dictate attachment work first, then I may begin therapy with the parent, working on trauma and regulation. We will include attachment work with children as soon as possible. If the child is a toddler or infant, there is an immediate need to work on attachment due to the child's age. In those cases, I refer the parent for trauma work simultaneous to attachment work.

Ordering Treatment Tasks of Attachment, Trauma, and Loss

When doing treatment planning for families whose children have attachment issues, trauma, and loss, the treatment plan begins with family stabilization and specific work on attachment (Figure 3.1). Then, using attachment as a resource, the therapist can move into

Tasks and Their Order over Course of Therapy

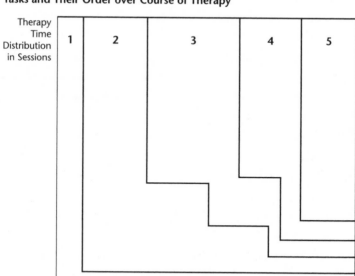

Figure 1. Order of Tasks over Course of Therapy
1. Parent Stabilization/Psychoeducation
2. Attachment
3. Trauma
4. Loss
5. Child's social skills, engagement in peer activities and daily life

Figure 3.1 Tasks and their order over the course of therapy

trauma or loss work. The treatment plan includes specific treatment for children's trauma. Otherwise, the effects of trauma or traumatic loss will continue their negative influence on overall development.

Both attachment and trauma work require emotional resources. The first tasks in therapy are focused on creating more capacity and decreasing overall stress. We look at ways to create a healing milieu for families. I like to spend time with parents to determine what stressors can be reduced without further upsetting the family system. This is a collaborative effort; the therapist does not take charge, telling the family what to do. Instead, after discussing the need for time and energy to do attachment and trauma work, I ask parents what they can drop or add. Often a realistic appraisal shows that the family is carrying too many burdens. Our early sessions may show that parents do not reach out to supportive people for help. When people have had a childhood with role reversals, they may be reluctant to ask for help during difficult times. Depressed parents tend to underuse the caring people in their lives. First sessions may be spent identifying strategies for improving the functioning of support systems or else creating supports.

During intake, I will need a developmental profile of children, with a life story from parents. I ask parents to send me developmental information: milestones, illnesses, overall health, assessments, medication, prior psychotherapy, and child welfare records. I also ask parents to write me a page or two describing the problems that they are having, what they have tried that seems to work, and what does not seem to work at all. If parents arrive without this, I will ask them verbally. In the first one or two sessions, I discuss a treatment approach with parents, coming up with an approach that makes sense to adults. That gives parents a big-picture way of understanding the overlapping issues of attachment, trauma, and loss, as well as how specific activities fit into an overall plan. With a consensus on treatment approach, I am able to bring children into a therapy session with a working alliance with their parents.

When children come in for their sessions, I develop a visual treatment plan for them (see Chapter 4). People who are struggling with attachment and trauma issues tend to like the predictability of a treatment plan. The plan needs to be simple. Within the initial sessions with parents and children I teach some relaxation techniques and identify calming and play activities suitable for the family.

Mourning and unresolved losses interfere with attachment. Especially when the loss is a traumatic one, the energy necessary to mourn the loss detracts from the energy needed to form attachments. When a parent and child have suffered a loss together, intake sessions will include ways to help bereaved adults to focus on their children's needs.

Children who have losses will need emotional connection with a known adult to complete grieving. Work with bereaved children includes building better connections with adults. When they can receive emotional support through these attachments, they are then able to process grief. Children do not have emotional resilience to work through the grief process alone. They are sustained during mourning through the relationship with a caring adult who knows them (Gray, 2012b; Pynoos, 1997). Attachment will provide caring parents, allowing children to mourn or complete their work on traumatic loss, or grief and loss together. Their ability to attach more securely, and with greater reciprocity, increases after their grief and trauma work have been completed.

The interplay between trauma, grief, and attachment is described to adults in families during the intake process. If families have a sense of the order of the tasks of therapy, it is easier for them to find hope, knowing that they are following a strategically laid plan. Anytime there is trauma or loss within a family, the presence of structure and planning provides valued predictability. They cannot afford more risks. As a type of secure attachment figure, the therapist is sensitive, capable, and predictable.

Attachment Capacity and Reciprocity After Trauma and Loss

Trauma and traumatic or complicated losses diminish the ability to connect in a reciprocal way to others. When individuals are coming in for help with trauma and attachment, as shown in Figure 3.1, the treatment plan typically starts with attachment, followed by work on trauma and loss, and then an emphasis again on healthy attachments, peer relationships, and areas of mastery. Children under 6 years of age may switch the tasks of loss and trauma, working with loss first and trauma second (Gray, 2012b).

People tend to be self-absorbed when processing trauma and loss. The reciprocity that is part of healthy attachments will be missing until trauma and loss are processed. Children and teens who are shown empathy during trauma and loss work become more empathic. While the therapist always works to keep people connected, it is only after the completion of some trauma and loss work that attachment flourishes. The treatment plan reflects this phased approach. Earlier therapy sessions will be about building capacity through connection and stress reduction skills. The next sessions will focus on trauma and loss, with final sessions focused on mastery and social relationships that include reciprocity.

Creating Experiences Within Therapy Sessions

Our clients' attachment and trauma schemas include explicit and implicit belief and memory systems. In order to access the implicit information, we create real-time attachment experiences, evoking clients' memories and schemas. Change often begins intuitively, led by either therapists or clients.

Some schemas brought into the therapy room are overt—for example, a person choosing to sit outside of social space of 6 feet, or a preschooler sitting with his back to his parents. Some are more subtle—a flat disconnect between children and parents, or angry expressions quickly covered up.

There is a balance between having sessions that are predictable and structured enough and those that take advantage of opportunities to work in the present moment. Therapists have the chance to work in improvisation. By noting the intersubjective flow of emotions in the room, therapists are able to intervene by asking for something different. We cocreate with our clients a change, often pleasant and novel, in their connection. Clients can also create a change in the minute-to-minute flow of information and emotions in the room. The changes become incorporated into our clients' schemas of how they view the world and relate to each other.

Our clients can enter therapy assenting to the value of closeness, physical touch, sensitive listening, and eye contact. Yet, in the moment, the unconscious beliefs about attachment belie their statements, as evidenced by body-based resistance. For this reason, the need for experiential work that incorporates mind and body is essential. This means that therapists may redirect clients. For example, a parent may want to reach out and comfort her child, but freezes as she reaches out. Therapists can feel the interruption of intent through their own senses. Our work within sessions is a melding of our knowledge of what we are seeing, our bodily senses, and our right-brain intuition. The work is in real time and feels like improvisation much of the time. It has the freshness of real time and the clarity of being fully present.

Therapists' Coaching of Physical Movement Within the Session

To signal availability to clients, I like to position my seat so that the distance from my face to my clients' will be less than 6 feet, but not closer than 3 feet, unless we are going to work on something special. For example, we move closer to draw together. (My seat is on casters so it can slide forward and back.)

Treatment goals for parents and children include increasing attributes of security in attachment: comfort, connection, attunement, repair, and playfulness. Therapists lead the movement toward these goals by suggesting physical closeness in the sessions, by preferential attention to topics that have potential to enhance attachment, though non-verbals that calm clients, through an attitude of playfulness and curiosity, and by modelling phrases or scripts that promote attunement and repair. Rather than relying primarily on talk therapy, I have found it helpful to use nonverbals in therapy. Going through physical senses, or through body work, creates powerful changes in interaction patterns. We then then reflect on the changing narrative of our clients. (Clients who have strong reflective capacities may help lead this activity.)

We therapists need to create experiences within a window of client tolerance. It is our responsibility to enter the room with enough capacity to regulate the affect in the room. Therapists should have a hopeful and curious energetic quality, as well. Reading this may cause guilt in some therapists. We all falter in regulation, hope, and curiosity in some sessions. But if there is slippage between our expectations and functioning, we have the chance to try something different or get help for ourselves. We may need to increase self-care, join a consultation group, or obtain therapy for ourselves. Or we may want to introduce some new props or activities that change our clients' patterns within the therapy room.

Sensory-Based Attachment Techniques

What type of touch feels good? Often therapists skip past that information. We normalize that basic knowledge, assuming that people and their families know the answer. This is a great investigation to make in therapy when working on attachment between parents and children. Coming up with a repertoire of preferred touches might involve finding out what feels best: light or firmer hand on the forearm, an arm around a shoulder, a circular stroking on the back, a firm hug or a light one. This is best done in a therapy office for people who might feel overwhelmed. That way, the therapist can help people to find their voice and keep them regulated if it starts to feel like too much, too scary, or "too close to you so that's enough for today!"

Touches or movements that are especially comforting for parents and children:

- Hand-holding—especially if the attachment figure uses their thumb to stroke the inside of the child's palm, which is called the well of the hand.
- Hair or head stroking—this is individualistic depending on hairstyles. Most children enjoy this if they are not using hair products that hold hair in a particular style.
- Foot rubbing, with parents massaging the bottom of the foot in the arch.
- Soothing by standing behind a child with arms around the child, face close to the neck, voice saying something soft or nice in a rhythmic tone. With permission, therapists can practice this with a parent, standing behind and modeling it. As parents try it

with their child, if the child is willing, I like to stand in front of the dyad, helping the embraced child to feel safe and regulated by modeling a relaxed body posture and eye contact. Rhythmic tones are hypothesized to be effective in calming lower neural networks originating in the brain stem, cerebellum, and diencephalon, helping more dysregulated people to become accessible for attachment and connection (Porges, 2009; Perry, 2006).

- Rocking together and swings. Rocking times help to connect people. The rhythm of nature is the rhythm of the womb—and comfortable rocking speed. People who sit on a rocking chair with a child, or rock in their chairs while sitting within social distance (about 6 feet), or sit together on a porch swing, are all getting in sync. Children who are swung on a swing can have their parents stand in front of them, catching their feet and singing made-up lyrics like, "You swing away from me and you come back to me" (Gray, 2012a). The rhythmic movement is especially helpful when people have endured trauma in the context of attachment. It helps to keep them regulated while enjoying closeness.
- Rubbing or lightly scratching a child's upper back between the shoulder blades.
- Stroking the cheeks or temples of a child who needs to be calmed. Young children can lie with their heads in their parents' laps, with the parent stroking their children's faces.

Physical movement that causes high excitement is an especially fun way to build attachment. To stimulate attachment, I suggest to parents that they take their children swimming. The skin-to-skin contact is a great cue for attachment. Fun happens when parents play in the pool. Kids dive out of their parents' arms, play with pool noodles, or ride piggyback in the water.

Activities of movement and excitement are favorites for attachment. For example, parents can hold younger children aloft, playing airplane. Children are zoomed faster and slower through the air, land in a particular city or jungle, and take off when there is danger. The children need to be a portable size, of course. They can call out some of the instructions, asking to move faster or slower. Other high-excitement games are horsey rides, with parents being the horse, and hide-and-seek. I look for activities that pair parents with fun while inducing positive physical contact. Sometimes we go outside during the sessions, trying out some of these activities. My presence, as a coregulating therapist, helps to make these games more successful, so children are less likely to move into hyperarousal. On the other end of the continuum, hypoaroused children may use pushing-away motions, clearing the air with their arms, as parents attempt to play. Parents feel rejected. I can help children get a drink, walk a little, and move into regulation. Then we play. I talk to parents about this being a brain-based issue, not a rejection of them.

Eating Together

Mealtimes are ideal for attachment formation. Attachment is enhanced with a languid pace, with time for dawdling and conversation. People seated across from each other are more available for eye contact. Reaching over to touch is easiest if one person is seated at the table head and another on the side. Parents can select seat placements according to children's needs. Mealtimes are to be times of shared enjoyment. Children's manners can be taught and reinforced at select meals. In general, mealtime is too valuable in attachment formation to be spent on table manners or a review of chores.

Because of the intimacy of mealtimes, people may quibble, argue, provoke, or dictate in order to maintain a pattern of emotional distance. When there is a sense of flow, joy, and connection, their alarm bells go off, warning them that loss or pain are inevitable after the good times. This is a great topic for therapy. What would happen if the good times were not interrupted? I like to prime people for success with their idea of an ideal meal enjoyed, followed by people separating to do the next thing without an argument. I ask how family members would feel. Or would they allow themselves to have such a pleasant and normal experience? If not, what is the underlying shame or fear that holds them back? Is it a memory of someone lost that prevents this experience? Practicing attachment-oriented activities is a great way to get into the actual state of mind toward attachment, rather than chasing symptomatic behaviors.

At times I ask clients to bring food to the session and share it, so we can enhance positives: commenting on taste, referencing family members' facial expressions, and commenting on selecting foods to enjoy together. I also bring simple food on occasion, modeling these qualities. People who are authoritarian or provocatively distancing tend to bring out these behaviors during therapy sessions with food. I tend to notice this, commenting, "Is this how it goes at your home during mealtimes?"

The answer can be "yes" or "I guess so," with nonverbal gestures or movement. I will respond, "Do you know that lots of people enjoy their time at meals? Do you ever feel like it isn't fair? Or that you are missing out?" (Children are alert to the phrase, "not fair.") After a pause for processing, I ask a parent or child if they want to change things, getting closer, or keep mealtimes the same, maintaining distance. I like to accompany the conversation with nonverbals. I use my hand to show distance, with two fists bumping into each other for the arguing behaviors, two hands very far apart for the provocative or avoidant behaviors.

I may or may not ask children or teens if they want to change. Sometimes they need time to process. Later in the session I ask them if they want something better in their lives. I might put it in terms of their narrative: "It seemed that you learned in one situation that you had to keep some space so that others did not hurt you. You could just keep that space" (hands wide to indicate distance) "or you could try enjoying a meal with smiles and good food with parents who love you" (hands together with fingers intertwined). "It's up to you."

Children may say with their fingers intertwined, "Which one is that?"

"Enjoying food with people who love you," I reply.

"I want that," they might say. Then we make a plan. Or we might try a snack in the office.

Because food is so tied to attachment, I keep a covered candy bowl in my room. Adults enjoy it as well as children. Children can choose one piece of candy anytime in the session, or two pieces at the end. (The reward for delayed gratification is an example to parents of building executive functioning.) I also give children juice or hot chocolate when they arrive and provide a beverage for parents.

When children or adults have had neglecting or dismissive attachment figures, I will ask about their favorite candy, occasionally including it in the bowl. I also have food available for people who arrive at therapy hungry—especially teens. This is simple: yogurt, raisins, apples, or snack bars. A client was running late and texted me to let me know. As she and her son arrived, I had her favorite tea and his juice ready. She commented, "Deborah takes care of us. It's nice, isn't it?" He nodded and grinned. This is an easy entrance to the attachment work in the session.

Changes in Client's Body Positions

I like to note and change body positions as part of the therapeutic work. I might ask for a child to sit beside the parent, or ask why a child has moved further away. Or I wonder aloud if it would feel good to place a parent's hand on top of the child's hand, or what it means if a child shrinks further back. And if the shrinking back is involuntary, would a child want to try it again after some reassurance? All of these actions follow therapists' appraisals of what clients' bodies are telling them. Therapists' in-the-moment timing tends to follow their own body-based reactions, determining what might feel comforting or provide closeness.

Therapists can model body positions with their clients. Of course, this is more appropriate for younger children. For example, Jerome, age 6, who spent his first two and a half years in many relative placements, was listening to his mother describe a 5-day trip away from him. Jerome inverted his body in my office chair, with his rear end out, bumping his head against the seat back. He was becoming increasingly dysregulated. Rather than telling him to settle down or stop it, his mother pulled him closer, touched his back, and then gently moved the chair from side to side in a steady rhythm. I complimented her technique as Jerome began to calm a little. However, I asked Jerome if I could show his mother an additional way to help.

"It's going to feel a little weird, since I'm not your mom, but I can show her and then she can do it," I said. I put Jerome on my lap, which he assented to, then turned and cradled him against me with his shoulder and knees getting gentle pressure. He sighed and relaxed. I passed him to his mother, who instead held him facing out, with his legs extended. She was tender, but cool in approach. I asked if we could try a more intimate cuddle, with more sensory feedback. She allowed me to arrange him against her in a cradled position. He calmed, exhaled, and closed his eyes a little, and then opened them as we talked. His mother noticed that the increased sensory feedback helped him to truly calm. I asked Jerome how he felt. "Love and good," he said.

We discussed how to show this posture to an aunt who would be caring for Jerome. He and his mom said that they would use that cradled relaxing time when he needed it, not just for the trip but at other times. Jerome's body was expressing the need for sensory feedback that increased attachment security. Rather than worry about reinforcing a behavior, the inverted posture on the chair, his mother met his need for connection and sensory feedback.

As we worked directly, Jerome and his mother experienced each other as successful in reducing distress and increasing positive affect, which changed their representational view of each other, enhancing the security of their attachment. We chose a bottom-up approach, moving from a body-based intervention to a cognitive discussion. The cognitive approach was not available to Jerome until he experienced comfort and closeness in real time. The beauty of the approach is that Jerome has motor memory of these events and will be more apt to seek out his mother's help in the future. Direct successes are easier for the brain to recall in similar situations. Over the next few sessions his mother said that, when distressed, Jerome began to look at her archly as if to say, "Why aren't you cuddling me?" His mom, and then dad and aunt, would scoop him up. Over time, he could simply look at his important family members, beginning to calm before the intervention. He was beginning to internalize regulation patterns and positive associations with parents and regulation. I describe this to parents as their child needing to "get Mom or Dad in the head and heart."

Drawing Time Lines for Narrative Work

A visual time line is an effective way to help with narratives. I use an artist's pad with cardboard backing. I draw a horizontal line across a sheet of paper. On the top side of the time line I draw or obtain pictures of the client as a baby, then toddler, child, or teen. Then I put words or images for care or loss experiences on the lower side of the line. Usually I draw faces and simple expressions. Then, at the bottom of the pages, I note clients' feelings or conclusions about attachment. The therapy discussion questions are simple ones that allow children or teens to decide what expressions to put on the faces of people on the lower half, or statements about how those experiences influenced them. For example, "What did the baby learn about whether parents will protect you or stay with you?" On one side of the line is a baby alone, with a sad face. Above the line is an irritated parent, or a parent leaving, and the client's belief, "I wanted too much from my mom."

Other questions for the time line could include, "When the parents separated and divorced, who helped you with your sad feelings?" Parents are on one side of the line, angry, and the child is on the other side with his or her thoughts and feelings. Or "What was it like for you when your parents were at the hospital, hardly home, and then so sad when your sister died?" Or "when you were abused, and when your sister told you not to tell anyone, what do you think that you learned about your parents?" Children can draw thought bubbles or I can draw them. Children might draw two or three expressive faces.

This time line can move from using the pronoun "you," for increased intensity, to "the younger child you were, a long time ago," when pacing and intensity need to slow. I also make comments about how vulnerable the client was as a young child, needing care. Parents in the room tend to react to the time lines with compassion and an increased desire to comfort.

The time line makes it easier for children to see their actions as having made sense in the past. They made the best choice possible. But the choice is not adaptive now. I might say, ""Well, you can keep acting like your parents are going to tell you "goodbye.' That did happen when you moved four times in foster care. But that part of your life is over. It seems that you suffered enough. Maybe you could risk having a happier life—getting as much love as other kids." If children agree, we plan an activity with parents. It could be sitting in a rocking chair while reading books, having a cuddle time every morning, or time to play soccer in the park with a parent.

Role-Plays in Session

I often use role-plays within family sessions. They help people assemble new attachment schemas, as well as play out themes of danger and comfort. In role-play, people's actual physical reactions emerge. An example would be a scenario that reviews a time when a parent let people into the home to do drug deals, with violence occurring. The child has continued to mistrust adults even though his living situation has changed. The child remembers the terrifying nights, loud arguing, threats, and occasional police arrests. In session, we set up the role-play, describing what will happen, and then give the child a signal that will stop the action at any time. We rehearse the stop sign a couple of times to be sure that the child has control over the events, and then begin. The role-play begins with my knock at the door. I hold up a piece of paper over my face on which we have drawn a face with a tough, negative expression. (If it is frightening to children for me to change to acting out a scary person, I can also use a big puppet with the expression taped on the puppet's face.) The parent in the session decides whether or not to open the door. "What is the child thinking?" I say, putting the paper down for a moment.

The child says some variation of these: "Please don't open the door. I'm afraid that person will yell or hurt me and mom. I'm scared." The parent can help supply the feelings and thoughts if children cannot produce language. The parent refuses to open the door. The parent says, "My job is to keep the family safe. I won't open the door." The child feels safe and relieved, showing a little smile or even cheering. The child might cling to the parent, showing relief.

Role-plays must be done with care so that therapists do not overwhelm clients or become associated with negativity. Children like these role-plays. First of all, they are lively and fun. But second, they are a way to demonstrate moving from fear to security. Often, previously unexpressed traumatic material emerges in these role-plays. For example, within the role-play a child might call out a warning: "Don't open the door. He has that knife!" It is powerful to have parents provide protection, even if they were the ones who did not previously protect.

Role-plays can be helpful when working with defensive, dismissing parents. For example, a busy woman cut off her son's description of distress, asserting, "I know that you were at the neighbor's house for almost a year. But stop and think of *me*. I was working 17-hour days. That's what it takes when you are doing a start-up."

Her son escalated, "It's always about *you*! When I talk about *me*, it turns to *you*." I established eye contact with the parent. Then, with gentle voice tones I asked if she could hear her son's feelings about his school problems, his embarrassment that he was again at the neighbors,' and his fear when alone at home during a snowstorm. He was not trying to attack her by sharing his experience. But his mother's dismissiveness increased when he tried to express himself. Responding with his part of the distance dance, he said, "Now she wants to ski together. Where was she when I needed her? Is she going to do it all over again? I'll start to get comfortable, and then, she goes to work."

Helping dismissive parents to hear pain is a necessary part of rebuilding connection and a narrative. I used a role-play with the mother playing the part of the child and asking for attention. I played the dismissive part with gestures. I asked the mother to play the part of a child, showing me pictures from her soccer game and showing me her trophy. While she did, I played out a parent who was looking at the phone, distracted, saying, "Just a minute," while using artificially bright facial expressions.

The mother said dejectedly, "You just played out my mother. This is worse than irony. I am my mother." The mother received support and compassion from me, and then was able to hear her son's loneliness. She said to her son, "I was passing on to you what I learned as a kid. It's not an excuse, I know. I'm ready to listen now." As was the case in this example, therapists can elicit memories of dismissing parents who were self-involved, busy, and insensitive. Since dismissing parents tend to be defended, this type of role-play has the advantage of side-stepping arguments. This role play opened intergenerational themes. I could elicit the parent's childhood pain as a source of empathy. Of course, this also required care and compassion on my part. (There is a section later in this chapter on coaching dialogues.)

Time Travel

One technique for helping to integrate attachment information is time travel (Lozier, 2012). I draw a rocket ship on a piece of paper. We place family members in the rocket ship as it time travels. (Children or teens have markers and help me with drawing.) We travel back to experiences, gaining information, and then return to the present. If we are close to tolerance, we may want to head home for the rest of the session. Family members who are in the session can say things like, "Welcome home! Want a snack?" They make gestures of welcome to the travelers. They show acceptance and care as the travelers come home.

These experiences contrast past attachment figures with more reliable attachment figures in the present. There are times when we are repairing with people who were in the original situation of threat. In those cases, there is a description of how things have changed. Using the scenario in the previous section, in which a frightening person comes to the door at night, the post-rehab adult says, "No way, I was tricked before! I need to protect my kids. They matter to me. I don't want them scared or hurt." Redoing the experience through role-play or time travel helps to update children's representational view of their parent as trustworthy. It also helps parents' determination to be trustworthy.

These therapeutic exercises activate attachment schemas, including the body-based information and emotions that interlace memories. They are activating—a necessary quality in attachment work. There is ample reparative potential, helping the change to secure attachment. A significant benefit is that I am able to reduce children's testing of their parents. Reenactments of attachment-trauma themes are reduced.

Modeling Behaviors With Follow-Up

Mirror neurons in our brains allow people to know what a certain physical action looks like or would feel like just by watching another person perform that same action. For example, by watching a person do "the wave" at an event, people know how to do "the wave" as it travels towards them in the crowd. People automatically know movement and timing by watching sequences of movements, since their brains recorded a brain firing pattern that mirrored the other (Cozolino, 2006). These mirror neurons can work to our clients' benefit in sessions where therapists are demonstrating a positive way of touching another family member. The clients know what the touch would be like through their mirror neurons. The therapist may have an easier time when modeling nurturing touch because there is no history between therapist and child of missed responses or ambivalent feelings about attachment. I can say, "I wonder if it would be OK if I laid my hand on your back? I can see that you are sad. What would it be like if someone sat next to you with a comforting hand on your back? May I show you what I mean?" Then the therapist shows the comforting gesture with a parent observing, with mirror neurons firing. Then the parent sits next to the child and repeats the gesture. The therapist talks about the original difficult topic, this time with the child or teen sitting beside the parent, receiving comfort through reassuring touch.

If this is too direct a path, therapists have the option of demonstrating touch on the parent. The touch can be a hug, a hand on top of a hand, an arm around the shoulders, and so forth. Children or teens who have been previously traumatized by attachment figures, and who are no longer with them, do well with the therapist demonstrating the action on the parent first. If the child or teen watches and assents, then the parent is able to provide reassuring touch.

A key quality of secure attachment is the parent's ability to regulate. What the therapist is building in these interactions is a regulated circle of communication: expressed need by the child, followed by the parent's comforting or coregulating behaviors, and then followed by the child's acceptance of comfort and coregulation.

It is typical that the children's expressions of need may be muted or ambiguous. When in distress, children or teens may shrug their shoulders and invalidate their feelings of loneliness or shame, saying, "I don't care." Instead of quibbling about the wording, the therapist's approach is to validate children's or teen's worthiness of care, providing physical expressions of compassion, like a hand on their shoulder, if it is accepted. This process is modeled in therapy sessions. I may make playful comments to them—"It's so new to get along with parents!"

Using the methods above, therapist can guide parents to place a hand on top of the child's hand, hold the child's hand, stroke his or her head, rub or squeeze a shoulder, or give a hug. We are helping children to make a paired association between comfort and physical touch. In the sessions therapists are building a cycle of parents noticing needs, children expressing needs, and parents meeting needs. Because children may be shut off from their feelings, or show ambiguity in expressing their needs, parent usually have trouble responding contingently. Parents frequently deflect, changing the subject or looking away. In these sessions, therapists build competencies in parents as they notice and meet needs. Children and teens become clearer in expressing needs and approaching their parents. It is important for therapists to note the completed circles of need and comfort, helping family members to integrate their improved relationship competencies.

Taking Photos as a Way of Anchoring Key Moments

When people are giving eye contact, sharing enjoyment, and relating warmly with coregulation, we will want to store those changes in their life schemas. An easy way to do this is by noticing it verbally, followed by taking a photo. I often take a photo on my camera, printing it or sending it to clients. Then they see themselves feeling better regulated in poses that are relaxed, intimate, and connected.

As mentioned earlier, people may have an expressed point of view about attachment, but their implicit beliefs, as expressed physically, may be at variance. In therapy, as people experience closeness as positive, they enjoy coherence in what they want to believe about attachment and their bodily expressions. Marking that with a photo helps them to retain their changes, updating their representational images of parent and child.

Parents, children, and teens find these photos meaningful. They look at the photos together, smiling and making jokes. I like to take several shots. As family members sort through the photos, choosing favorites, there is potent symbolic meaning in the choosing. They are selecting representational views of themselves and others as caring and worth care. I often lay a hand on people's upper backs or arms as they leave the room after these sessions, further accenting the intimacy of the session's work.

Client Hugs From the Therapist

Because of the emotional intensity of sessions, often people feel that they want to give or receive a hug. If people want a hug, and it is appropriate for the clients, I do hug them at the end of the sessions—or at the start if they reach out. Younger children who get to know me will often hug me. I stroke their heads a moment, making eye contact with parents. I am careful to include parents in this interaction. The parent is the attachment figure and is preeminent. I model the warmth and positive aspects of attachment work—with boundaries of course. If people want more contact than is appropriate, we talk about their legitimate needs for physical contact, making plans to obtain it from friends or relatives.

Assignments at Home

When working with families on attachment-producing behaviors, we see stronger and sustained progress when they practice at home. The homework varies by age ranges or need, from a nighttime back rub accompanied by prayer and a chant for a 9-year-old, to a teen and parent eating popcorn as they sit together watching their favorite television program. I often suggest active play. A play homework assignment could be that four times a week parents and kids play soccer in the park or backyard. The assignments may include a mixture of high activity and close, snuggly moments. Families can help pick out what brings them shared enjoyment and or closeness.

I like to warn people who have considerable avoidance that they might feel contradictory impulses to ruin the moment or interrupt it. We can discuss or role-play what people might think or feel that would make them want to draw away or interrupt the closeness that is being built. For example, "I don't deserve your attention," or, "I reached out before and was ignored," or, "It's probably not going to turn out well anyway, so why try?" Using a mixture of humor and encouragement, I challenge people to show courage, by allowing themselves some joy and happiness. Some families and I compose songs, with moves, with lyrics about "believing in the power of love" (reminiscent of Aretha Franklin with some regrettable decrease in quality). We discuss in simple terms that it takes strength for people to believe that they are worth loving and are capable of loving well. This is a motivational pitch. I also discuss with families that it will take some time for closeness to feel natural, so we will take one step at a time.

Sometimes families revert to old patterns within a couple of days after our therapy sessions. In these cases I ask families to leave a message for me so that I know how things are going. Sometimes I ask them to take pictures at home for me to see. For more guarded family members, I normalize their desire to both get close and move away. The homework may start with something like 15 minutes of rousing play every day, or 20 minutes of reading aloud, or singing together, followed by a time of separation. That way, they do not have to have conflict to get a separation.

Feelings of Disgust and Helplessness in Parents; Countertransference in Therapists

I meet alone with parents in order to help them process their mixed feelings toward their children. I offer periodic sessions as needed. I also meet with most parents for the first 10 minutes of the 55-minute session, unless one client is a teen and this makes confidentiality too difficult. Sometimes parents are discouraged or feel ill-used by a child or teen who is rejecting them. Parents who have had a role reversal with their children feel threatened as children or teens develop more autonomy. Part of keeping parents emotionally available to their children includes giving them a place to process pain and shame.

Many times parents describe their treatment by their child or teen as one more situation in which they are relating closely to someone who does not honor them as worthwhile. This is especially true when parents have histories of emotional or physical abuse. They are looking for their children to give them affirmation, which places a dependency burden on their children. While I do want to encourage positive and contingent responses in children and teens, a parent's approval rating needs to be generated from within themselves and from other adults, including from the therapist. It helps to explore these issues, with empathy, in individual sessions. I support parents by helping them to process their feelings of shame, anger, and disappointment. After processing, parents have more willingness to keep trying.

Some parents will grimace and make expressions of disgust when their children are asking for care. This arouses countertransference that the therapist must own and handle carefully. The discrepancy between the feelings that parents want to have and the feelings that they do have now, is important to process. If parents want their therapist to take sides, therapists may refer parents to do their own therapy. But it is still essential to have compassion for the struggle that a parent faces. The therapist must avoid taking the false stance of being the good parent who shames the actual, other parent as being the bad parent. Parents may treat their children as peers, competing for the therapist's approval or attention. Within this dynamic, therapists can easily find themselves favoring one "child" over the other. Watching these tendencies in ourselves is part of good practice.

In the process of exploring disgust or helplessness, parents often make connections to their life story. Simply by processing feelings with a regulated therapist, parents often show better regulation of those feelings. After this exploration, we can talk about how parents will get the resources and support to meet the needs of children or teens. I offer myself as a person who will help parents as they nurture. It is difficult to make connections with children who have attachment and trauma issues. Therapeutic parenting is challenging. Some parents will say, "You would have been proud of me, Deborah. I did not argue with my son. I stayed calm." In later stages of therapy, parents outgrow me. They become confident that they have good parenting skills or a parenting approach that fits their children.

This has roots in the concept of being held in another's mind. As a parent sees me delighting in her as she delights in her child, she accepts herself reflected as a nurturing parent. Parents who have been slighted in their early years welcome this approach. For parents who have tendencies toward narcissism or extreme sensitivity, nurturing the nurturer has some success.

Dealing With Shame in Therapy

Parents commonly have shame about the poor relationship that they have formed with their children, and in-the-moment shame at the feelings evoked as they struggle to relate. When people feel intense shame, they tend to withdraw or lash out in defensive postures or comments. Often they shame in retaliation.

The therapist who is demonstrating ways to be close to children, and who unwittingly taps into shame, may exceed the client's tolerance. The therapist may be surprised by escalations or withdrawal. For this reason, I recommend specific questions around shame during intake, with periodic discussions around shame, helplessness, and competence.

When shame comes up in the sessions, I like to think about its function. Are parents defending themselves, saying that they know the needs are unmet, but just can't do any better? Is the teen shaming the parent, asking for change and repair? Children may make shaming comments because parents are now presenting themselves as sensitive, but have not always been so. Were hurtful comments made? Can the parent stay connected and apologize (repair)? Did the child get hit or left? Will the teen shame the parent, testing to see if the parent apologizes or gets angry and withdraws again? If the child is being raised by different parents, mistrust and shame issues may be replayed with current parents.

The therapist who includes shame as part of therapy, accepting that it is hot but keeping it at tolerable levels, is able to help dyads move into successful patterns despite issues of shame and helplessness. Children or teens can share their feelings and thoughts, usually in words spit out, choked out, or whispered through tears. Parents and children listen to each other and then connect authentically.

It may help to meet children and parents separately first, reducing activation to a tolerable degree, and then facilitate an exchange. The resolution may be nonverbal, with a hug, kind gaze, or reassuring body posture.

The therapist can help coach the dialogue as necessary. Then the therapist could ask them to use a sensory-based technique, touch, gaze, or proximity, placed in this relational context. In families who have not previously been relating closely, we ask for touch when people are open to a change in the pattern of connection. The emotional ebb and flow within the session guides the timing.

Helplessness is associated with fear or shame. Parents often have blockages in their narratives of care that connect to when they felt helpless or fearful. An intake narrative from adults may reveal these times. But often the blockages emerge during the sessions, since our work on connection evokes their feelings around care, fear, and shame. If I feel that the feelings and related issues need to be explored with the parent alone, I meet with the parent only. That way, he or she has been affectively modulated to some degree prior to sessions with a child/teen. For example, a parent described that her daughter was being groomed for sexual abuse by a relative. In a session alone, the mother spoke chaotically about being groomed by a neighbor as a child. Her parents overlooked the undue attention. Her helplessness as a child, knowing that something bad was about to happen but unable to talk, was recurring. In the session with me, she was able to see the intersection. In the following session she was organized and outlined a plan with her daughter, saying that she was getting a no-contact order.

Since the stress systems of children and teens are less developed than those of adults, I do not want them to be exposed to overwhelming adult dysregulated states with no possibility of repair. That will simply cause more disorganization in their pattern of relatedness. Shame is such an early, hot system that it needs particular care when doing attachment work (Cozolino, 2006).

Therapist's Help in Creating Dialogues Between Family Members

Many clients have trouble finding words when working on attachment. This has a logical connection, since attachment relationships are integral to the development of mind-body connections and recognizing and putting into words a person's feelings or needs. Many clients who are asking for help for attachment have missed the type of attachment relationships that would incubate developing self-skills, which include talking about feelings. Coaching people in noticing and speaking about their physical and emotional states is part of creating healthy connections.

I have found the task of putting language to needs and internal states a humbling one. I ask if certain phrasing seems to fit, and how children or parents would say it better. I ask if I am reading the situation at all correctly. In spite of this clumsy approach, I work to create a language around needs for family members. Children are more likely to use my words as a springboard for ones that fit them better. When I say something, they are able to discern that it's not correct for them, and come up with what is correct. This is a welcome development as they are experts on themselves.

Many times clients correctly say, "I don't know," when asked how they think or feel. One girl told me, "I got locked. I felt a lot but could not find words. This is helping." In her case, we started in a basic way. I had her feel which felt most accurate, choice A or B. As she chose, she actually wrote down the phrases to use with her parent in the future. Her mother said, "I thought that she did not care for me much. Now I assume that her orphanage experience impacted her ability to communicate." When children or adults move into hypoarousal, it is hard for them to think or to communicate with words (Porges, 2009). Rather than insisting that children respond, it helps to change therapy practice to fit their physiological state, providing acceptable touch, caring voice tones with rhythmic cadence, a drink, or a little walk. Then we can return to the process of finding words.

As we work together to find words, I ask clients to practice saying the words within the session. We work on voice tone, simple expression of needs, and a contingent response by parents. Lectures, qualifications, snotty tones, and descriptions of past failures are normal pitfalls.

It might sound like this: "I am worried that you are too busy to pay attention to me. Like, I am a bother to you." Answer: "I did not know that you felt like that. I will stop texting and concentrate on being with you. You are important to me." At that point the therapist would note what a great job they did, risking opening their hearts to each other. I might suggest a time that would work every day for their time together. Or I might explore when they shut each other out and how to avoid these interruptions, as when they bring the phone or tablet to the dinner table or text during a walk.

The successful dialogue above typically has earlier renditions like, "You never have time for me. Your work or your friends are more important to you." The former answer: "Someone has to make money. You are the one always asking for name-brand jeans. Maybe if you helped once in a while I would have some time for you. I don't get any appreciation from you."

We might talk about the shame behind these statements. Then we cocreate the dialogue, trying again. Children and parents needs to be able to state their attachment needs in simple ways, such as these:

- I am afraid. Please go with me.
- That person scares me. Please keep them away from me.
- It embarrasses me when you criticize me in front of others. Please stop.
- I need help with something.
- I am lonely. Please spend time with me.
- I don't know how to solve this problem by myself. It is too complicated. Please help me by finding some help.
- I need food, clothes, or transportation. Will you provide for me? I can't do this much on my own. (This is suitable for a younger person or a person who has limitations.)
- I do not have a path to a hopeful future. I am not successful in school or friends. Please help me to find a path to success.

- I am depressed. I need help.
- I am scared all of the time. I need help.
- I am afraid that you don't love me . . . that you wish you could trade me in. Do you love me?
- I am afraid that you will leave me. Will you stay with me?
- I am afraid that your feelings will be hurt if I want to spend time with friends.
- I get confused when my parents compete to be my favorite parent.

These are simple combinations of feelings and thoughts. By asking questions or stating concerns, the clients are taking risks. It is the therapist's job to support the client in helping to phrase and ask the question. If the parent gives a qualified answer, then the therapist may describe the impact on the child. With close questioning, as above, the therapist may say, "You see your child's hurt, but you have changed the subject and looked away. Is that actually how you want to leave it?" The point is to help parents see the dissonance between what they just did and what they value. Then we rework client responses to move toward security. This is no smooth process. It can involve tears, the need to take breaks, the use of angry defenses, my request that they lay aside the defense to try something new, and so forth.

Sometimes a parent is not willing to meet needs. The therapist can help to process the answers in terms of how children can believe themselves worthy of love and care, even if their parent cannot provide it. At that point, the therapist will ask for time alone with the young person.

Many family members may tend toward answers that are concrete and literal, missing the implied concepts. The therapist, using executive function, can bridge to answers to important core issues around needs and worthiness.

Child: I don't have money on my lunch card at school.
Parent: Get a free bag lunch. I can't stop now to load your account. And I don't have money until I am paid.

Child: I have had a free bag lunch more than anyone in my class.

Parent: It's not my fault that you forget to tell me about your lunch card until I pay bills.

Therapist: Notice the look on your son's face [pause]. What do you think he is feeling when he doesn't have lunch?

Parent: [looks at son with her shoulders slumped, and then with chin up and neck stiff] That he shouldn't put off telling me?

Therapist: Of course it would be better if he reminded you. But the big meaning is that he feels on his own. That he has to remind you of his needs. Is that how you want it? He feels shame in front of the other kids, shame that he is hungry because he doesn't remember your payday.

Parent: [turning to child] Is that how you feel? Like you think you don't matter? You are the best thing in my life! I am embarrassed to be out of money, not to be able to fill your card. [She blinks several times and looks at her son, her eyes getting softer. The boy and mother both lean toward each other.]

Therapist: So the smaller problem is something we can fix, getting you a lunch. The big issue is that you have a stressed parent and you are stressed as well. It makes you [points to son] feel that you are not worth much. [Turning to mother] Your son needs to feel that you care about him, that you two are going to be OK. You do a great job of keeping up with bills and providing for the two of you, even when it is tough. Why don't we come up with two ideas about how to solve the lunch problem?

In the dialogue above, the parent's high stress showed up in defensive postures, distancing from her anxious son. Her helplessness and shame are masked through minimizing his needs and blaming him. Executive dysfunction, with its detail-oriented perspective, is making the situation worse. The dialogue above shows a way to connect, discuss the larger issue, and then problem solve. (For the detail-oriented reader, parent and child used leftovers from dinner and a thermos to take warm food to school.)

The following is an example of another dialogue that helps with attachment security, which starts off with an overly literal response.

Child: I am afraid that you will leave me.

Parent: [with a heavy sigh] Everyone needs a break now and again.

The therapist helps by putting the comment into context, deepening meaning.

Therapist: Your 10-year-old is afraid that you will take off, abandoning her. Are you able to give reassurances? She is not asking you to wear her. She wants to know if she will lose you as she lost her father.

Parent: [Responding with a dismissive shoulder shrug] Of course I won't leave her. I would miss her too much. I would never do that!

Therapist: [Engaging parent with eye contact to increase emotional intensity and connection] Take a look at her face. See how tense your daughter is. Would you repeat that you won't leave her?

Parent: [Looking at her child's eyes] I am here for you.

With a nonverbal cue, the therapist indicates the parent should move closer and hug her daughter.

Therapist: [Speaking quietly] See the relaxation on her face. Thanks for making that clear. Your daughter was helped by your answer. . . Of course she worries because she lost a parent.

As the parent moves close and hugs her daughter, the therapist inhales and exhales, modeling helpful breathing.

Therapist: [Speaking in low, rhythmic tone] It feels good to connect.

Parent: [Continuing without prompting into verbal reassurance] I'll come back. It's only one weekend. I love you. I need to keep some adult friends in my life. But you are my family, forever.

I noted in the first exchange that the parent was able to access her own feelings, saying, "I'd miss her too much," but not her daughter's distress. But the combination of minute-to-minute alterations in the session and physical connection allowed the parent to move into a comforting mode, concentrating on her child's needs. The new cognitive information was embedded in a dynamic interaction within the dyad.

People with dismissive and insensitive behaviors are able to use these dialogues to become more sensitive. As the dialogues unfold, they are faced with a stark choice of being sensitive or dismissive. The hurt caused by the lack of sensitivity is startlingly clear in the sessions. Rather than an automatic defensive response, in which they brush past the other person's hurt, they are held in that moment, facing the hurt caused by their comments and behaviors. They decide that they do not want to cause pain. This type of clear communication, within a nurturing setting, allows people to practice making choices that move them toward security. The positive words and choices are then noticed through the therapist's body posture, facial expression, and words.

In this third dialogue, the attachment conversation is between the family adults. I asked for this meeting without their child, Janessa, who is 12 years old.

Mother: You say that you want a better relationship with Janessa, but you only argue and lecture her when you spend time together.

Father: [Looks away with a negative head shake and then responds] The kid is irritating. She baits and annoys me. Then she raises her voice to get your attention. You come to the rescue and give me dirty looks before taking over. So I find something positive to do. I have better things to do than argue and then get second-guessed.

Mother: [Ignoring his complaints, his wife describes her own feelings and thoughts] You leave when things are tough. I am so mad at you. I'm alone parenting a daughter with mental health problems. I feel alone in this marriage. I wonder if I should even be in this marriage!

At this point, the therapist assists with some regulation and common ground.

Therapist: So you both feel left out and alone in various ways.

That statement causes each parent to slow the escalation of argument, moving to shared disappointments over their inability to rely on the help and regulation of the other. After a pause, the therapist turns to the father.

Therapist: Do you feel that your wife likes you?

Father: [Eyes down, and then raising them to therapist he replies.] No. Not lately. There's no evidence.

The therapist then introduces hope and an anticipation of movement.

Therapist: But there was a time when you two really got along.

Both parents began to speak over each other a bit with an exchange of eye contact and nods in assent to the other.

Mother: Before our daughter's problems got so severe.

Father: We saw things the same way.

Mother: We used to be fun people.

The therapist continues the progression into hope.

Therapist: So you two were able to talk, laugh, and be friends?

Father: Sure. We helped each other. We planned and finished projects. We built our house. We had each other's backs.

The therapist is able to circle back, with both parents recalling their sturdy teamwork, to approach the problem with hope.

Therapist: It seems that you have lost your connection and your teamwork in parenting. Why don't we start restoring that?

Mother: I resent Janessa for what has happened to our family.

Therapist: [Speaking to the father, with full eye contact. The eye contact with the father allows his wife to observe him, arousing some sensitivity and compassion.] What is it like for you? Do you feel special to your wife?

Father: No. I feel like a big incompetent oaf.

Therapist: [Speaking respectfully] You would like to feel competent and respected . . . and treasured.

Father: Yes. Any time something goes wrong it's, "What did you do to Janessa?"

Therapist: Let's leave Janessa for a minute. What do you need your wife to say, her face to show, for you to feel special?

When young people have difficulties, it is easy for parents to use them as a scapegoat. It is also easy for the parents to be at odds over parenting. This is especially true if children or teens have a background of attachment issues, including a problematic connection with one parent in particular. The resulting triangulation can jeopardize a parenting plan. While therapists can and should refer out for couples counseling, as needed, it is a normal part of treatment to help parents protect their own relationship. In the case above, coaching parents with scripts and movements will help reduce conflict. We might role-play Janessa, played by me, doing something that the Father finds annoying. Barring abuse, scripting could look like the one below.

Janessa: [played by the therapist] Mom, help me. Dad is making me really upset.

Mother: Work it out. I love you both too much to keep taking sides.

Father: Janessa, what do you want? Do you want your mother's attention to help you to feel in charge? You can relax in this home. I'll help to keep you safe.

Therapist: [playing Janessa] I don't know what you are talking about. Mom, he's talking crazy! Come here!

Father: [coming up with his own script] I'm sorry that you are kind of stuck in this drama, fighting me and getting Mom to rescue you. I'm going to stay in this room. I'm ready to show you something funny that I saw on YouTube. Check it out if you want.

Therapist: [still playing Janessa] Mom! Mom! Mom's not coming!

Father: That's because you are fine with me. You can start with staying relaxed around me. We don't have to connect much. But, I don't want to argue. No one is leaving this family. By the way, mom just took a walk.

In therapy, Janessa could be helped with scripting and role-play to help her with her request to be saved by her parent. Her pattern could be a reenactment of a past situation or a triangulating approach that has been rewarded by parents due to their family-of-origin issues. The point would be to stop the ongoing damage to relationships. Often one parent has to stop doing so much in order for the other parent to step up. It is normal for the parent who is trying to become more engaged to struggle when establishing an individual relationship pattern. I am frank when talking about this. For example, in talking to the mother I could say, "You have been handling Janessa's escalations and problems alone. You are tired of it and also feeling good about your skills in helping her. Janessa's father will have to find his own approach. And he won't have as much practice. He won't get better until you step out. And he won't sound like you since he has a different personality. Think what else you'd like to do with your time instead of intervening." Some parents go for a walk or take a long shower, where the sound of running water will block the conversations of the others.

Celebrating Accomplishments

In optimal development of attachment, parents amplify expressions of joy and enthusiasm throughout infancy and on into the early years. Joy and happiness are hallmarks of early, healthy attachment relationships. Therapists are encouraged to point out and show enthusiasm as families make gains in attachment, problem solving, or mastery.

When parents are seeing gains, I may recommend adding a reward, which helps to emphasize the pleasure in accomplishment of parents and children. Accomplishments in attachment might include giving hugs, noticing expressions on another's face and responding with care, eye contact, repairing a relationship problem, and so forth. The therapist responds with a joyful description of how well they are taking care of themselves and their family member, or, how great they are at loving the other person, or, how emotionally intelligent they are. The wording changes to suit the age or family culture.

Rewards can be a food treat, with a family cheer as people talk about this accomplishment. Other rewards could include renting a movie to watch together with popcorn. Often we choose a reward of shared food, simply because eating together has an attachment aspect. Other preferred choices are play choices, such as going to the park to shoot hoops, attending a soccer game, buying dress-up clothes at a thrift shop, or heading to the batting cage.

Creating a Dialogue Within the Self

A goal of attachment work is to create a positive internal voice for the self—one that both values and regulates the person. For those with secure attachments, these positive voices abound. Many people say things to themselves like, "It's OK. Don't worry. You are loved. You will be fine." These soothing phrases are almost exactly what they heard from parents in early life.

I like to create opportunities for some of these phrases to be spoken and internalized. Sometimes I have parents say these reassuring phrases to children. I may repeat them, drawing them to the children's attention. Later, I might have children/teens imagine themselves in a certain stressful situation, thinking about what a parent would say that would soothe and boost them. If children cannot come up with words, parents can lend them soothing words, which the child repeats. Over time, these voices become part of the person's internal resource. Some children tape their parents saying soothing and encouraging phrases. They listen to them on their phones when they are establishing self-soothing.

My part in the internal dialogue is to be certain that parents are hearing positives from me. I can say, "You are a caring parent. You are a perceptive parent. You are a sensitive mother or father." Over time, I look for ways that children or teens can become gratifying in their words to their parents. They might say things like, "Thanks, Mom, for helping me. You are a great dad or mom."

Realistic Expectations When Trauma and Loss Are Present

When people are entering treatment, it is helpful to tell them that their attachment work will necessitate work on trauma and loss. The treatment plan discussion includes the reality that therapy will be complicated and worthwhile.

It seems to work best within treatment plans to have a couple of specific goals for a few sessions, meet those goals, reflect on the success, and then take on new goals. For example, a couple was struggling with the attachment needs of their daughter, who was 6 years old. The daughter had been adopted at 3 years of age. A relative did most of this child's care postadoption, since her mother became severely depressed. Her father described himself as planning to relate more as his daughter became "able to talk and discuss ideas." Then the little girl received even less attention from her mother, as the mother dealt with the final illness and death of her own mother, encountering her childhood abuser at the funeral. They came into therapy with great concern since the child's caregiver was moving.

We discussed the need for help for attachment, trauma, and loss in two intake sessions. I met with the parents alone and then with the child for part of the second session. I spent time with the mother in determining what attachment-producing activities would not trigger her trauma. We also spent time getting the 6-year-old's needs in focus. We practiced some of the activities that would encourage attachment formation, including, rocking while reading a book, a cozy time with snuggles, and singing in the morning and after school. The father was to comment positively when he noticed sensitive and contingent responses, rather than remarking on unmet needs. (The father's suggestions reminded the mother of her critical and brutal father.) The father was to either try to meet some of these unmet needs or bring them into the therapy session for discussion. I referred the mother for work on trauma.

We did some short-term work to help with some of the intrusive symptoms until the mother could begin with her therapist. I referred the mother for a medication consultation, which resulted in some relief for anxiety and depression. I helped the mother with processing her loss, giving her ideas about using art and poetry to hold on to positive memories of her mother and reduce her identification with her mother's helplessness.

This mother worked on techniques, as did the father. She developed a much greater connection with her daughter within 3 months, and more sensitivity, skill, and confidence in attachment and parenting tasks within a year. We were able to process the child's trauma and loss issues, while maintaining work on attachment over the following 25 sessions. Fortunately, the relative had created a relational base for this little girl, which we built upon.

At that point, the parents came in asking for help with their marriage. I helped them to celebrate their parenting accomplishments thus far and then spent a couple sessions helping them to define what they wanted from professional help. I referred them for marital work, which was also successful. I maintained the family with visits once a month for years, and then saw them yearly for 8 years at the mother's request. Both parents made a point of coming and engaging in therapy, although the mother always asked for some time alone just for herself. I finally told them that since they were being asked to lead a parenting class at their church, they had to admit success.

This example illustrates the process when addressing complex issues. The parents had an adequate therapy budget, which helped a great deal. The family had previously made unsuccessful attempts at receiving help for attachment issues. One earlier treatment plan did not include complicating influences of trauma and loss. Another plan was all behavioral and just resulted in despair. The more complex approach that these parents and I agreed upon helped them to enjoy their successes within a 60-session treatment course.

Pacing Within the Session

Therapists have the task of pacing both within the dyad and with individuals. During intake, I often tell clients that I will intervene to make the sessions feel tolerable and safe. I intervene if people begin to dissociate, attack each other with name calling, or bring up too much activating material in a particular session. Clients and I may work at a comfortable pace right up to the edge of tolerance for about half of the session. We work on less activating material, like mastery, relaxation, social skills, or plans to cope with stressors during the rest of the session. When we go past tolerance, which is not planned but is a part of treatment, we do extra work on repair.

Attachment work presumes that some of the family members may not have developed a sturdy regulatory system, or that this regulatory system has been overwhelmed by trauma or loss, or both. Since regulation is typically developed through an attachment relationship, most people struggling with attachment will show that developmental weakness. In my working model for families, I like to have a sense of what happened with their attachment figures when they needed help. I can help them with pacing by letting them know what will be different in our sessions. They might hear that they are allowed to say when pressure feels too much for them, without being shamed. They are allowed to call or email me if they are having trouble after the session; they are allowed to reach out for help. They can tell me if I hurt their feelings in the session; we can repair.

When therapy exceeds the threshold of tolerance, with the therapists remaining available emotionally, clients learn that they are able to tolerate dysregulation, finding their way back to regulation (Schore, 2012). Therapists stay present and available, providing non-verbal reassurance. Exceeding tolerance, followed by repair, stretches the ability that clients have to risk venturing further into difficult emotional material. The therapist does not plan for these experiences. However, they are not a therapeutic failure as long as they are not too frequent or disorienting. Instead, clients learn that their therapist will engage over problems, owning their part of the problem. Or, that their therapist will provide more support if client's move into dysregulation. These missteps help clients to believe that repair is possible both in their therapeutic relationships and in attachment relationships.

When families want to exceed the tolerance of one member, and we have already had some success in session, I typically ask the family member to stop without addressing the overwhelming situation. We can take on the problem area in the next visit. In almost all cases it is best to have clients leave the session with a sense of flow and connection. Since family members vary in their capacities, I want people to begin to recognize the shifts in each other when family members are at maximum tolerance. In attachment relationships, family members can learn to note the body signals or verbal expressions of others. Pacing in the session may include prompting a parent or child to inhibit, waiting to bring up a topic until the other has enough capacity to hear it.

As mentioned earlier, I spend approximately 10 minutes with parents first, during which I help parents to become better regulated. We may come up with topics for the therapy session. Then, when we bring in the child, parents are in a better place to both connect and regulate their child.

At times, I see children or parents alone during treatment, even though the work is typically dyadic. Examples are when parents are weeping in an overwhelmed manner, parents are attacking or threatening, or parents are sensitized to trauma issues and begin to dissociate during their child's trauma work. It provides no benefit to child or parent to have them together in the session. However, I will summarize what occurred in therapy for the parent letting children take the lead if they wish. I also interrupt sessions during which people persist in a threatening or unsafe manner. This does not tend to have a dramatic, negative impact on my relationship with people, although the boundary setting within the session can seem dramatic. There are also occasions when I am sure that some information is missing. I ask to speak to children and parents in turn, so that I can understand what is happening. Sometimes I ask people to separate, simply because I am confused. It helps me to give myself some space, reducing the many variables in the dyadic relationship. I usually tell parents what I am doing and why.

When things are escalated in the therapy room, I ask people to get quiet, breathing with me or calming with me. If things are quite escalated, I set physical boundaries. I say things like, "Would you please go out and meet us in the waiting room?" "It would be easier for me to help one person at a time right now." "I can see where you get stuck. Let's separate and then come back together." "This is a safe place. Those words [threats] can't happen here. Please wait in the waiting room. I will come to check on you in a little while." "Threatening isn't helping us. Please take a walk around the building. I will come find you in the waiting room."

There are times when a family member's actions toward another person are unsafe. I do make Children's Protective Services reports, according to statute. This is not a common occurrence. If I need to make a report, I try to discuss this with clients so that we may continue to work together.

While working on attachment evokes some lovely sentiments, it also brings up defensive aspects of the self and the other. Very angry people may expose others to risk. I take seriously my role in providing both support and safety.

Methods to Increase and Decrease Emotional Intensity

Some specific techniques to help with regulation, intensity, and pacing are part of the therapist's bag of tricks. I like to use techniques that clients are able to replicate in their own relationships, or within themselves.

Change tenses and envision the future. We can change tenses from active to passive, or future. This allows people to shift focus and emotions before becoming too dysregulated. For example, "You were looking hopeless as you were sitting in the waiting room. But let's imagine you and your son moving past this hard time, laughing, jumping on the trampoline, and playing a game."

Move between senses or from cognitions to senses. Using visual and olfactory senses will tend to heighten affect and memory. Asking what people said and what they thought tends to cool things down. Moving from the senses to cognitive conclusions is a normal way to store work as therapists and clients conclude a section of therapy. But sometimes we can move into these conclusions even though we know that there is more information in the senses to process. It denotes some work done, some yet to do. Children's sexual abuse is an example of a topic that lends itself to this approach.

Exaggerate or minimize distance and time frames. For example, "Many years ago, when you were very young, and lived in another country. [Pause]Think back to what you felt like as a 5-year-old in your apartment by the park. You were living with your grandpa and your mom . . ."

Talking speed and off-topic asides. The therapist can increase or decrease talking speed. When people have done something noteworthy, I may want to increase talking speed and inflection. When children or teens use negative attention-getting behaviors, I may want to talk more slowly and with little inflection. I usually want to provide more emotional response for positives. If clients describe an important insight, I can use a slower, dignified, and thoughtful speaking style, in response. As client's reference accomplishments, I reflect their pride by responding with voice arcs, with a rising inflection at the end of the phrase.

If people are becoming overwhelmed with shame or are uncomfortably activated, I can also divert conversation with a distracting subject and then come back to the main point. If challenged, I can explain what I'm doing. Sometimes family members begin to follow this model by distracting for a moment, and then ask if we should get back to the main point. These are helpful techniques to model in real time. It does not mean that you will not come back to address the issue, but that you are controlling pacing.

Use a third object. Drawing with a client allows for enough divided attention and energy to help with pacing. Introducing a connecting game will do the same. The therapist and family are practicing some flexibility in approach when doing activities together.

Time. For some children or teens, we make a plan for the therapy hour. For example, I might spend 10 minutes discussing the week (teens) or with a parent (child), 30 minutes working on a problem or problem solving, and then 15 minutes talking about the week ahead. For some children, we make an agreement to work on some hard aspect for a set period of time. This helps children to feel a sense of predictability and control. After that period of time, we may make some type of a plan. So, in those cases we say, "Let's discuss this for 20 minutes, and then see if you can come up with a plan." Making a plan tends to be engaging. For example, your grandparents are coming for a visit. What is your plan for what to do together? How about when they discuss people we never met before? What is your plan? What do you want to share with them?

Generalizing versus specifying. Generalizing tends to cool down the intensity of sessions. Specifying increases intensity (Briere, 2002). I tend to be more specific for dismissing parents, and more general for anxious parents. In trauma work, I move back and forth between specific and general, depending on the capacity of clients.

Stories. I tell stories that shape people's feelings or points of view. My stories do not tend to elicit defenses, so I sidestep the defense systems of well-defended people. The stories prime people in the session to experience certain affects. They often show a way to tolerate or reduce shame. (I use stories from composites of other clients or benign stories from my own life.)

Eye contact. I will sometimes ask kids to stand in front of me, looking at my face. For younger children I gently hold their hands, perhaps rubbing their palms. I offer reassurance, kindness, and care. I ask them what they see, besides my physical features. "When you look at me, can you see that I like you?"

They might say, "I see your nose."

I will say, "Oh no. Did I forget to tell you that I really like you? Oh, what a mistake! Well, here goes. I really like you and want you to see it in my face."

Sometimes kids get a half grin, look at me, and then turn their faces to the left, saying something like, "Yeah. You do like me." Then they look back at me. (The left side is their withdrawal side, or shy side, for right-handed people.)

I say, "I won't let things be too hard. Tell me when you need a little break. Do you need to sit on the therapy ball or have some bubble gum?"

Drinks, books, or walks. Sometimes people need a break. I will read a story (or three) go for a walk, give the kids another juice, or give two pieces of double bubble gum to chew at a time, lightening up the sessions with laughs. When there is not much capacity, I try not to push people. Over time, they become better at describing their capacity without defenses or irritability. This is an extremely useful skill within families.

Freeze-Frames to Connect Thoughts and Feelings, Mind and Body

In optimal early development, parents amplify and name their infant's and toddler's body signals and thoughts and feelings, responding contingently. This helps infants and toddlers with their mind-body connection. This process is replicated by therapists in some degree. I want to capture body signals just before people use a protective strategy. I use the concept of a freeze-frame. We stop for a moment for a feelings check, exploring what people are feeling, what their body is doing and telling them, and perhaps why they stopped processing the flow of information at a certain point.

An advantage of using this technique is that therapists and clients have integration opportunities rather than an automatic defense. For example, if a father reached over to touch his daughter's shoulder, but she shrugged away, the therapist could ask for a freeze. "Notice what your body is doing right now. What are you thinking and feeling?" Or perhaps in session a boy looks away vacantly, twists his body away, and then begins to scratch his arm, painfully hard, as a parent talks about a sibling and ignores the boy's body signals. The therapist could say, "Let's stop right here. Your body is showing you something. What are you feeling, right now?"

Our discussion often starts with a denial: "Nothing! I don't feel anything." Together we notice that nothing. What were the body-based reactions as the client disengaged to reduce stress? When did the client stop integrating body and mind? In one example above, it might be that a parent elicits shame in the boy, using warmer voice tones when talking about the sibling, irritation when talking about the boy. We also have the chance to have a repair for issues that are being expressed on a nonverbal level.

Since freeze-frame is in real time, it helps with in-the-moment integration of thoughts and feelings. In defensive moments, clients do not have to access working memory to work on issues. And since they may be reacting to implicit memories or dissociated material, this technique bypasses the need for clients to first recognize body or emotional states and then use a cognitive-behavioral approach. Instead, it is a bridge until people are able to do so.

Narratives of Hope and Endurance

The best books, the greatest stories, all have episodes of pain, love, loss, tragedy, and courage. This message serves my clientele well. Most of my clients do not enjoy lucky lives. In theirs, endurance and courage prevail. As people are coconstructing their narratives in therapy, they need a framework for their experience. In sessions we do not minimize misfortune or the pain of loss. But we also credit their gumption to create meaningful connections despite the odds.

I do not like to interject a rah--rah false cheer in the midst of pain. Still, there are times when clients' courage shows up, when they prevail, and when praise for courage and endurance are earned. In trying to love well in spite of rejection, or attempting to soothe a person who is terrified, a person who persists and stays positively connected should be commended. It helps in building a life story that includes a sense of mastery or commitment in spite of obstacles. The emphasis shifts to values rather than outside appearances or short-term outcomes.

When making sense of their life experiences, clients seem to appreciate help in constructing life narratives that credit their resilience. Finding that there are other people on the same road gives them a sense of belonging to a group that is moving along in spite of rocky terrain. I point families to support groups that help families acknowledge the pain and difficulties that they face, but also team up to solve problems and to support each other.

CHAPTER 4

Treatment for Children

Children are biologically driven to form attachments. So why does the development of security in attachment falter for some children? When parents are asking for help with attachment with their children, their children's issues tend to fall under one or more of these major headings:

- Children have changed homes and parents. They are being parented by a secure attachment figure, but are relating in a pattern formed with another parent.
- Children have unresolved grief or traumas, including domestic violence, which impede secure attachment.
- Children have had excessive separations from their parents, resulting in feelings of abandonment, with resultant defenses.

The above list includes serious reasons that families seek out specialized attachment help for attachment. Attachment relationships may be impacted by high stress or temperamental difficulties. These families also ask for help, but the treatment plans are often shorter. Children have longer treatment plans when they have been maltreated, have backgrounds of institutional (orphanage) care, or their parents have died or cannot parent them. Yet even with these children, therapy is often effective in increasing attachment security.

Effects of Children's Maltreatment or Losses on Parents

When children are showing insecure-disorganized attachment patterns, even secure parents need support. Because children's reactions are inconsistent and trauma driven, they keep parents off kilter. Parents begin to feel some of children's high arousal, alarm, or hypoarousal, which is disorienting in a way that parents cannot easily put into words. As children respond or cue parents in an inconsistent and confusing manner, parents become indignant or mixed in their own response patterns. Parents expect, but inconsistently receive, a contingent response to their nurturing and comfort. When children have been traumatized, parents find themselves revisiting their own traumas or losses, issues they thought were safely in the past.

It is in this state of confusion that most families reach out for help for their children. Sometimes parents recognize the part that they play in perpetuating children's defenses or in exacerbating problems. Oftentimes they do not. When parents feel shame because they cannot connect to their children, they can veer into blaming their children or blaming themselves, depending on their abilities to tolerate shame and problem solve. As one father said, "I never failed at anything before. Not in my career, my marriage, my parenting . . . until now. I am failing with my daughter."

Leading With Compassion to Parents: Activating Empathy

Even emotionally sturdy parents feel dejected when they begin to parent children with attachment issues. It is important to normalize attachment problems as being common after maltreatment or losses. Zeanah and colleagues (2004) assessed the number of infants entering foster care who have attachment disorders at 38--40%. Of course, this not a lifelong diagnosis for the great majority of children. But it points to the importance of addressing children's reactivity around parents and in social arenas. From the first requests for therapy, parents and children who are trying to smooth out a rocky start will need ample encouragement in addition to skills. Therapist empathy allows access to parents' limbic system–mediated emotional processing, as well as their right-brain cortex. This socioemotional processing is critical in attachment work. When I establish empathy, I include myself, with my attachment capacities, as a resource, enhancing the regulation and emotional resources of parents and children. I provide support for emotional processing of factual information about trauma, neglect, and loss.

Unmet expectations are painfully common when parenting foster and adoptive children. I frequently hear professionals say, "What did they expect?" Actually, parents expected more of the joy that is part of raising children. That is not wrong-headed, which is what parents are left feeling after off-the-cuff judgment. They simply did not integrate what their emotional responses would be to their child's rejection, control, or trauma in the context of the placement information on loss, trauma or discipline. They are surprised by the emotional toll of forging an attachment with a child who has emotional dysregulation and who is wary of attachment.

Some parents are given lectures on the effects of trauma and loss in such a manner that they feel guilty for having any expectations of their children. This blaming only complicates connections. Parents may also respond to trauma and loss psychoeducation by confining it to cool facts that they know. The trauma and loss information that parents learn does not include an understanding of how their children's trauma and loss-related moods and behaviors will influence parents' own moods and reactions. When attachment, which is a hot system, is activated, the cool facts are not integrated into their schema of parenting.

In beginning with parents, I want to hear how hard they have worked and how they feel about their successes and obstacles. Meeting with me and getting support is a way for them to get recharged, not so alone with the problem. Then I give hope: other families have surmounted these problems; there are specialized parenting approaches that help; and their children can change and learn. Rather than viewing the problem as being the child, I recast the problem as being the effects of maltreatment. These painful experiences have influenced relationships. As we increase attachment security, parents and children will connect better, and parents will help their children with trauma and loss. With a caring approach to psychoeducation, we discuss the emotional and physiological impact that children's maltreatment has on parenting and normal emotional responses to these impacts.

The annual ReFresh conferences from 2013 through 2018 in Redmond, Washington, showed the positive result of this approach. The conferences started out with nurturing and refreshing experiences for parents. The parents heard and experienced that they were not alone, and that it is normal to feel confused and dejected at times as they try to love their children. The speakers in the conference first connected to the emotional experience of parents. Then, after parents received nurturance, they were provided with a series of workshop choices to help them with attachment, sensory issues, trauma and loss, educational issues, and self-care. It was all done within a caring context. (More information can be found at ReFresh.org.)

Michele Schneidler, the cocreator of the conference, described that on the first day of the conference, the organizers access the parents' right brains with compassion and sharing (personal communication, May 20, 2017). Parents share that they share similar reactions or problems. The conferences give techniques the second day. By helping to reduce shame and isolation, and by increasing nurturance for parents through emotional connections and support, including food treats and fun activities, parents are ready for techniques later in the conference. The annual conference has become an extremely well-attended foster care, kinship care, and adoption event in the United States.

Tasks of Treatment and the Ordering of Those Tasks

In the previous chapter, I provided a figure that described the order of the tasks of therapy. In this chapter, I will be elaborating on that task. The figure is repeated for ease of reference (Figure 4.1).

During the first intake session, 90–120 minutes just for adults, I ask parents the history of care and attachment. I also want to hear where they feel that they have made gains. During the session with the adults I obtain a history of breaks in attachment, evidence of childhood trauma, developmental issues, and overall family support or stress. I prefer to hear the story of their relationship in person, because it gives me a sense of how parents put their narrative together. I listen for themes of nurturance, stressors, dependence, repairs, approaches to problems, and limit setting. The narrative gives me insight into parents' theory of mind about their child. It also gives me a glimpse into their abilities to reflect, cope with emotional stress, and organize their thoughts.

If children are with a biological parent or were adopted at birth, I ask about early life. A developmental history includes information about the pregnancy and developmental milestones. I include attachment-informed questions like these:

- When did your baby first smile at you?
- How much support did you receive during pregnancy and in the first months after birth?
- When did the baby seem to need you the most?
- What were the toddler years like?
- What phase for you or the baby or toddler seemed especially gratifying?
- Do you think that your baby and toddler was easy to soothe or more difficult in temperament?
- Was there a time when you thought that your relationship changed?
- Was the relationship between the two of you always difficult?
- When does your relationship seem to go well?

Tasks and Their Order over Course of Therapy

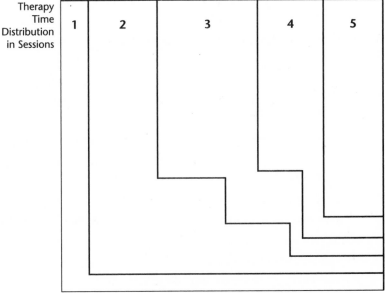

Time Spent on Tasks over the Entire Course of Therapy

Figure 1. Order of Tasks over Course of Therapy
1. Parent Stabilization/Psychoeducation
2. Attachment
3. Trauma
4. Loss
5. Child's social skills, engagement in peer activities and daily life

Figure 4.1 Tasks and their order over the course of therapy

These are all more open-ended questions that encourage conversation and a focus on the way that people think about relationships. It also allows a look at variables that may be significant in treatment, hospitalizations, domestic violence, parent absences, or periods of high stress in the family.

The early history will be sketchy or unavailable for many foster or adoptive parents, or when custody has changed due to a parent's addiction. After obtaining basic developmental information, I ask for the parent's parenting story. Using a conversational manner, I ask for information on these 20 topic areas:

1. Were there past attachments, with losses? If so, what happened that caused the loss? At what developmental stage was the child at each loss? Was the child moved suddenly?
2. How was the child fed? Was there food scarcity? Did the feeding involve emotional closeness?
3. Were the other physical needs of this child met, and met promptly?
4. Was this child traumatized? How did this child attempt to keep safe?
5. Does this child go into states of overarousal, hypervigilance, and immobilization or dissociation? If so, when? What helps that child regulate?
6. Where is this child developmentally? In a stimulating environment, is this child gaining, staying on a normal curve, or maintaining a slower curve in cognition, language development, and perceptual reasoning?
7. What seems to be the child's social adaptive level with peers, self-care, and family chores?
8. What does the pediatrician indicate about this child's health? Is there evidence of prenatal exposure to alcohol or drugs, or other toxins? Is there evidence of ADHD? Are there other health concerns that inform the treatment plan?
9. Where is the child open to cueing that leads to attachment (e.g., food activities, singing, eye-to-eye contact with responsive smiling, touch, play, shared activities with positive affects)? What qualities that promote attachment can be intensified?
10. What qualities listed above are in parent(s') strength areas? Are there qualities that the parent plans to withhold? What do I need, long-term, to gratify parents as well as their child?
11. What is weakening attachment now that could be avoided?
12. What is this child doing that diminishes family self-esteem? What can be introduced to help raise family self-esteem?
13. How can parent(s) find and use community support in raising this child?
14. What did the parents most hope for in their parenting experience? Can parents be strengthened to grieve the loss of the

wished-for child if this child's problems represent a loss? Can strategies that the family has used before to deal with difficult times be adapted to this situation?

15. What temperament does the child seem to have?
16. When does this child use more control?
17. When does this child relax control and show less anxiety?
18. How is this family perceived in their community, culturally and ethnically? Is this a transracial family? If a minority, how is the child's sense of self as an ethnic or cultural minority member being strengthened?
19. How do the parents regulate their own emotions? Who has influenced the child's stress system before, such as teaching comfort, calming, and soothing?
20. What are the areas of mastery for this child (Gray, 2012b)?

In our intake interview, parents and I focus on issues that our treatment plan should address. The treatment plan may take more than one intake session for parents who are dysregulated or who have a number of family members and considerations. Before a child enters my office, I like to have a consensus about the therapy process. I begin with children only after we have a basic agreement on therapy goals and the approaches to reach those goals. Sometimes parents will decide that they want a plan that does not address all of their child's needs. While not ideal, this gives me a chance to reduce goals rather than having children leave halfway through the treatment plan. For example, parent sometimes want help with attachment, but want to wait to do trauma work.

Treatment Planning: Talking to Parents About Tiers of Problems

In discussing treatment, it is helpful for parents to hear my thoughts on the relative significance of problems. My observations, shared with parents of an 8-year-old boy, sound like this.

Liem is showing effects of toxic stress and trauma resulting from his first four years with his first parents. I am noting the following as significant: his bad dreams that keep him up almost every night, his extreme startle reactions, his mood variations, his shutting down when reminders of scary events occur, and his fear of getting close to you—as well as extreme fear of losing you. I am also noting his feelings of missing his first mother and his fear of her. I hear that he is controlling, anxious, oppositional, and friendless. Your son sounds like he is a miserable little guy, and your empathy for him and frustration with him makes you feel miserable, as well. I will work alongside you to help.

Let's think of tiers of problems. We have two first-tier issues. One is his attachment to you, being able to feel close and safe with you. The second is traumatic grief, which makes him too sad and frightened to relax in your care. We will work on attachment first so that he can reach out to you. Then we will move into trauma work after he feels more safety and connection with you. His trauma and grief overlap. They seem to be standing in the way of a better attachment to you. We should see a rebound in attachment after we work on trauma and grief.

A second-tier problem is relationship building with people. We will work on friendship skills after we make gains with attachment, trauma, and loss. It will be easier for him to practice friendly behaviors at school after he feels calmer and safer. During this phase we will work on lying, stealing, and controlling behaviors, replacing them with friendlier behaviors.

The third-tier work will be mastery areas, with Liem believing in himself and connecting to the world in a positive manner. He is shame filled, with core feelings of worthlessness. Shame will be reduced through our attachment and trauma work, which was the first tier. We will work on ways that he can enjoy his life more during the third tier of work, finding areas of mastery and ways that he fits into his world.

Throughout the work I will be available to have separate sessions with you, problem solving about behavioral issues. We will also spend the first 10 minutes of our 55-minute session talking with parents only. That gives me the chance to listen to you and support you emotionally, as well as help with behavior and discipline in your home. I would like one parent to be in the sessions as we work on attachment, friendly behavior, and parts of the trauma. During some of the trauma work we can decide whether you stay in the whole time or just come in at the end.

The parents may ask, "How long will treatment last?"

I reply, "When there is complex trauma with behavior and attachment problems, the treatment plan will take about 50–70 hours of therapy. Usually that plan will take about 15–18 months if children do not have language processing issues. With language processing issues it may take longer. The attachment work will be about 15 sessions, the trauma and loss sessions about 30–40 hours, with friendly behaviors and mastery for the remaining sessions."

When working on attachment, the activities in the session are hands-on. Throughout the work with children, careful attention includes nurturing parents. It is exhausting for parents to provide sensitive, regulated care for children who are dysregulated and ambivalent. An appreciation of parents' reality is essential in supporting their efforts to nurture and steady their children. Therapists add their own attachment-savvy emotional support to the family in order to see best progress. About once a minute I will note and comment on parents' positive gestures, tones, time devoted to care, and skills in relating to their children. That noticing can be verbal or nonverbal.

Using Attachment-Producing Techniques in Therapy and Home

In the intake session and throughout the attachment-oriented treatment, I describe to parents the need to increase the time spent on nurture. This might entail one-to-one nurturing and playtime for half an hour a day, in additional to more sensitive care throughout the day. Often this means a shuffling of tasks in order to carve out the time. This one-to-one time includes:

- rocking and singing together,
- storytelling,
- baking or cooking together,
- active play with a chance for eye contact and movement (soccer, playing catch, swinging on the swing)
- nighttime stories and cozy tuck-ins,
- dancing together, and
- hide-and-seek or other play activities that parents and children find enjoyable.

I ask parents to increase positive touch, warm voice tones, pleasure at shared mealtimes, and friendly eye contact with smiles, and to include fun activities in the home. I like parents to provide a positive-to-negative comment ratio of 7:1. (Parents are asked to put seven pennies in one pocket, moving a penny to the other pocket for each positive comment, touch, or eye contact. They can spend a penny on a negative comment or look when they have a positive balance.)

Often the list above means that parents stop spending time with their children on discipline issues of lying, stealing, chores, homework, and sneaking. As I point out to them, their efforts in these areas are not working well anyway, so they should simply reduce energy spent there. Parents often argue with their children over organizational tasks associated with executive dysfunction or sensory issues: messy school binder or room, homework lapses, slumping or inverted postures, fidgeting, leaning against and touching walls or objects, being off task, and negative nonverbal gestures.

I talk to parents about taking a break from parental emphasis on children's misbehaviors listed above. For several months I suggest that the parents reduce their efforts on eradicating bad habits of lying, stealing, and so forth, spending more time on positive, attachment-producing activities. Children may be accustomed to getting the majority of their attention from misbehavior, so parents take the lead in preferential attention. We associate parents with positivism and fun instead of disapproval.

Since executive dysfunction is so closely linked to maltreatment and prenatal exposure to substances, often parents are irritated by behaviors that show that these factors influenced a child's brain. I am most interested in helping children to regulate themselves by using a regulated parent as a touchstone. Research is demonstrating that connection to a regulated parent is a route to improved cortisol levels and executive functioning in at-risk children (Tinienko et al., 2010; Dozier et al., 2008; Lewis-Morrarty et al., 2012).

Many parents are desperate to stop the external evidence of their children's problems. I ask them to work from the inside out, instead of trying to force change externally. We do work on behaviors, but only on a couple of items at a time and as secondary to attachment. Often this means dramatically simplifying and slowing down daily life.

When working on attachment, we are building the children's capacity to reach out to parents and trusted others, who will help them when they have overwhelming feelings and images. It is crucial that trauma work does not retraumatize children. To prevent this, there need to be people who can help them feel as safe and regulated as possible when they are working on trauma and grief. Children need to experience a sense of safety, or return to felt safety, if they temporarily lose their safe feeling during therapy. During the attachment phase, the therapist is helping children to build connection with parents, with a reduction in stress. Children learn to move toward parents, first at the therapist's suggestion, and then automatically.

As we move into trauma work, children turn to parents, as well as the therapist, for help with anxiety and grief. Most children have felt alone, or have been alone, without a protective parent as they faced trauma or traumatic grief. They are obviously reluctant to revisit trauma or grief if they expect to be alone with it again. Therapists can explicitly address this by telling parents to remind children that when afraid, overwhelmed, or sad, they need to go to parents. Parents will give a hug, sing, talk, or just be there, putting an arm around their children. I am intentional about building motor patterns in sessions. When children feel negative feelings, they physically go to parents, or parents reach out to embrace them. In sessions I ask children to note the decrease in their negative feelings after a hug and calming time with parents. They experience that stress reduction in real time. Parents begin to anticipate that need, drawing children in automatically.

Intake Sessions With Children

When children come in for first sessions, I ask them to bring three things that they are proud of, or things that they like. This start is a nice way to relate around their successes or interests. My responses to children are purposefully a bit heightened in the opening sessions. I provide an easy relational map with my face, tones, and gestures. I make it simple for them to connect to me so that they can begin to use my nonverbal cues for emotional information and regulation.

In the first session, as we begin looking at the items that they brought in, I have an entrance to subjects that are meaningful to them. With their parents in the session, I model a brighter way of relating. As the parent catches the positive affect, I ask the child to look at the parent and say, "Notice how your mom [dad] looks when she hears us talk about your soccer trophy [picture, Lego structure]. What do you think she is thinking and feeling?" Kids might say, "She's happy," or "Good."

"I think that you are right," I say. "Let's see if we are right." Then I say to the parent, "What are you feeling or thinking while you watch your son?"

"I like looking at him so happy," the parent might say. Or "I am feeling proud when I look at his drawing."

Then, I go back to the child, saying, "How does that make you feel?"

"Happy," the child might say. Or the child may have already moved on, ignoring the parent and breaking off contact. If the latter is the case, I might say, "Oh, so that's something that makes it hard for you to be happy together. When your mom is happy, you turn away. We can work on that. But, I'd like to talk to you about myself and what I do."

I will ask children, "Why do you think that you are here?"

"Because of my problems," they say. Or "I don't listen." "I get too mad." "My past."

Some parents will interject, saying something like, "We all have problems. It is not just you who needs to change." Other parents may give a little summary of their favorite lecture on behavior to the child at this point, raising defenses. Our tiered approach in intake sessions has been forgotten.

I promptly move the conversational ball back to my side of the court if lectures or shame are occurring. I may give a little more time if the conversation is positive. But, speaking directly to the child, I say, "I am meeting with you because my job is to make your life a lot happier. I don't think that you are as happy as you could be. What I do is to help kids to have a happier life."

Visions of new electronics may start to dance in their heads at this point. I might say, "You are right, a new video game might make you happy. But I am interested in your heart. Didn't you ever wonder why it is so hard for you to feel very much love in your heart? Or why your heart has so much mad and sad? I'd like to show you with a drawing if you will help me."

I will ask kids to sit beside me, with a pillow in between us if they need that distance, helping me to draw on an art pad. I ask them to draw, or help me to draw, a picture of a heart. I have a number of gel markers ready, so I can ask them to pick a color.

I say, "The thing that I do is to help kids whose hearts have been hurt a long time ago. My job is to help you get happier, to help you

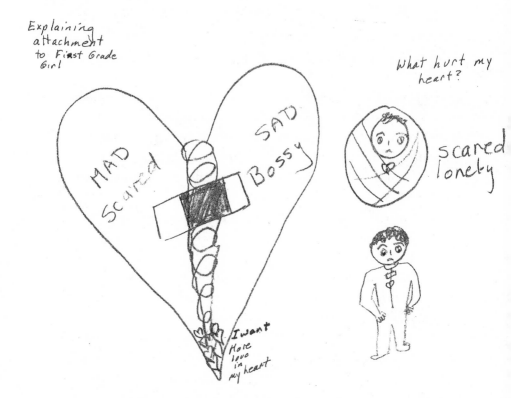

Figure 4.2 Heart drawing

with your heart." While saying this, I draw a heart with a jagged crack down the middle. I ask them if they know what things break a kid's heart—not the beating heart but the feeling heart.

"I don't know," they say.

Then I will refer to one or two items from their lives. "Losing a mom." "Being really scared of people coming in the night." "Being really, really hungry and not having anyone help you." I might write the words beside their hearts as we talk. Or I might draw the feeling face that conveys the emotion. Figure 4.2 is an example of a first grade child's heart picture.

At this point, some children blurt out, "I got hurt, and so did my mom!" Or "I got in trouble. I was really, really hungry. They wouldn't get out of bed." Other children engage without words, but put faces on the hearts or decorate them.

I say, "The kind of work that I do is to help kids' hearts." Then I draw a looping stitch to close the heart, with a Band-Aid on top. "I've done this kind of work for lots and lots of kids. Do you know why?"

"So their heart doesn't have that crack?" they might say.

"Right. When your heart has that crack, it doesn't hold much love," I say as we draw. I put a number of little hearts in the bottom of the heart shape. "Most kids have a lot of hearts, filling up their love tank," I say, with a hand patting my heart area, which causes them to direct attention to their own heart area. "You do not have as many hearts in yours. It fills up the space with big mad and lots of scared and lonely feelings." At this point, I write symbols or the words "mad" or "sad" or "scared" on the empty spaces of the heart. "We'll work together to help your heart to hold more love, more safe feelings, and more friendly feelings."

Some kids wiggle a little and agree. I say, to the parent, "Will you put your arm around him [her]?" I direct the child to look at the parent. "Can you see how happy that would make your parent to give you more love?" At that point, kids will nod and capture some of the parent's engaging facial expression. Other kids will get dysregulated, so I put them right on the exercise ball. "Take a little break. Sit on the ball and take a drink of your juice. You are doing great in this session. In a few minutes we'll come back and make our heart plan."

Other kids will shut down the display of adult emotional expression from the parent and therapist. I talk directly to this: "Are you showing me that heart work worries you? Maybe scares you?" Kids may respond at this point or may simply take this as information. Because of the earlier work, I already have information about the impediments to connection in the past. I can say, "It sounds like you are not sure about this. That maybe you shouldn't get too close to parents. I have helped lots of kids who weren't sure that this would work. I'll help you, too."

At this point, I am eliciting buy-in from a child to work with me. I prefer using an additive rather than deductive way of conveying information. (Children with processing issues do better with additive processing, less well with deducing.) I am providing a conceptual frame of the topics of our work together.

Kids might say that they did not think about why they got mad so much. "I just didn't think about it." Or they might say, "If they gave me what I wanted then I wouldn't feel so mad."

I give a different answer depending on their statement. If it is about parents and limits, I say, "If parents gave you what you wanted, it would probably work for a while. But there is going to be a time when parents can't say yes, and then you will have the same problem. Too bad. I know. It would be so much easier if parents just wouldn't say 'no!'"

I include visual images of the heart because the right brain is rich in processing emotional meanings and images, including trauma images. Visual processes are also more interesting to children. And they are a better modality for children with prenatal exposure to toxic substances and executive dysfunction. I add the verbal discussion right after the visual imagery, because I want to move to a cooler way of relating. I want them to slow emotional memories until we have more regulation.

I continue, "My job is to help you feel more love from parents, and also to be able to hold onto love. I also will help you with the scary and sad parts of your life. But we won't do the sad and scary parts first or else it could feel too hard. We will work on the good feeling of being with parents and being loved first. First, we will fill more of your love tank." I point to the heart picture as the love tank. "We will make a plan for what we will do when you come to see me. And every time that you come in, we will work on some of that plan."

At this point, I may give kids a juice box with a straw that they can chew on, offer bubble gum that they walk across the room to get, or let them bounce around on a therapy ball for a few minutes so that there is a sensory break and a deceleration in emotional intensity. Then we resume by making a treatment plan together.

Visual Treatment Plan

The treatment plan for children is set up in squares. I might have four, six, eight, or nine squares, depending on the complexity that children and I choose, constructed like a patchwork quilt. I tell kids

Figure 4.3 Positive identity, attachment, and grief visual treatment plan

that this will be our plan for how we will work together. That way, they do not have to wonder what is going to happen. I have included two plans made by children. The first was for a child who had formed an insecure disorganized attachment (Figure 4.3). She was impacted by grief and neglect. She indicated her first parents in one of the squares. (They were farmers, who had bees.) She included an area of interest and mastery, horses, as well as what she wanted to work on in sessions—grief and liking herself better. She did all of the drawing.

The second visual treatment plan was done by a child diagnosed with reactive attachment disorder, who experienced severe abuse and neglect with her first mother (Figure 4.4). She drew most of the faces and made decisions about which symbols to use. She had not benefited from intensive, in-home work with cognitive-behavioral approaches. She had not developed affect regulation. Since she had a high score on a childhood dissociation scale, as completed by her

Figure 4.4 Attachment and complex trauma visual treatment plan

adoptive mother, we agreed that she should use symbols rather than more evocative pictures.

Kids can pick out the colors, doing the amount of writing or drawing that they want. I use the choice of color or type of markers or pens to slow down pacing and intensity. A typical plan includes squares about closeness with parents, friends, anger, sadness, scary stuff, mastery and interests, and hope for the future. Each square has an evocative picture or words in the square. I describe to children that we will start with the closeness square, which is marked with a sketch of a parent with an arm around the child. I ask for children's consent to begin working with them. Then I show them the therapy room and ways that we could use the materials in the room.

First Sessions

In the beginning sessions, we work on closeness to parents. I help children to approach parents for regulation and care. As children come into the session, I greet them, and then we define what we will work on and what materials to use.

Sometimes, children and parents have made some progress on attachment, but trauma hinders the development of better attachment and regulation. In those cases, I ask parents to increase nurturance and the meeting of dependency needs, but our treatment plan moves directly to trauma or loss work. While I expect that attachment is impacted negatively by unresolved grief or trauma, there is still enough attachment that I see the following:

- Children are looking for and guided by the expressions on their parents faces.
- Children are reaching out for parental closeness and accepting some closeness.
- Children are expressing dependency needs and accepting parental help in meeting those needs.

Even if a secure pattern is just emerging, I will ask for an increase in nurturance in the home, before moving into trauma or grief work. In fact, until we work on trauma and grief, it will continue to diminish attachment security.

I use parents in the attachment phase, exploring with their children ways that they feel open to closeness. We experiment by finding out which type of touch feels good to kids—light touch on the arm or firmer touch on the shoulder, for example, or a stroke on the head or light scratch on the upper back. Sometimes I make an outline of a person, showing on the picture which areas of the body parents will not touch. This reassures children who have been sexually abused, yanked, or slapped around by other parents. If the parent in the session has been rough or even abusive, therapy includes an explanation of how things have changed. The therapist leads the parent to promise to touch and cuddle only in safe-feeling ways. (If abuse or harshness is ongoing, therapy immediately moves to better self-control for the parent. The therapist would not ask a child to drop defenses necessary for living with a harsh or abusive parent.)

Parents and children compose some goals for how they will spend special nurturing time together, with the therapist providing suggestions. In the session, attachment-producing home activities are tried out to the extent possible. For example, for parents whose cozy time will be sitting next to a child, reading, we will practice this activity in session.

What seems to be a fine idea, in concept, instead pulls up children's defensive reactions from their implicit memory systems. I may see motor movements with elbows out, knees digging in, feet drumming, and "clearing the air" arm movements that push parents back. Occasionally children even start moving into dissociation or immobilization. I stop and help children notice what is happening to their bodies. I say things like, "Your baby brain is remembering times when you were not safe when you got close. Waving your arms and getting your feet up to kick helped you back then. But that parent is gone. You are 6 years old now and in Deborah Gray's safe office. I want you to get all the love that you deserve. Let's try again getting close for a shorter time. Let's practice how you can get up when you feel uncomfortable. No one is going to trap or grab you." As they start to get distressed, I will say, "You can move. It's fine." With permission to move and get up, children find that they are able to stay closer.

I might have the child try sitting next to me, with the parent promising to keep the child safe. Then we alternate back to the parent, while I adjust positions in a kind way. Those adjustments often include putting an arm down so a child does not poke, or providing a blanket for a child's lap if the child feels exposed. I try to interrupt too much intensity by saying, "Great," or "How nice," and then, "That's enough." These breaks occur before children feel the need to arch away. Then after a little break, we try again. This time I might film them or take pictures with my cell phone. Parents, children, and I look at those pictures in session. I may send those photos to the home for them to look at later. Then we make a plan for them to practice closeness during the week.

It is important for children to feel some agency. If children have prior experiences of immobilization, not being able to move away from danger, I am especially interested in their motor expressions of fear. We will practice having them get up and move away from parents or me. We work together to try closeness in way that sidesteps some of their intense feelings, such as sitting on the floor at an angle instead of side by side.

Working on attachment schemas often causes visceral feelings, a sense of alarm, or a feeling of falling apart (Schore, 2003b). Talking to kids with compassion about this feeling, and letting them know that it will decrease over time, helps to encourage them. If I see the physical manifestation of these sensations, I talk about it to children. I say, "When we work on getting close to parents, some kids say that they feel upset feelings in their bellies. Or they feel like they have to go to the bathroom when they just went. Some kids feel these feelings, and some do not. Are you having some feelings like that, or feelings in your chest?" I put my hands on my body on the places that I am indicating—chest, upper gut, and lower gut. "Your brain is trying to decide whether getting close is safe or not safe. We need to send it some signals that it is OK now. I promise that I will keep you safe in here so that your brain gets the signal. If you get more than a little scared, we will take a break. I am proud of you for trying so hard. Taking a break is fine."

The goal is to begin desensitizing them to parents. Parents need to be desensitized, as well. When parents are just trying to be close and instead experience their children's trauma symptoms, parents are leery of getting close. My steadying presence helps parents to stay in regulation. I make little reassuring comments as we work on parents and children sitting together, reading together, and so on. Soothing and rhythmic voice tones, which I initiate and which are copied by parents, can keep children from moving into dissociation or immobilization.

During this time, I ask parents to make little alterations such as moving a hand to cover their child's hand, sit closer, or tilt their bodies so that children may nestle. The list of parental behaviors in the secure attachment behavioral checklist in Chapter 3 gives many behavioral options that will bring parents and children closer. Often I will try a couple of these, asking children and parents how it feels. Reactions range from "good" to "different."

Children who have backgrounds of neglect have not had the chance to cling, get cozy, sit closely, and receive eye contact. In addition, their tolerance of body-based attachment signals is lessened because neglect has impacted their sensory systems. Their systems are easy to overstimulate. Simply discussing this reality helps children to feel better about their reactions. I tell children that they have missed out on early experiences. But it is not too late to have those experiences now. Still, it will take their bodies a little while to get used to touch, eye contact, and closeness. Some children have had sensitive parenting followed by neglectful parenting, and now have sensitive parenting again. Those kids will get comfortable again, but it takes a while. I tell them that their body needs to get used to being safe and loved again.

The description I give to children sounds like, "You were a beautiful baby and toddler. But when your eyes looked up and your arms reached out . . . lots of times there was no one there to smile with loving eyes or to pick you up. You got used to not having what other kids were getting. But it wouldn't be fair to you to say, 'Too bad, you had your chance.' Instead, we want to give you some of what you missed. It may feel weird at first, because you got used to not getting the smiles, hugs, and nice looks. I would like your brain and body to get used to being loved and close. Would you work on that with me, even though you get weird feelings at first? It will feel normal pretty soon, just like a new pair of shoes feels normal after you wear them for a couple of days. People are more important than shoes, so it takes more time than shoes, but not too long." I provide many nonverbal cues and pauses throughout this discussion.

At all times I am aware of sensory sensitivities. I will not ask children with sensory sensitivities to desensitize to well-meaning but ill-advised cues that are outside of their sensory capabilities. A good evaluation by an occupational therapist will help to define the range of stimulation for touch, gaze, sitting, movement, excitement, motor play, and voice tones.

First Session With Highly Controlling Children: Framing the Conversation

During intake with more defended children, they often will make demeaning comments about goals of closeness with parents, blurting out, "Ewww, get close to her?" "Blah, blah, blah, I've heard this before."

While my responses to kids are individualized, I try to decide what is important to defended kids. Many kids want friends. I hook them on the concept of practicing friendliness with parents as helping them make friends of their own age. Or I bring in their jealousy of a sibling to whom the parents show affection. "It seems like you are telling me that you don't need the attention and fun that your mom and dad show to others. Kind of like," I take on a haughty expression, "you are above it all and better and smarter than your parents."

They may agree, saying, "I think I am," while laughing at my posturing.

I use mime to advantage. The laughter brings down defenses a little so that I can slide in important information. "But I notice that you are jealous of your brother when Mom snuggles or when she takes your cousins to the movies. Maybe you just have decided that you can't trust a parent enough to get close. Or that you need to be in charge of parents, and not let them know that you need them. Too bad. Well, I'll work with your parents today. You can wait in my waiting room while we make our plans. I don't want to waste your time and mine." I remain friendly, but matter-of-fact. I am not sarcastic. The bravado typically fades at this point, since kids are decreasing their anxiety with control and dominance. Sitting in the waiting room while the "real" adults make plans tends to be disconcerting. They are more accustomed to adults debating them as peers.

I go on to tell them, "The work in this room is on closeness right now. If you want to talk to me about why that is hard, I would be glad to hear it. I think that it is scary for you and different to work on closeness. I also hear that you feel bad about friends some of the time. And that you have really bad dreams of being alone and on your own. I don't want you to have to work so hard in life, taking care of yourself. Do you think that we could draw together, so that I could show you some pictures?"

If children hesitate, but show attention, I move into drawing a time line for them, showing what worked in the past and what would work better now. I might go on to say, "I am glad that you worked so hard to take care of yourself back then. That was a great choice. But it would be a bad choice to try to be in charge of everyone and everything now. And even if your parents put up with it, it won't work out for you at school. Other kids won't like it. They won't invite you to their birthday parties. It is lonely. Being in charge and kind of bossy was your only choice back then. You have other choices now." This is said slowly, with pauses.

This conversation is right-brain, empathy-led and has some exaggeration in nonverbal signals. Then I say, "So, you can stay or go, either one. But the people in this room are working on closeness today." Often kids will see if I will actually escort them out. I will if it is not too rough feeling. On the way out they might say, "OK. OK. I guess I'll stay." If it seems like a rough control battle is going to occur, with resistance at the door, I might say, "I will be working with adults only. You can sit here with this puzzle or the stamps while adults work." Then I set them up, just outside of the social distance, with an activity that allows them to listen. During that activity, I talk to parents about attachment and the impact of neglect and trauma on kids. The dialogue is directly spoken to the parents, but simple and tailored to the child in the room who is listening. I give examples of kids who have had negative reactions to beginning work but who have done very well. This gives resistant kids some hope and predictability. Kids may begin to interrupt, saying, "I hear you," or providing corrections.

I say, "Oh. I am just working with parents. Pardon me, but I need to work with them." If they persist, I say, "Come over and join us. I'd like to hear what you have to say." Then I begin to work with them as well. I need buy-in, at some level, to begin working.

After we have made progress on attachment, and after I see children able to use my help and their parents' help in regulation, we can open up other areas of need. This work is described later in this chapter. Secure attachments are an amazing way to increase regulation capacity in children. They have the advantage of pulling parents in to become insightful and sensitive, helping their children through painful material.

Physical Description of the Office and Use of Materials

When working on attachment, having an office space that invites the work makes for easier sessions. The materials need to have themes that include safety and dependence, aggression and anger, symbols of attachment through food, symbols for moves between families, scary figures that are not too overwhelming, people figures that include some symbols of people in their family or past families, places of safety, items to contain scary people, space for movement or role-play, and places for children to sit closely to their parents with feet tucked up. I also need items that will help children to stay within sensory regulation, including exercise balls (small and large), gum, floor space to stretch, and fidgets.

My office looks like a place for people to relax and relate. I have a love seat that angles and faces a sofa, with a swivel chair off to one side and a child-sized table and chairs on the other side. My love seat is on casters, so that it can slide back and forth, giving me more floor space for play, or intimate space for work on family closeness. As stated before, my seat allows my head and my client's head to be within 6 feet, or social distance. That indicates, nonverbally, a familial relationship. I have therapy balls so kids can move on or off the correct-sized ball for sensory reasons. I keep one high, one low and within easy reach. I have closed cabinets that contain other play materials.

I have plastic food for issues of food and attachment. I also have some real, wholesome, snack food for any child who arrives hungry. I dip into this stash about twice a week for children. Children who have had food scarcity as part of their trauma may express anxiety as hunger. Feeding them helps them to reduce their overarousal,

bringing them into a working range. At some point we make meaning of the connection between the feelings of hunger and their story.
Chewing also helps with sensory regulation, so I might suggest some
gum as a transition.

I have a woven blanket that is nice for helping kids nest with a
parent. Additionally, I have two quilts, gifts to the office from former clients. They lend a cozy tone and can be pressed into service to
make a fort or to insulate kids from touch or contact.

Puppets are super in play therapy. Mine include a scared scallop
that opens and closes to protect its satin inside. I have a small and
large turtle. The small turtle can tuck under the shell of the parent turtle, looking out. It can be used in a variety of metaphorical
ways. I have a crying kitty, fierce lion, lion headpiece, spider, adult
and baby opossum with attaching tails, a large-mouthed and loud
duck named Big-Mouth Duck, an intrusive and nosy Pink Panther,
a long monkey with a tail that hangs down behind and resembles a
penis, a little rabbit, a larger rabbit, a dolphin with flower wreath, a
cowboy shark, and a pig (comic relief).

I introduce the puppets with younger children. Depending on
their level of imagination, I give no hints to several hints as to their
possible meanings. For children who need some help moving out of
the trauma reenactments that are so hopeless, I may introduce a figure as an ally or magical power figure once I see that children need
that figure. I keep a powerful puppet figure (magical bear) out of
sight to introduce, if needed, for this purpose.

I have two dollhouses and ethnically diverse people. I have a lot
of babies. I also have family options with two moms and two dads.
Having two houses helps children who are demonstrating home
transitions or events in a former home or with other parents and
people. I also have a jail, which is often occupied, police cars, fire
engines, an ambulance, hospital staff, and medical equipment. I
have rescue and medical figures, all helpful for trauma and grief
work. We can introduce positive, helpful figures, as needed, if children are stuck in hopeless replays.

In yet another cupboard I have dolls, along with play food and
baby care equipment. A number of children like to have their par-

ents help them with tender child care, expressing their desire for care. Or they may hit the baby, telling the baby to stop crying and being a bother, describing their parenting.

I include the fidgets close to the seats. A favorite is a Mickey Mouse koosh ball. Another is a flexible yellow pot scrubber with half-inch long silicon spikes. Children start to look around for these items when we are working on intense materials. After a short time, the parents notice when they need these fidgets and will reach for them. (I do not use fidget spinners, which are distracting.)

I also have a library of children's books on topics related to attachment, fears, regulation, abuse, friendship, limits, divorce, changing caregivers, death, and adoption. These books help children relate to emotions that are hard for them to describe. I may read to children who are tired or overwhelmed, when they need a cooler session. I include some funny books with no therapeutic value. At times we will read these books to take a break. It helps kids to trust me when I say that I am not sneaking in a meaning with a book; it is just a funny book.

I provide spiral-bound art sketchbooks that sit nicely on a lap. I draw some of the ideas or concepts with children. The visuals are easier for them to relate to and retain. As one boy said to his grandmother, "Deborah Gray helps me fix my feelings with pictures." In fact, I am creating right-brain-led imagery that helps reduce traumatic imagery that is making them miserable. For example, I will draw a box at the top of the page. In that box is a smiling child whose smiling parents have arms around him. I say, "This is real." Then we might draw some of their bad dream that includes domestic violence. We may superimpose an end to that dream that is cocreated by the child and parent, with my help. That solution might be drawn over or taped over the scary dream. Or we might tear the dream monster off the page, placing this monster (which resembles the person who was violent) in a locked container in my room. The monster asks to be let out.

The parent says, "No. I don't let scary people into my house. You are locked out."

The child chimes in, feeling some separation and mastery. "Poopy head. You are done!"

I have large rolls of paper that look like shelf lining paper (available at art supply or craft stores) Children and I use those scrolls to write and draw out life narratives. Children choose a setting, draw who was there, have thought bubbles for their thoughts and feelings, describe what happened, include what they wish had happened, and their current thoughts. I scribe, if needed. Often children want to write down the most important aspects. For children who have had multiple experiences that need attention, those scrolls are unrolled so that we are working one section at a time. Children like to look at the completed roll. Other times they like put a rubber band on their work, providing a sense of containment.

I have a family of anatomically correct dolls that may be used when working on sexual abuse. They are in a restricted area and used with kids for trauma work with sexual abuse. They also help with sexual information for developmentally delayed children. I can use a doll of the same gender to show genitals and care.

I have hats that allow for some personas, including prince and princess crowns, police officer hats, and cowhand hats. I also have a medical staff smock that can fit a variety of sizes. I encourage children to imagine other parts of the outfit, encouraging executive functioning development.

I have more advanced art supplies for teens, producing them as needed. Some teens enjoy coloring a complicated picture with gel pens as we talk. I have games that I play with kids. Using a suggestion from Richard Rose (2017), I use Jenga, but write feeling or identity questions on the blocks. I use other feeling or expressive games on the market, often adapting them for various children. When answering the games' questions about their feelings or those of others, I use tokens and real money, rewarding for thoughtful answers. That makes the games especially meaningful and costs about a dollar.

Some children leave the room with me, going for a walk and talk. Most of these children are older. Getting out of a confined space is a relief to active children. We might walk, talk about a topic, and then return to finish the discussion in the privacy of the therapy room.

The playroom has a candy dish that is large and covered. The treat dish is popular. It leaves a sweet taste at the end of sessions. I am not under the illusion that this is minor in children's economy. Kids mention the candy dish as a top factor in my status. "That Deborah Gray really understands kids," one child said, unwrapping his Jolly Rancher.

A few children have great difficulty with regulation. I have gum that they can chew during the session. I put one to three pieces on the table for those children to take as they need it. Initially the need is great. After a while, they ask for it less, ask to take it for their stash, or leave it behind. Periodically, I have a large, covered tub of bubble gum replacing regular gum. Again, children take it as needed. They need to walk across the room to get the gum, which helps with needed mini breaks. (I tell kids that I wanted bragging rights, so I got the big tub.)

In order to work on attachments that have included grief or trauma, I will bring in photo albums for children or teens, sliding the pictures and letters that we draw or compose into the photo sleeves. For example, we may use photos of people who have died or photos of themselves at earlier ages. I like having the trauma or grief book in this portable format, since they may want the books in the future. In the book, we can slide very frank pictures or letters into the plastic sleeves, writing a summary on the outside. For example, we might have a picture of a child with bruises. We cover it with a sheet that says, "Under this is a picture of what a really mean guy did to me. I don't need to look at his face. He is in jail and I'm glad. He's the one crying now. Not me." I can also take a photo of their play setup, printing it and sliding it into the pages.

I have swords, helmets, and shields on top of a tall shelf. I use the armor and swords when children are doing trauma work. They may tape a drawn face of an abuser on the monkey puppet, whacking the monkey with their swords and telling it how they feel. More generally, we may enjoy some sword play as a physical way to end the session. For some children, we may work on staying friendly even when very excited. Rather than trying to eradicate me with the sword,

I remind them, "friendly," cuing them as their bodies become too aggressive. Other times we work on stop-and-go impulse control using the swords.

I include parents who may enjoy crossing swords. The activity builds reciprocity. I like to take a photo of kids in the helmet, with the shield and with the sword raised, showing their strength. We look at the photos together, with parents enjoying the moment. I think that it helps kids to feel their power and show me their strength.

I will buy special materials for particular child or teen issues. Kids like opening these supplies or helping me to pick them out. For example, a teen wanted to work on large paper, using graphic art pens. We walked to the store and bought them. Her mother called later, saying, "My daughter told us at dinner, 'Deborah spent a lot of money on me. She must really like me!'" In fact, the amount of money spent was about a quarter of the cost of a therapy session. The benefit was high.

Organizing Therapy Sessions

In my therapy sessions with children, I begin with a review of the week. With children who are able to wait in the waiting room, as mentioned earlier, I debrief with parents, helping those parents to regulate and set goals for themselves or their children. Goals might be spending 15 minutes a day in active playtime with their child, or playing a game daily with a child and sibling practicing compromises instead of them hitting each other to conclude the game, or including 10 minutes of singing and rubbing shea butter into their child's skin at bedtime. I briefly review what larger issue we are working on but continue the process of attachment security. In another example, if we are working on grief, we would review what the child has processed at home and suggest some comforting rituals at home.

When children enter the therapy room after getting their juice or hot chocolate, I ask about their week. I find out what pleasant things are happening, as well as what seems to be working for attachment and de-escalation. If we are working on trauma or traumatic loss, I ask about their fear level, and what part of their story we want to work on, giving them choices about time and materials. We agree on materials and what to work on, as well as when and how to get breaks.

Some children move easily among play materials as they need to. I follow them. Other children avoid the themes of therapy, scared of their feelings, and need lots of support in pacing. I will suggest moving to cool modalities to limit the amount of activation. I suggest being very clear about this with kids. I tell kids that I do not want them to go home from therapy and have a really bad night. I want to work on enough so that they feel good by the next day. When moving to cooler techniques, I ask them to transition to paper and pencil, away from rescue and police cars. I remind children that they have a signal to use if they start to feel overwhelmed. They can ask for breaks, sit on the ball, or play with some cars, stamps, or figures that are not part of the expressive therapy materials. As we work on trauma or grief, we may set a time limit on how long we work. For example, a boy said to me, "I think that I can do this for 30 minutes." We agreed on that amount of time.

I summarize at the end of the session, with a discussion of the tasks at home and support that they need for the coming week. This is often written out. Sometimes we cut a card from the art sketchbook to make reminder cards with 3 o 4 pictures or words about "what to do when." The what to do might be calming skills, fun things to do, or closeness goals like getting 7 hugs a day. I may turn this into a laminated card.

A summary is especially helpful for children with executive dysfunction. They have a harder time organizing information and storing it in memory systems. At the end of the session, if we used pictures and writing, we send the sheets home to share with the other parent in two-parent families, and to review. Not only does this help children retain information, it helps them change their mental representations of themselves as they review and explain the sheets to another parent.

Using Then and Now

As mentioned in Chapter 3, Dan Siegel (2010) describes how using the concept of an intervening variable helps people to drop defenses. Using a time line or role-plays, we can show children what has changed. What was necessary at one time is not necessary now. The following is an example of a child who was sexually abused at the age of 4 when he was in a Children's Home in Russia. He had no person to whom to turn for help at that time. He was adopted when he was 5. His parents requested help for attachment, anger, and dissociation when he was 10 years old. The following conversation occurred a year after some attachment work was completed and with trauma work underway.

"When you were in that Children's Home, those people were just going to do what they wanted to do. There wasn't really anything that you could do to stop them, except freeze. That was what your body was made to do to survive." I paused, providing a moment to hold him in regulation with my eyes, body language, and caring voice tones. Quickening my language and increasing pitch slightly, I continued, "But things are different now. You are older and bigger. You can speak and yell. You can report them. You have a whole team of people around you to help you. Can you name some people on your team?"

"Dad," he said, hesitantly at first. "Mom, my brother, Uncle Chad," and, looking straight at me, "you." He looked at his mother, who nodded, nonverbally showing an erect posture of strength.

I continued, "Your life has dramatically changed. You have backup—even when you are in trouble and it's your fault. Sometimes that's when we all need our families the most—when we've made a mistake. Families help you to figure out how to fix the mistake instead of freezing and hiding from it." I added the information about mistakes since he tended to move into hypoarousal with shame.

That is a more sophisticated example of an 11-year-old boy who freezes and hides, when afraid or after making mistakes. Shame is a big issue for him. For a younger child, we can make simpler before-and-then descriptions. For example, "When you were little, you did not get enough food. You needed to save some in your bed so that you had it later. Now you have lots of food and your family wants you to enjoy eating with them. You still use the old way of running off with food, eating and storing it." While talking I will draw, using a line down the middle of the page with an empty cupboard on one side and a full cupboard on the other side. "Which side of the page fits with eating with your family? Which fits with not enough food?" The child will point to the respective sides. I'd continue. "You did a great job taking care of yourself before. But now you want to be in charge of food—like your parents can't do it right. I don't think that you are being fair to yourself to stay on the scary and hungry side. Do you want to stay on the scared side or the side of enough food?"

The child will point to the side of enough food.

I then say, "Point again where you would like to be and draw some of your favorite food." The child points to the ample food side again and adds some food. "I think that's a good choice," I say. "Do you want to play it out?" Then we move on to use the play food to act out the trusting scene. I might supply some raisins or trail mix to make it more realistic. We laugh and enjoy the picnic. Then we make a plan for the new way.

Shame and Attachment

Most children feel a sense of shame around attachment. If they had previous parents they could not stay with, they are afraid of rejection. They question whether they will end up rejected and shamed after opening up to parents.

One boy, age 12, had improved attachment to his mother, but avoided his stepfather. He was discussing this with me without his parents in the room. "I feel like it is too much. I already had a dad. He beat up Mom. She left me, taking my sister. When I was at school, he locked me out. It was winter, but he went out drinking and forgot about me. You are asking too much."

I nodded, listening with my face and heart, saying little, but absorbing his pain.

I agreed with him that it was too much to trust all at once. I asked if he would allow himself to enjoy his new father, playing with him for just 15 minutes every day. We began there. I also told him that he had already done a good job of loving parents who were hard to love. He cried. "I did love them," he said. "But they didn't love me back."

I quietly said, "So you are wondering if there is something about you that people see? Something that makes them feel that they can treat you badly?"

He nodded. "Yes."

"I know you pretty well," I said. "I don't see anything about you that would make people want to treat you badly. But let's take it slowly. That way you can always back away and check out something scary."

Shame can infiltrate a person's core self. Phrasing it in a child-friendly manner, I begin a conversation about shame and closeness. The tension between trust and shame is part of the human condition. But it is especially potent after relational trauma. Some children like simple stories about shame and trust. These stories normalize the mixed feelings that people have, with a gradual growth of trust. Usually I pull parents in so they can relate their stories. These examples only take 2 or 3 minutes in a session, but give parents a template for storytelling rather than lecturing. Bruce Perry's work has demonstrated the power of storytelling (Perry & Szalavitz, 2006). I have seen the effectiveness of this in my work with children and teens.

Neglect's legacy, shame, has infiltrated the core of many children. They agree that they were not worth care (Gray, 2012b). In part, this is due to the brain development occurring at the early ages during which neglect occurred. When the brain is running its emotional wiring in the ages 18 months and up, shame is being developed (Sroufe, 1995). There is an overdevelopment of these structures due to the negative reactions that people have to children's needs and the helplessness that toddlers experience. In addition, there is a typical feeling of shame at the helplessness people feel when they are in abusive situations. Children incorporate into the sense of themselves the behaviors shown to them, that *they* are the degrading neglect, sexual abuse, or physical abuse.

Secure attachments provide brain-to-brain connections that are very intimate, in the same way that abuse is intimate, but convey different messages. Children sometimes are afraid to respond because of shame. When we are asking children to get close, it evokes for some children this question: "They saw something in me that caused them to reject or to abuse me. Will my parents see the same thing?"

I like to talk to kids about this, with social stories and thought bubbles, if needed. I convey these messages over a series of sessions. "Lots of kids wonder about that. After all, you were a child. Every child thinks that what happens to them must be because they caused it." With adoptive parents and children, I could say, "Your second parents have lived with you 6 years. They see you as precious. And it is not just because you are theirs, or because that is the way that adoptive parents are supposed to feel. It is because that guy who abused you was really wrong. Our whole country disagrees with this wrong guy. Judges send to jail people who do crimes like this person did to you. The reason it is so wrong is that it makes kids feel awful. Our job is to help you say back to him, 'You were wrong. It was *your* problem, not *mine*.'" We may make a picture of the abuser, putting the face on top of a big puppet, helping the child express his thoughts at this point. The process is one of making the shame of abuse external to the self, something that happened to the child instead of part of the child. I may bring parents into the room, if they were not already there, asking them to hug their child, and to express their thoughts and feelings. This example does not include the shame issues of lack of protection, dealt with in another session.

Shame is pernicious because it makes children want to hide themselves from close relationships. They do not want other people to see the mysterious something that caused notions of abuse to enter the mind of the abusers. We usually try to attribute simple causes to the people who maltreated, like addiction, being overworked, or mental illness. That way we have less polarization in the way children think about people. (This is true past the age of 5. Under that age, polarized categories of big versus little, good versus bad, are age typical.) The exception to a nuanced view of maltreatment is with sexual abuse of children. That type of maltreatment tends to stand in its own category, without mediating considerations until children are further into adolescence.

In sessions with children, we emphasize the options that they have now as opposed to the limited options they had before. "What would you do if you saw the person who abused your son trying to speak to him? Would you help your boy or freeze and stare?"

"I would help you! I'd call 911," parents say, speaking to their child and not to me.

"If you had to, would you hit, kick, or fight them off?" I say.

"Yes," parents say. "I would do what I had to do to keep you safe."

Kids might want to linger here, asking, "Would you be really, really mad?"

Parents fill their chests and almost shout, "Yes!"

Children look at parents, taking in new emotional information, with strong nonverbal cues, demonstrating that the children are worth defending, vigorously and physically. Sometimes we role-play situations, using a four-foot-long monkey puppet as the bad guy. Children may use a sword and helmet, taping a simple bad-guy face on the puppet. They whack at the puppet, expressing some of the information that they learned. For example, "You said that I had to do the touching thing before I got food and the video. You were so mean!" With more protection, they are able to process the dissociated material.

As children display motor expressions with feelings, they are able to express what was previously inhibited (Fosha, 2004). They also feel a sense of strength, autonomy, and mastery. They separate their sense of self as the victim. They reengage the memory with outrage at the assault on their sense of self, backed up by a parent and me. Sometimes they return to the parent and cry a little, with sorrow for themselves, that something so grievous happened to them. Other times they feel quite good. As one boy said, "It felt good to whack the bad guy. I always wanted to do that." Often we return a few more times to the whack-the-monkey work as they use the attachment support of parents to separate their sense of self from the toxicity of abuse. The expression of anger in play is not because they must "get anger out." Rather, the therapy gives permission for previously inhibited motor impulses, meant for self-protection, to come forward. Children do not feel immobilized by a mixture of fear, shame, and helplessness.

If children have bonded with a predator as part of the grooming process, we address this confusing aspect. "He was kind of tricky. He acted like a good friend, but then did something that made you feel icky and special at the same time."

Children may eventually respond, "That was so mean! He pretended to like me and be my friend, but made me feel scared, and like it was my fault if anyone found out and he got in trouble." We talk about how it makes kids wonder whether other people will get the same feelings when they get close. Or whether they will dare to get close to adults in case the same things happen again.

Children who were sexually abused are quite prone to acting themes out, sexually touching as part of their testing, or sexually touching because a previous disorganized attachment schema paired sexual behavior with closeness. In these cases, we tend not to use the puppet initially. Their feelings of closeness and anger will take more processing as they discuss the complexity of being asked to take an adult sexual role in a former attachment, instead of being protected and treated as a child.

Shame and Connection

Shame tends to be a prevalent theme in attachment issues. Some children have an overdeveloped shame circuitry, as mentioned earlier. Other children feel a sense of shame from not being able to stay with birth parents, as in the case of adoption. Of course, the therapist carefully addresses these issues through stories, discussion, or play. Throughout therapy, the message is explicit: You are worth loving, even with difficult behaviors. You are worth care, simply because people are valuable.

Parents who use shaming are encouraged to use cooler reinforcement systems instead. There is an emphasis on restitution, making things right, and making it up to the person offended. Children who do reasonable restitution feel much better about themselves, once again within the good graces of the family.

Self-Talk by Parents That Reinforces Attachment

When parents have children with attachment problems, they can use some help with self-talk. Because they are feeling a mixture of feelings about the relationship, those feelings result in an internal dialogue that blames themselves or their children. Replacing that voice with a more helpful internal dialogue can provide some peace. For example, "I am doing well in getting help for my child. We are making progress." "I may have had difficulties because of depression, but I am working hard now to enjoy my child. I am making progress." "I am parenting a child who had many losses before he came to me. Of course this will be hard for him and for me. I am doing the things that I know to do to help us. I am a good and caring person, even if he can't believe it yet."

These internal dialogues are often lifted from what the therapist says during the session. It is important to convey these messages of hope. The therapist acts as an attachment figure to the family, providing expressions of their value and an enjoyment of working with them. Some people do well with written affirming scripts. Particularly for people with a history of abuse, writing a few affirmations on a note card during session will help them to access positive comments when stress levels are high. I might say, "This is what I think of you as I watch you." I make the note card a size that will fit in a pocket, writing it out with first-person pronouns, with expressions such as, I am a caring mother. I am frustrated, but that is a normal part of parenting. I am doing what has been asked of me at this stage of therapy. I am imperfect. I am both loveable and imperfect—like my child. Today I can enjoy my child just as she is. I am a good-enough father, right now.

This section on self-talk is intentionally placed just after the child's section on shame. Maintaining a positive sense of self and building in learned optimism assist families to sidestep the shame trap. Too much shame makes parents and children want to fight, blaming and making the shame external, which is common in avoidant attachments, or give up, internalizing shame, which is common in anxious attachments for parents with preoccupied attachments. Positive self-talk helps build a pattern of hope and positive activation.

Daily Activities and Routines at Home That Enhance Attachment

Maintaining consistent and positive patterns in the home will make space for attachment. I like to look for a certain time of the day during which I can enhance security and encourage play.

The work of Bruce Perry and Stephen Porges describes the need for better attention to the regulation of the sublimbic areas of the brain, as seen in Figure 4.5.

Upper level cortical functioning is dependent on the smooth networking between the upper and lower brain areas. However, after childhood maltreatment with prolonged high stress, there is a tendency for the lower areas to be less robust in organization or function. The lower areas on the diagram are prone to a disruption in the flow of information between upper and lower brain levels. In Figure 4.5, this is symbolized by a rupture marking. When this happens clients will function out of primitive, survival-based parts of the brain, which tend to be organized like a turtle's brain, without mammalian warmth, empathy, or affection (Porges, 2009). When under high stress the flow of information between higher and lower brain levels may be suspended, as the figure displays. When in this

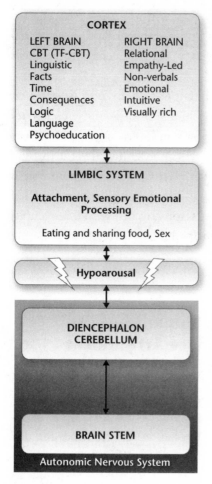

Figure 4.5 Matching emotional activation levels to therapy approaches

state clients are temporarily unavailable for connection or language-based therapy, since both capacities are within the limbic system and the cortex.

If clients are responding on a primitive level, then expressions of love and care, or prompts to use skills, will not be helpful. Instead, chanting, empathic phrases with cadence, touch that is wanted, kind voice tones, songs with lilt and rhythm (lullabies), or drumming can all cause the integration with the limbic system to resume. Then, reassuring nonverbal cues and empathic expressions allow for a resumption of information flow to the right cortex, and finally on to the left cortex. The information flow between all levels resumes.

Many of the sensory-based attachment approaches in this book are helpful in increasing the brain's organization between lower brain levels and the limbic system. The methods of reassuring children who are losing connection (limbic) tends to be through touch (welcomed), cadence, or soothing voice tones. I also tend to offer a drink or an exercise ball to sit when children are beginning to lose connection.

It has been a long-standing practice of mine to suggest an hour of physical activity for children every day. I did not know that physical exercise had specific benefits to underdeveloped brain systems. I simply noticed that children were healthier, with behavior and mood improvements. Bruce Perry teaches us that this emphasis on physical play enhances brain organization and functioning, especially after complex trauma (Perry, 2006a).

Figure 4.5 shows the therapies most associated with the right and left cortexes. (Please note that that right and left will be reversed for left-handed people.) When highly activated, clients may be unable to access their left brain's linguistic capacities. Cognitive behavioral therapy depends on access to left brain dominant abilities. Instead, therapists must use right-brain dominant approaches of empathic voice tones and non-verbals, in order to help to regulate clients. Once better regulated, therapists are able to access left brain capacities again, using psychotherapy that includes linguistic processing and cognitive behavioral approaches (Schore, 2012).

Our brains like predictable, consistent patterns. Children will show gains almost immediately with a daily schedule that includes time for nurturance and play with parents. They like to have the day listed on a chalkboard, if they can read, or in a series of pictures if they cannot. The pictures can be drawn, or photos can be taken of daily activities, copied on the printer, and then placed in order for the next day. There would be a photo of bedtime, teeth brushing, the soccer ball, and so on (Gray,2012b). Order calms children. Parents who have two or three children will say that the schedules help all of the children, not just the child who was maltreated. Predictability decreases anxiety. It also helps children to know when they will get play and attention. They do not have to act out to get parental attention.

The day might look like this:

- Get up, sit with Mom or Dad for a cozy time, talking about the day.
- Breakfast—unhurried with talk and enjoyment.
- Get dressed, with clothes laid out the night before. Make funny faces in the mirror as hair is done in front of mirror.
- Goodbye ritual and commute to preschool or school.
- Pickup from school or afterschool care with a greeting and singing time on the way home, or physical exercise on the way home from school or day care.
- Snack time, snuggle.
- Playtime with parents.
- Dinner prep with child helping.
- Dinner.
- Free choice time.
- Chores and stories.
- Bedtime ritual.

This would be the routine on a typical school day. Chores might be moved to a less challenging time of the day. Often children who have been maltreated have an inverse cortisol level that makes them more lethargic in the morning, thus more in need of regulation in the morning. This schedule accommodates that child's biorhythms, with chores later in the day.

The point to the schedule is that parents can calm children's brains by letting them know what is next. Additionally, play and closeness are prioritized rather than left for free time. Dinner or breakfast time would be times of shared enjoyment and positivism.

This type of schedule allocates parental time and energy. Some parents are simply moving too fast. Children may feel dismissed, with parents devoted to the to-do list which never gets done. Stopping one task and moving to connection and play on schedule helps with a positive home life. It allows children and parents to feel more hopeful about their worth to each other.

Every family in treatment does well to have a go-to list of things that they can do to enhance attachment in the home. Megan Clarke, Jill Dziko, Laura Stone, and Jill Fisher, and I wrote a book that provides many suggestions for play: *Games and Activities for Attaching With Your Child* (Gray & Clarke, 2015). That book describes games and activities that are suitable for children of all ages and includes activities that are fun for children with fetal alcohol syndrome or who are on the autism spectrum.

Some families will need to experiment in order to find activities that are mutually enjoyable. Being curious whether the family would enjoy the beach more, or a walk in the woods opens them up to think of themselves as a group. Some children will shoot down various ideas. I say to them, "Saying no is making your life too small! We need to give you more space to enjoy life. How about letting yourself enjoy 30 minutes of the time? Then complain as much of the rest of the time as you need to." Some sessions later I might ask them to spend all but 5 minutes of the complaining, complaining in their heads only. I say, "It is OK with me if you need to push back some of the time. But I don't want you to ruin your own day."

In that way we change the expectation that it is an all-or-nothing proposition. They can both enjoy and push back some. Because negative behavior has been proscribed in a gentle way, there is less need for children to make their point through obnoxious behavior.

Time Frames With Tolerable Separation Spans for Children

Children can have attachment stress simply by spending too much time away from their attachment figures. This has been a quite a problem in custody situations. The court may rule equitably from the point of view of parents, with children left in a state of attachment loss. Similarly, parents may be able to arrange child care for a long day or for business trips, but that does not mean children are able to tolerate those hours or trips.

Children have unique histories, so I individualize their tolerance for separation, looking at these factors:

1. Has this child had earlier attachment losses or traumas?
2. Has this child struggled to maintain connections with attachment figures?
3. Has this child a more resilient personality, or does this child show sensitive characteristics? These sensitive children need more buffering since they are more susceptible to changes or challenges in their environments.
4. What is this child's age?

Depending on the answers to these questions, parents and I are able to discuss the length of time children are able to tolerate separation. Typically, the advice is to keep infants with their attachment figures, without overnights away, unless they are staying with a well-known person who has spent ample time with the infant, such as a grandparent. The residential schedule for infants typically does not include overnights away from the primary attachment figure, with switches between homes, even if parents have joint custody. Children tend to have one primary home residence or "nest." Their need for stability also includes time in this nest as opposed to away from it. For toddlers, the time away from a parent and their home nest, is only one or two overnights. Children 3 or 4 years old only spend that many nights away from attachment figures. Children 5 to 8 spend about 5 days. Children 8 to 10, about a week. Children 10 to 13 can go 2 weeks. Children 13 to 15 can expand to a month. Parents have to be more protective of attachment, ensuring attachment security after foster or adoptive placement of a toddler or child, after a child's or parent's lengthy hospitalization, after a parent's in-patient treatment for addiction, or after the death of a parent or sibling.

It is also important for children to have tolerable periods of separation. From this they learn that parents return. Some parents keep babies and children with a parent virtually all of the time. Attachments, although precious, are not fragile, requiring these extraordinary strictures. In fact, getting some breaks can help parents have time to rejuvenate themselves, coming back to their parenting roles with enthusiasm. Children endure minor frustration and anxiety, learning that parents do return.

Repairing the Connection After Relationship Problems or Absences

When we hurt our children's feelings, stay away too long, act insensitively, yell at them, or overdo the consequences for behavior problems, there needs to be a repair. Sometimes parents will say, "But they were part of the problem!" While that may be true, parents are always expected to act as parents, not peers. I encourage them to take responsibility for their part of the problem, regardless of whether their children take responsibility.

Any time that parents frighten children, it is especially important to debrief children, apologize, and make a plan so that there are not repeat occurrences. Parenting is hard. Apologizing after hurting children's feelings models how to maintain healthy relationships. When parents apologize, it does not mean that children have the burden of making parents feel better. Parents, instead, focus on moving children back into regulation, restoring their feelings of worth, and restoring their confidence in their parents.

A script might sound like this: "Liem, I am sorry that I raised my voice and went on and on about missing assignments. I sorry that I made you feel so bad. Next time I will go calm myself down before talking to you about a schoolwork problem. I do want you to do your homework. But you are a great kid. I don't want a homework problem to mess up the way that you and I get along."

Liem might say, "I forgive you" and accept a hug.

Then the parents might say, "I wonder if we should talk about the homework now or after dinner. Either is fine with me. Do you need a little time or should we work on the problem now?"

In this script, the parent is modeling a continuing need to work on the problem, but that relationships are the biggest priority. Notice that the parent does not let go of the need for an improvement in performance. The parent also inquires as to whether or not the child might be calm enough to work on a problem. That demonstrates the reality that there are good and bad times to approach a problem, depending on regulation abilities. (The script above would have pauses between sentences, with Liem providing eye contact or gestures, to ensure that Liem tracked the mother's information.)

A script for an extended absence sounds like this: "Esther, I am so sorry that you missed me as much as you did. My trip took two extra days because of a snowstorm. I did not plan this. I am sorry that you were so angry and sad." The parent either hugs or stands close to Esther while saying this. "If I have to be gone this long in the future, I will take you with me. And I will look at the weather next time before I fly out."

Esther might push her mother away, whining, resisting, and accusing. "You left me. I don't want you now. You are a bad mom." If the mother can hold out her arms a little longer for an embrace, Esther may come close, begin to weep, and express her feelings of despair. Her mother can soothe, hug, or rock, as appropriate. This is the process of repair, with recognition for the hurt endured and responsibility for comforting and restoring the relationship.

If an insult to a child is more profound, then parents may have to approach over the course of several days. If the child had previous experiences of loss, then therapy around the evoked memories should be arranged.

Repair is one of the necessary components of secure attachment. Teaching children to repair is easiest when it is first modeled. Once modeled, parents can teach their children to use the process of repair as the issue comes up. This entails having children listen to a description of distress they have caused and how they hope to make things better.

In therapy, sometimes therapists help with this process. Earlier in this chapter I suggested relegating work on lying and sneaky behaviors until some attachment progress was made. The following is an example of dishonesty, which is ripe for intervention, since the parent and child have completed work on attachment. For example, Julian age 11, sneaked off with his mother's cell phone, ordering apps for his phone. He lied to cover it up. His mother spent extra time with their internet provider, untangling the mystery of data charges. In therapy, Julian heard his mother's frustration and hurt that he took her phone and charged her account. I asked him to listen without interrupting. At the end he said, "Mom, I'm really sorry. I got carried away."

His mother, rather than lecturing, said, "Julian, I forgive you." She patted his back. "You will need to pay for the data. I know that you want to make things right. I know what kind of kid you are. I would like you to wash all the inside windows of our home on Saturday. That will pay off the debt. And let's talk about when you are tempted. How could you either make some money next time or avoid taking my phone? Let's talk about this."

Julian says, "But you forgave me. Why do I need to do a job?"

Mom responds, "A great parent makes certain her son grows up to be honest. If you do something hurtful and sneaky, you don't want your brain to figure out that it is no big deal, that you can take a shortcut when you want something. Part of my job is to teach you how to care about others' feelings so that you don't take shortcuts that are wrong or hurtful."

This is the type of exchange that I outline with parents in their time alone. Then parents use their own words, helping their children to take responsibility, repairing the problem and relationship without feeling overwhelming shame.

Anger as a Cue for Attachment

Anger is a normal reaction when we need help and receive none—especially from the people to whom we are attached. When children have not had consistent care, they tend to assume that parents are going to fall down on the job. They are angry at parents before parents have the chance to respond to needs. The ABC project described in Chapter 2 noted that after maltreatment children may give contradictory cues and be confusing when signaling that they need help.

Many parents describe little gain from using behavioral consequences for children's anger when it is related to much deeper issues. Instead, it is more helpful to assist children in learning to express needs to their parents. Parents respond with an emotional tone of warmth and care, with the therapist's help. This means that parents learn to see past the literal meaning of what children are requesting, thinking instead, "What does my child need? What are they worried about?"

Parents need to develop a theory of mind, or a working model of children's day-to-day stressors or priorities. A boy who yells at his parents because they did not get him new soccer shoes might be expressing that he has one area of mastery, soccer, and that he played poorly because his feet hurt. He may have mentioned tight shoes only in passing, not feeling that he deserved a parent's care. Then, he yelled and threw something after the game. While therapists do not want to dismiss the issue of parents being yelled at, it is most helpful for children and parents to look for the dependency need that was not met.

First, with the therapist's help, inquiry can help children express their needs. As Dan Hughes points out, children who have attachment issues often need therapists to help phrase their thoughts and feelings (Hughes, Golding, 2012). Over time, as children practice talking to their parents, they improve in noting and speaking about their needs. Parents can respond contingently, with a therapist's help, as needed.

Levi: Dad, my soccer shoes were too tight. I couldn't run during practice. My coach yelled at me. He said, "Levi, get the lead out!" Everyone laughed at me.

Dad: I'm sorry that happened. I can get you new shoes. I didn't know that yours didn't fit. I did not know what you needed when you said, "I want to stop at the sports store, but you're probably too busy."

Therapist: Levi, could you say to your dad, 'Please get me new soccer shoes. Mine don't fit.'

Levi: Would you please take me, Dad? My shoes don't fit. [Levi struggles to ask for this need.]

Dad: Sure thing. I know that you are growing. No problem.

In the situation above, Levi unwittingly set himself up for failure. His automatic response was to protect himself from rejection, which confused and annoyed his dad. Most parents, approached as if they are inept, have a hard time responding to their children's needs. Children's requests tend to be confusing and expressed negatively. Parents can be taught to cue children in this way: "Will you please ask me again, remembering that I'm the parent who cares about you?"

Reducing Children's Escalations Around Separation

When children start escalating fears around separation, parents may further escalate these fears. Therapists can maintain regulation in the room, guiding children and parents through separation fear. These conversations might occur many, many times for children with fears of abandonment, as in the following example.

Emily, age 9, was separated her from her mother during her mother's lengthy and successful rehab program. She now has anxiety around being separated from her mother and begins to accuse her mother of being selfish. "You like to go off with your friends. You do not care that I am crying and scared."

The mother defends herself, saying, "You are not being fair. When is the last time that I did anything for myself?"

I catch Mom's eye, signaling her to join me as I breathe out, pause, breathe in, pause, and then breathe out again.

Then I say, "Mom, would you please put a hand on Emily's shoulder? She looks lonely."

I say to Emily, "It was hard when you had to be away from your mother. You remember those feelings."

Emily turns to her mom and cries a little.

Then, I lead her into change. "My job is to help you with some calm-down tricks so that you don't feel so bad when Mom goes."

Emily tries again. "But I don't see why see has to go. She sees lots of adults at work every day. Why does she go off with her girlfriends all of the time?"

Again, I cue the parent, with a little head shake, helping her to resist rebutting that once a month is not all of the time. I respond, "I know that it is hard to understand. But you can't trap Mom, like a butterfly in a net, so you don't have those feelings." I pause. Emily pretends that she has a net and moves around the room chasing imaginary butterflies, and then Mom. Her mood shifts a little with this. I continue, saying. "I have two ideas for ways to feel better when Mom goes out in the evenings." Pause.

Mom says, "I want to know what they are."

I say, "Emily, do you want to stay in the stuck spot of being upset when Mom goes out, and then arguing about it? Or are you ready to try a new way?"

I draw eye contact, which is friendly, but not overeager.

Emily says, "OK, OK, I will listen to something if you're not too boring."

At that point I give her the choices. One is to create a box for the nights that her mom leaves. In the box will be a letter from Mom promising to return, a picture of the two of them, a maze to do, and a picture to draw of what Emily did while Mom was gone. The second choice is a video, made on my phone and sent to the parent, in which Mom promises to come back and Emily practices breathing to stay calm. Emily and Mom agree on a reward for Emily if she doesn't yell or tantrum when Mom leaves or returns.

When I am working with children with anxious clinging, parents feel trapped. That exacerbates the problem, since children perceive their parent's desire to escape. Instead, we want to have times in which their parent is mindfully present. Children can use emblems when parents leave. Pictures in their pockets, or a parent's sweater or scarf to wear are emblems that remind children that their parents have not disappeared.

Hypoarousal, Hyperarousal, High Arousal, and Techniques That Match

Most strategies for regulation are centered on de-escalation. It is problematic when children move into their autonomic nervous system, unable to process normally or even to feel the love or care of their parents or therapists. The limbic system, which connects upward to the cortex, goes off-line. Children cannot feel mammal-like feelings of connection. Instead they use a primitive way of responding that is similar to that of a turtle—a cold withdrawal or attack (Porges, 2009).

What seems to have the best success is to use calm, rhythmic voice tones, gentle touch (invited), poetically spoken lines, or singing, chanting, or drumming (Porges, 2009; Perry, 2016). These will help children to regain connection with parents, accept empathy, feel feelings, and then speak and process linguistically. Figure 4.5 describes therapy practices that best match the state that children are in. In the words of Bessel van der Kolk (2013), "When in doubt, always go to the body."

Empathic voice tones and nonverbal body messages are essentials in order to reestablish limbic system–based connection in children and families. I use calming voice tones and facial expressions to prime parents, matching my nonverbal cues with their children. I will model first and then cue parents, saying, for example, "Oma, will you turn to your son so he can see the caring look on your face?" Then I might say, "Levi, can you see the love and caring on your mother's face? She cares how you feel." At that point, Levi might nod, getting tears in his eyes. I can cue again, saying, "Oma, do you think that you could hold your boy for a little bit? He seems to need you." Then, they embrace. I might ask Levi if he would like a light blanket. If Levi nods, I would get a light blanket, draping it over him as he sits next to his mother or upon her lap. Then we would sit quietly for a couple of minutes, with Levi's mother loving and coregulating him.

All of these practices are best done real time rather than through psychoeducation. I use enough psychoeducation that parents are informed and in agreement with what comes next. But modeling and coaching the patterns of coregulation through real-time experiences demonstrate the pacing and phrasing of the music of coregulation. My experience mirrors the research findings of parent training in meta-analysis—it is most effective when parents practice these skills with their children. Researchers also see a stronger treatment effect for traumatized children when using attachment-based models (Berlin et al., 2016).

Role-Play That Allows Parents to Be Prosocial Protectors

Therapy goals often include prosocial identification with competent adults, with repair of the social contract: society protects and benefits them; they should conform to societal values and limits (Pynoos, 1997).

Children with attachment losses, especially traumatic ones, tend to see the world in terms of power. They will identify with powerful people in their lives—often those who have been abusive. Even if they express that they hate them, there is an implicit belief that the powerful are mean and brutal, and those with self-control are the ninnies, likely to be exploited.

I play up parental strengths, introducing parents as strong and kind. Children and I will compose scenarios that help them to connect their fears and with kind, strong, and competent protective adults. For example, "What if Grandfather came to my school? He told me that he had a gun, and I saw it!" We might role-play the scenario. (I would use a puppet for Grandfather to reduce activation.) The school front desk attendant calls security and the police (played by Mom or Dad). The school locks down. The police come and arrest Grandfather. (I play the police role the first time through. The child might want to have a parent play this role the second time through, with me switching to be the front desk person or principal). We move the role-play on to the grandfather sitting in jail (played by a puppet) and saying, "I guess it only worked to scare him when he was little and living with someone on drugs. He has protectors now."

Or, in this continuing role-play, a mother might go on to testify in front of the judge, asking for a long jail sentence. To help with pacing, role-plays like this can move between people playing parts, to paper-and-pencil sketches, or therapy room figures. I have made paper dolls when I need to use figures for several sessions. These are simple, but have an actual photo of the child's face as the paper doll's head. (Children are so literal that a distorted or hastily made face can make them feel devalued, so I use a photo.)

These role-plays may include public places that are worrisome to children. For example, a child described his fear of being approached in a restaurant by a former abuser. We played out the scene but boosted both protection and affiliation with prosocial concepts and people. The antisocial figure (a puppet that I handle and speak for) gets too close to the child, saying, "Chrissy's my buddy. She's like me. Aren't you, Chrissy?" The abusive puppet reaches out for Chrissy. The parent puts up a spirited defense. "She is not like you! You were tricky and taught her wrong! Now she has me. Get out of here before I call the police." The parent scoops up the child and calls 911. The puppet says, "I'm scared," and leaves.

Chrissy might say, "What if he keeps coming and the police aren't there yet?"

The parent will describe getting into the car, driving away, or yelling, "Call 911!" The parent may even say, "I'd punch him in the nose." In role-play, a child may stand behind the parent, popping out from behind to yell, "Mom will kick you where it hurts! Get out of here."

Children enjoy these role-plays. Sometimes they want to cast a parent in an abusive role. I intervene with a recasting suggestion. I might move that role to myself, using the monkey puppet with a mask. Or I might play a former parent figure but make certain that I have a signal so that clients know when it is me and when I am in play. I can put on a cape to show that I am the figure, then take the cape off to return to my therapist persona. In fact, due to transference issues, some of the abusive parent issues are loaded onto me in therapy. As I told one boy, "If it seems too scary, then it will make it too hard for you to come in to see me. If you never feel some of the scary feelings from thinking of me like your first mom, then we don't get much done." He got tears in his eyes and said, "So when I am feeling really safe, I never see you again?" I assured him that he could stop by. I'd be around. (He did stop by as a young adult.)

Children find it affirming that they are worth fighting for. Since parents, hopefully, are not typically seen in fighting mode, kids need to know that parents are capable of protection. Various role-plays allow children to incorporate this concept of adult protection.

For example, a woman who naively allowed a predator to babysit her protesting preteen was in therapy with her daughter. The girl had contempt and conflicting impulses to get close to her mother and to hit her. In working through this conflict, she approached her mother and punched toward her, although not connecting with her. "I wanted to punch you for being so stupid," she told her mother.

Her mother said, "I wanted to punch me, too. You can punch me if you want." The teen moved forward but stopped with her fist lightly bumping her mother's collarbone. "But I will never be tricked again," her mother said. After holding each other's gaze, and with tears streaming down their cheeks, they embraced. Then the mother went on to describe herself as strong, able to protect her daughter into the future, and having learned from her experience. The last section of the dialogue was led by the therapist through questions. The mother and teen were gazing at each other, speaking to each other. I would not have suggested the punching, but their work showed the power of expressing inhibited motor movements.

Grief Work That Includes Parents

Children do not have the emotional stamina to move through grieving an attachment loss by themselves (Pynoos, 1997; Gray, 2012a, 2012b). They need the emotional support of others to process grief. Especially if grief is traumatic, children will require ample help. Children who readily accept help are children who have secure attachments. They are accustomed to moving toward trusted adults when they need comfort, buffering, or questions answered. And certainly there are many questions after the loss of a parent, including foster parents or stepparents to whom children were attached. Children with disorganized attachments tend to become overwhelmed, chaotic, or avoidant in therapy. They believe that remembering the loss will result in the same feelings as the ones at the time of loss— shock and overwhelming grief, without comfort or emotional regulation from others. Of course they are leery of the therapy room.

For this reason, I prefer the treatment plan to begin with an increase in attachment security with parents. Some parents expect to opt out, especially if they are foster parents. I explain why I want to engage them in the process. I have some success in gaining their help once they understand the value of their participation.

Parents may ask, "Why do the work if it is so difficult? Let's let well enough alone. Why open a can of worms?" I describe the Adverse Childhood Experiences Study results that demonstrate more vulnerability in mental and physical health unless such losses are supported (Anda & Brown, 2010).

A second reason to do the work is that otherwise children make themselves central to reasons for the loss. As one boy said, "I keep losing mothers! One died, one uses drugs, and the last one gave up. Who is the common denominator?" Another child said, "I am like a national (sic) disaster to parents!" The current crisis of opioid addiction makes this discussion particularly pertinent.

When beginning grief work with children, we review several realities:

- Getting a hug, snuggle, or encircling arm can reduce pain.
- I make a "before and now" comparison. Before they were alone with their pain and had to push it away. Now they will have help and will not feel the pain without comfort.
- I will observe children's pain levels and try to work within tolerance and their level of understanding.
- Pushing down the pain does not answer their questions. They deserve to know the truth of what happened.

I provide a simple description of how unresolved grief keeps intruding, and the reason why we do the work. I mention issues common to children, often in the form of social stories or a cool list. I also give them examples of children who have similar situations, and what seemed to help them. This allows them to follow the emotional shifts within the story, without triggering defenses. The stories also give hope. Most children are sure that they did something that caused the losses. They simply do not want that confirmed. In other cases, if the person lost to them is still alive, children would prefer to be the reason for the loss. That provides some hope that the lost parent has parenting abilities and could return to parenting them.

When moving into grief work, I suggest a slower, daily pacing within the home. Grief work takes space, time, and sensitivity. Parents may want to avoid grief because it evokes their own losses. I will talk to parents about having a person to support them as they support a child—sister, best friend, or therapist. I also reassure parents. This emphasis on grief is a stage of treatment. I am not asking them to focus on grief indefinitely. The goal is to prevent grief from intruding on everyday life. As one boy said, "Whew. I was glad that I got it out of the way so that it wasn't always bothering me!"

Children need certain essentials when working with grief.

What Happened?

Children need facts about the people they lost: siblings, parents, foster parents, stepparents. Whether through death, child welfare intervention, or custody changes, children want to know what happened—in concrete terms. These facts are literal. Children's processing may be part-oriented, rather than big-picture. They need to assemble the parts, or information about the loss, to make the picture, what happened, why, and their part in the loss story. The following is an example, with changed identifiers, from my work with a child.

"This was the layout of the house, as you remember." We were looking at a sketch and a picture of the house that he lived in with his mother. "You were in this room, and your mother and brother were in the second bedroom. Your mom took OxyContin. She started that drug when she hurt her back. That was before you were born. She got addicted. She swallowed lots of pills a day for a year, not the two pills for just 10 days that the doctor gave her. Too many pills made her breathing slow down, and then stop. She died. You and your brother were taking naps. Your mom's roommate yelled and woke you up. Then the sirens came." We pause and connect. "Why don't you sit closely beside your mom for a minute?" The child tucked into his mother for about 3 minutes. I said, "Do you want to keep going or not?"

"Keep going," he said.

"They tried hard to blow air in her mouth, but she was already dead. They took her body to find out why she died. They found all of the drugs in her body. Now her body is buried beside her mother, your grandmother."

At that point the child cried a little. "She was stupid! It is her fault. She was a bad mother. She forgot to feed me. She took drugs that killed her. I don't like her!"

The facts about the parent's death were concrete. The child then drew a picture of his mother, dead, and wrote under the picture, "No breathing." He was assembling facts in order to understand what happened. This picture was placed in a memory book, as we called it.

Anger is a normal part of grief work—a realistic processing of mixed emotions. A few months later, this child said, "I love my mommy, Amalia, and know that she loves and sees me. I am sorry that she can't see my good life." That was the concluding page of his memory book.

Children who have lost parents before the age of 6 often have their sense of self merged with the lost parent. Grief processing helps them separate their identities from their parent figure (Gray, 2012b). An unexamined identification with lost parents may propel children toward their own early death or loss of family. Facts are a necessary part of knowing what happened and how their lives can be different.

Typically children want to disallow certain facts. They need emotional support when hearing certain facts. They may need help when facing the finality of their loss so that they are able to grieve. Adults may unwittingly give false hope. I worked with a girl whose mother was dying of cancer. This girl asked people, "Can my mother get better? Is she going to die?"

She received confusing answers that included, "There's always hope." The parents were dealing with this girl's extreme anger issues. In a family session I said, "Your mother will probably die in the next 2 to 3 months." Then I asked her dad to put his arm around the girl and hold her. She pulled away from her mother. We were able to talk about what to do with the time left. She said that she was too angry to say goodbye to her mother. Her mother and father affirmed her anger. They recognized her impulse to start pulling away before the death. In the next sessions we discussed what she wanted to do before her mother entered hospice. She was able to choose a couple activities. We also made a concrete plan for her support. Stating the finality of loss allows us to provide support for children's feelings of grief and despair. In a recall appointment 2 years later the girl said that every night she looked at pictures of her mother, remembering her mother's wishes for her. That picture book with wishes was an activity done prior to her mother entering hospice.

How Was I Involved in the Loss? What Was My Part?

Reality testing of guilt is part of the grieving process. Some children or teens believe that they do have a part. For example, "If I weren't such a hard kid, my mother wouldn't have hit me, left me alone to get a break for two days, and then said she couldn't parent me anymore." In cases in which children are no longer with parents, it is as much of a loss as death, but much more confusing. The ambiguity of having a parent who is alive, but not available, can cause mourning that is ongoing rather than finite.

Children are often told, "It's not your fault." I wish that this global assurance worked. Children may do better with this approach: "Tell me what you worry about. What things might have been part your fault?"

Children will tell me of times when they ran away, hit their parent, or heard their parent say, "If you don't shape up I will leave!" "If you tell anyone that I twisted your arm, you will get in big trouble. It will be your fault." These events will need context and careful processing for children to move through grief.

A visual aid can help build a context when issues are complex. I might use blocks of color to mention each factor:

- Red means drugs in the house and fighting (domestic violence).
- Blue means no one to watch the child when adults were sleeping in the morning.
- Yellow means getting hit.
- Purple means the child's behavior of hitting the parent and running off.
- White means something that no one knows.

Children and I color a square with the amount of color for each factor. They can see that their event is a small part of the whole. I can talk about one of the factors, the red part, being enough that Child Protective Services had a pickup order. I tend to use a visual to help children keep all the parts in working memory. I can also simplify the exercise above, showing amounts by my hand position. Their part would be a small distance between my hands, with domestic violence a wide spread of hands, for example.

In the same session as the work above, I might talk with the child about what happens to children who are not getting enough structure and care. It sounds like this: "How do you think a 4-year-old feels when it is bedtime, but there are loud and scary people in the house?"

The child might say, "Scared. Maybe tired."

The therapist can respond, "When kids are scared and tired, and they don't get dinner, do you think that they are in a good mood?" I point to one palm to indicate that it's the good mood. "Or are they in a bad mood?" I point to the other palm.

When kids point to the bad-mood palm, I look them in the eyes, holding them in my empathic expression, and say, "Yes. You are right. They will act out. That's how kids let us know that something is wrong. That is the way kids are made. And even if you did not act out, it would not have made much difference. Your mom had a letter from the judge. She had to go to court to talk to the judge about the fights and drugs at her house. She was going to have to choose. She could choose living at rehab or going to jail. She could not take you with her either place."

At this information, kids often exhale. Sometimes they cry with frustration that no matter how much they change, they cannot undo the loss. Finality helps them to process grief.

In discussing his grief after getting more facts, a teen boy said, "I have felt guilty for 10 years, like I was just too hard. But it was actually that my mom chose a real asshole and she couldn't get away from him. He beat us both. She left me with my aunt and then caught a bus out of town. I can't imagine any kid putting up with as much as I did! When we lived in a van, I never complained at night. I slept cold. I was, like, the easiest kid ever! And I have been feeling guilty, like *I* did something wrong. I was 4! How could a 4-year-old be responsible?" By getting more information and then supporting the processing of the information, he was able to make progress.

This is an example of helping a teen's grieving, with progress on issues of guilt, responsibility, and sense of self. In this scenario, his sense of self was shame infused, his self-image still joined with his birth mother's. With therapy, he was able to free himself from some of the guilt around his losses. Indignation, a defense of self, emerged naturally. He went on to talk about his love for his mother but looked more realistically at her parenting problems. Before that, he was blocked by shame, saying, "I don't want to talk about it." The trauma and grief, until worked through, made it difficult for him to attach securely or to have hope. He doubted himself and others. The example shows his view of himself as a worthy person.

Feelings Toward the Person Lost to Them

While the examples above have already dipped into this area, I am breaking it out as a category just for clarity. Most children will have ambivalent feelings about the lost person. Some of the work on grief, especially traumatic grief, includes recognition of these mixed feelings. For example, in the teen example above, the boy felt joy at hearing from his mother during the course of therapy. "She loves me and thinks about me every day." This accompanied his wry comment, "She's a wacko," when he heard that she took her abusive boyfriend back several times.

It is normal for children or teens to have fantasies, mixed feelings, and logically inconsistent thoughts about people lost to them. Part of therapy includes emotional support as they examine these thoughts and feelings. Frequent observations that I make in therapy about lost attachments include, "It sounds like you love them, but can't trust them. That is always hard." "They were hard to love, but you loved them as best as you could." "They did not have many good choices. Of course you are frustrated that they didn't see a way to stay in your life. It leaves you with a lot of pain since they couldn't find a solution." The latter is particularly apt when dealing with children adopted internationally. Some children need to see photos of poverty in their countries of origin. They cannot understand the concept of not having enough food, for example. Children and teens often convey their mixed feelings through letters, which, may be sent or may just be part of therapy.

In working with children, it is helpful if they are able to hold on to their first parents' positive attributes. "They loved me" stands out. They hold on to some of the positive memories and wishes of their parents. In spite of difficulties or loss, children or teens develop a more optimistic view of themselves if they have a representational view of the first parent as an affirming figure who wishes a good future for the child or teen. A teen talking about what his deceased father would say to him said, "Get your diploma. Stay away from drugs and you will be OK." This was a source of strength for him.

Typically I have parents in the room for grief work. Kids may veer away from having parents in the room if they feel they must choose to love one attachment figure or another. I address that loyalty issue directly. I tell kids that almost all adults know that kids need people to love on a daily basis. They want their kid to have as much love as any other kid. It doesn't take away from the first attachment figures. Teens typically do not have parents present when working on grief, but may ask for their comfort toward the end of sessions.

Meaning of the Loss to Their Identities

The consolidation of the loss information allows for personal questions and conclusions. What does it mean about me to have a parent who has died? What does it mean to me to have a parent who is in this world but who is not able to be my parent? What does it say about me that I have a parent who expects me to parent him, supporting his addiction?

These identity conclusions are part of an integrated, but complicated, narrative. Children who work on these conclusions at a more literal age will return to them at more abstract developmental stages, updating their narratives. The processed narrative moves children to have secure attachments when they have opportunities. I look to the next generation as these young people become parents. Their abilities to form secure attachments with their children will be invaluable.

Using Parents in Therapy Sessions on Grief

A benefit of working on attachment prior to grief is that parents can comfort their children during grief work. I describe traumatic grief in the later section on trauma.

I am able to ask parents to put an arm around their child, comforting them. Because attachment is not primarily cognitive, parents' value in the therapy room can be underestimated by therapists who are cognitively oriented. The encircling arms and soothing voices of parents trump my ideas. I help bring children to the place in which parents may provide solace. The parents and children are the ones creating a reinforcing cycle of children expressing needs, parents meeting needs, and children showing relief and restoration.

Some children do not want their parents present during grief work. I do not argue about this, but do question whether children have decided ahead of time that their parents will reject them or act insensitively. Sometimes this is the case because of past experiences. Sometimes it is a fear. I prepare parents so that they are more likely to succeed. I might say to a too-talkative parent, "When Johanna gets sad in the session, I will ask you to put your hand on hers. You do not have to say anything. I will ask you if you care about her sad feelings. You can answer that you do. You do not need to distract her or say anything wise. She needs your comfort more than your thoughts." Or I might say to the parent, "I know that when your niece cries for her mother, it brings up how much you miss your sister. Are you able to be there for your niece, putting an arm around her and letting some of your feelings show? Of course, you do not want to take over all of the feelings in the room. But it feels real if you show your sadness, letting her know that you feel your sad feelings with her."

Equipping Parents to Assist Grief Outside of Therapy

Grieving children are irritable. It is an about-face for parents to react with sensitivity and compassion rather than a consequence. Letting parents know what to look for can help them to help with grief, instead of dealing with a chronically irritable child. Depending on the situation of the child, major reminders of grief include Mother's Day, Father's Day, the anniversary of loss, certain places associated with the lost person, school events around issues like addiction or disasters, and so forth.

Parenting plans for grief could sound like this: "Sharon, I know that you are sensitive right now. Little things might feel big because you are already feeling bad and missing your dad. For the next week at dinner, let's light a candle, remembering your dad and the things that you want to remember about him And, let's you and I have a little time before school sitting together, reading *Calvin and Hobbes* cartoons. We could use some extra good things in our lives during this next month."

We include other ideas such as these:

- Making up a song about the lost person, and then singing or dancing it.
- Writing a letter to the person who is gone with an update on the child's life.
- Contributing a memorial gift such as food to a food bank or a nice shirt that the lost person would have liked, given to a homeless shelter.
- A picture of the lost person placed in a pleasing setting. For example, a picture of the child in a pleasant park and a cut-out figure of the lost parent looking down from above, saying, "I want you to have a happy life, but it is not time for you to come up here." This type of picture is particularly helpful if the last visual memory that the child has is a traumatic one.
- Routines in the family are slowed. The family takes a week off from all appointments or activities except for therapy. This conserves energy necessary for moving through grief.

Many adults are not resolved in their own grieving process, so would rather avoid children's grief work that will trigger their own painful memories. (This includes therapists.) I can help parents in a short-term way with some of their grieving, or else refer them. But if they are not able to come in for therapy, they can review the grief work done in therapy in a compassionate way. I will talk to children about the reasons that the parent is not in the room. It is not that the child's grief is so potent, but that the parent is still getting help. The parent is well aware and accepting of the grief work. Often these parents will come in just for the end of therapy to supply hugs and expressions of care. Children tend to understand explanations of parents in progress.

Interweaving Trauma and Attachment

Many of the cognitive-behavioral models for trauma include a focus on attachment. Sometimes the attachment work is deferred to the end of treatment, bringing parents in for connection and affirmation, hearing the trauma narrative toward the end of treatment (Cohen, Mannarino, & Deblinger, 2017). Other models include attachment work from the onset of trauma work (Blaustein & Kinniburgh, 2007, 2010). I enjoy reading the bright lines that seem to connect these models in effectiveness, beyond the inclusion of a therapist who lends attachment capacity to families:

- emphasis on parents acquiring sensitivity and theory of mind toward their children,
- repair after problems,
- regulation and coregulation skills taught to families,
- de-escalation of traumatized youth prior to solving problems,
- parenting skills learned and applied in real time,
- bonding between the therapist and parent,
- support and positivism shown by the therapist to the parent,
- specific targeting of trauma symptomatology and trauma reminders, and
- encouragement of areas of mastery and competence (Cohen et al., 2017; Blaustein & Kinniburgh, 2007, 2010).

The National Child Traumatic Stress Network provides the following list for trauma work:

- Motivational interviewing (to engage clients)
- Risk screening (to identify high-risk clients)
- Triage to different levels and types of intervention (to match clients to the interventions that will most likely benefit them/ they need)
- Systematic assessment, case conceptualization, and treatment planning (to tailor intervention to the needs, strengths, circumstances, and wishes of individual clients)

- Engagement/addressing barriers to service-seeking (to ensure clients receive an adequate dosage of treatment in order to make sufficient therapeutic gains)
- Psychoeducation about trauma reminders and loss reminders (to strengthen coping skills)
- Psychoeducation about posttraumatic stress reactions and grief reactions (to strengthen coping skills)
- Teaching emotional regulation skills (to strengthen coping skills)
- Maintaining adaptive routines (to promote positive adjustment at home and at school)
- Parenting skills and behavior management (to improve parent-child relationships and to improve child behavior)
- Constructing a trauma narrative (to reduce posttraumatic stress reactions)
- Teaching safety skills (to promote safety)
- Advocacy on behalf of the client (to improve client support and functioning at school, in the juvenile justice system, and so forth)
- Teaching relapse prevention skills (to maintain treatment gains over time)
- Monitor client progress/response during treatment (to detect and correct insufficient therapeutic gains in timely ways)
- Evaluate treatment effectiveness (to ensure that treatment produces changes that matter to clients and other stakeholders, such as the court system) (NCTSN, n.d.).

As described earlier in this chapter, when children have significant attachment issues as well as trauma, I typically start with attachment, and then move on to focus on trauma or grief, depending on their age. Throughout treatment I will continue to enhance attachment, working with attachment and trauma in an interwoven manner, with active use of parents as resources within the sessions. This is not abstract, but appears in practical requests like this one for emotional support: "Would you please put your arm around your son?" Or this request to increase sensitivity and theory of mind:

"When your daughter was so irritable this week, do you think that it might have been due to the sexuality class at school with its section on sexual abuse? Would you turn to your daughter, asking her if she had problems with this?"

After the parent turns and asks, getting a yes nod from the daughter, the therapist says, "What do you wish your daughter had asked you? We want to know what to do next time something like this comes up."

Often the parent will turn to the child and say something like, "I am so sorry that I did not think about the abuse part of the class. That must have been hard for you. Let's think about whether or not you want to be in the class during that discussion."

In the example above, I would work on the specific reminders of trauma that came up for the child. However, the work on attachment sensitivity proceeds in a natural manner as part of the increasing family capacity.

When working on attachment issues, there are necessary trauma activities:

- psychoeducation for parents that includes an increase in sensitive parenting and theory of mind;
- positive parenting skills, selective attention, and behavioral consequences rather than escalated emotional parenting;
- teaching children regulation skills including relaxation, perspective taking, and ways to calm or distract themselves;
- describing a trauma narrative, with work on correcting distortions in self-concept development and processing feelings associated with the trauma;
- facts about the trauma and the failure of societal protection, with rebuilding of the social fabric;
- desensitization to trauma reminders;
- plans for safety and prevention of reenactments;
- practice in reaching out for help and the use of social supports;
- encouragement of strength and mastery areas; and
- a plan for return to therapy, if needed.

While this book is not primarily oriented toward trauma treatment, complex trauma is so associated with attachment that it is important to discuss essentials of trauma in a book on attachment.

The more active use of parents in the therapy assists in trauma treatment. Parents describe that sitting in therapy sessions while I am discussing trauma with their child gives them the opportunity to use similar words, pacing, and emotional tones when addressing trauma issues. They say that it is extremely affirming when I teach their child to reach out to them for support, and their child begins to do that reaching out spontaneously. Parents tell me that they recognize a trauma reaction in the future since they have been in sessions, observing the changes in their child when describing trauma reminders.

Teaching Parents to Help Regulate Their Children

Healthy parts of infancy and early childhood consist of parents providing soothing and buffering when little ones are overstimulated, play and attention when little ones are understimulated, and being in a brain-to-brain connection with normally regulated stress patterns of parents. As many authors have described, this sets up the template for a regulation of stress, which is further developed through life. Many children have missed these experiences or have had them disrupted through trauma and losses—their own or experienced vicariously through their parents' experiences. Therapy gives space for children to learn relaxation experiences through the soothing, comforting, and coaching of parents.

Neglected or traumatized children may be older but still need special buffering. They may never have had soothing from parents that would help them to internalize calming and stress regulation. Parents are tempted to instruct, with increasing urgency, "Calm down. Act your age. There will be a consequence if you don't stop now." Parents may get more frustrated as children cannot respond by calming. Parents may signal threat with words or nonverbally. This either escalates children further or pushes them into immobilization. Psychoeducation helps parents understand why an early childhood approach of staying with and helping children to soothe will provide long-term gains in emotional regulation. Of course, this should be demonstrated in the session.

I like to have parents as models, demonstrating soothing in the session so that children are able to see what we have planned. We demonstrate it first because it helps children to see that the postures and intent are not threatening, but helpful. Earlier in the chapter I described the parent soothing as they stand behind their children.

Calming can also be done with parent and child sitting side by side. After I practice with a parent, the parent practices with the child. I may say to a child, "You did not get the calm-down in your inside self when you were little. We are giving you that inside calm-down now so that you are more comfortable. It also helps you so that you don't get mad and in trouble so much."

Recognizing Change

Children may have changed enormously without altering their view of themselves with others. It is fun to spend a session from time to time to reflect on children's gains. A boy was grumping about going to see me. After all, he was doing quite well. As he came in, I said that we were on our way to Starbucks to have a treat and to celebrate his great summer. We went over his changes. I told him quotes from his family that made him smile. He asked if we could meet once a year. He said, "This could be our tradition!"

Parents start reporting things like, "My son is now coming up to me, saying, 'Mom, I'm really sorry that I did that. Will you forgive me?' This is new."

I'll say, "So your son's attachment is improving. He is trusting you, caring more about your connection. How does that feel?"

"It feels like there finally is some hope," Mom might say.

I continue, "I think that you are seeing him trust you more—especially after he revealed abuse to you and you responded in such a caring way."

Mom says, "For so long we had no idea why he was so disconnected and mean. I feel like I understand him better."

I reply, "You are showing a lot of insight as you parent your son through grief and trauma. It is a difficult parenting course. It's a privilege to watch you as you guide your son."

Mom says, "It's been no easy road, that's for sure. But I see him as he really is now. I didn't realize how hurt he was. I feel protective now, instead of burned out. He's coming to me for help instead of just asking for things."

At this point I might nod, showing nonverbal assent. The final statement, the parent's description of change, rests as the ultimate comment. I am mirroring, reflecting back, her changed view.

Changes in Worldview

Changing attachment patterns are not just reflective of the connection between people, but also change how people view their relationships within their world. I like to find out the beliefs behind a person's worldview. With children, these are often beliefs like these:

- You lose people you love.
- Everyone lets me down.
- Just when you think that you are safe, something seems to hurt you again.
- I need to be the one to take care of myself. Adults mess it up.
- Adults are broken. They fall apart when you need them most.
- Take what you can. The relationship isn't going to last anyway.
- I am reacting to an unfair world. I need to connive to survive.

Some of the key pieces in reestablishing a prosocial way of thinking are to examine those beliefs, determining whether some gradation is possible. These are critical pieces of work when children have moved between families, from an unsafe one to a safe one, or when parents have recovered from mental illness or addictions. This moves a step beyond the relationship with parents. It includes the way that children see themselves in the world. For example, a boy whose favorite character was a negative, brutal cartoon figure decided that his world was different. "I will be the protector of babies and little kids," he announced. "And my mom will be so proud of me. I will be her knight." He was holding a play sword at the time. "She moved me to a house with not very many mean guys around her. It is . . ." He struggled to find a word and then smiled as he exhaled and concluded, "very relaxing." His phrasing incorporated some of the nonverbal gestures and concepts that we had developed over the previous month. His fighting at day care had decreased. He changed not only his environment, but his worldview.

A worldview in which children bond and connect to trustworthy adults is a bonus of secure attachments. It opens children to look for adult friends and mentors. It helps them to believe that classroom curricula or rules might be to their benefit. I tell children that their wiring to respond to dangerous people will always be there to protect them. But they need to work on enjoying the life that they have now in a protected setting with protective adults. There are rare occasions where this is not the case. In those cases, I predict that they will be able to make decisions someday to be in a safer place. They can start to pick out more reliable people now. We work on skills to determine how to find and connect to such people and places. Almost everyone has had contact with great people. We are able to select attributes to look for in the future, as well as unreliable or dangerous people to avoid.

Role Reversals and Control as Aspects of Attachment Work

After losses or maltreatment, children or teens tend to be highly controlling. Parents will describe their elementary-school-age children pushing for control with expressions like, "She is 8 years old, going on 15." Control helps children decrease anxiety over whether their parent will disappear or fail to provide protection. If control is taken away in one arena, children often look for new ways to control rather than experience high anxiety. And even if children begin feeling more secure, the desire for control may not dissipate. Some children do not like giving up their illusion of power.

Over time, parents weary of control battles. Some parents do not maintain boundaries by setting and enforcing them reasonably. Instead, they become involved in protracted discussions, with high emotion. Their child describes how the parent failed to meet expectations. Parents mount a defense, debating the child as if they are peers, and as if children are owed elaborate explanations. Parents seem to mislay the information that children have neither developed abstraction nor can think about the long term. The underlying message from the children is, "I am afraid to trust your care and that you will be there." They convey, "I will control my parents, critiquing their performance when I am dissatisfied and monitoring their movements so they do not leave and so that my needs are sure to be met."

Parents' underlying response is, "I am doing a good enough job. I'm outraged. Why are you questioning me and telling me what to do?"

Parents tend to swing from proving their love and competency to getting angry and distancing. Of course, this further dysregulates their children. Some parents distance, saying, "He sucks the life out of me!"

Children, in turn, feel more anger and despair. Other parents become highly emotional, complaining, watching for arguments to start, and behaving irritably. Paradoxically, this gives children the nonstop attention that they crave after earlier neglect. After neglect, children tend to elicit the most attention even if it is negative, and even if that leaves their self-esteem in tatters.

Framing the Discussion Over Control

In simple terms, I like to begin developing some insight and theory of mind for parents and children. As children are picking, criticizing, or eye rolling, I like to construct a conversation method in which parents and children can better understand each other. As mentioned in earlier sections, I do help children to see the difference between before and now. Using pictures of them earlier in life, and in different homes or circumstances, I describe what used to be adaptive. For example, "You needed to cry and whine, and keep at it, to get attention when you lived with a depressed parent [or busy foster home, or international orphanage]. That was a super choice to get some attention. But you are here now." I point to a picture of them now, which we have drawn.

I point to their parents and ask children to see the love in parents' faces. "Now, it is just confusing everyone. You are asking them to help you as if they are not going to help, or as if they don't care about you. Don't you know that you are their precious child?" At this point, children may look at the parents' faces for confirmation. "Just sit a minute, thinking about what would be different if you believed that. Would you have to remind Mom about food for lunches, or to have a birthday party for you, or to spend time with you?" At this point, some parents who are activated and finally feeling some backup, might want to sermonize, saying things like, "That's what I keep telling Julia. She doesn't have to nag and control me every minute. She even tells me how to drive." The parent takes a breath, preparing to say a great deal more. I move the discussion, saying, "That must feel bad and annoying. But, it must be *really* sad for you to realize that Julia is afraid that something will go wrong: that you will leave her, forget about her, or make a big mistake like other adults who took care of her. What could you say to Julia about how important she is to you, and how you take care of her?"

Julia's mother catches on to the context and tender voice tones, and reaches toward Julia, saying, "I got ready for you. I changed my job and moved into a bigger place with kids in the neighborhood. I think about you all of the time."

I ask, "Did you imagine having a daughter like Julia? What was it like when you first saw her picture?"

Julia's mother says, "I was over the moon! I emailed your picture to everyone. I was so excited that I could hardly sleep! Poppi and I went shopping for books, toys, and clothes for you."

I say, "Do you have enough love, food, and stuff for this girl?"

"Yes," Julia's mother states with assurance.

"When she starts arguing and reminding you how to parent, are you able to help Julia calm down and feel secure?" I pause, waiting for Julia and her mother to think about and feel the transition. "Are you able to breathe out, saying, 'Julia. I love you. I have enough for you. I am a great parent and you are a loved child. Don't worry. I have it covered?"

This is an example of a script that reframes the control battle as an anxiety reaction, which it typically is. In some cases the issue is complicated by ADHD. Children have a hard time shifting focus. In these cases, we describe the need to teach their minds to shift. As one little boy said as we practiced in therapy, "First I get mad. I blow away the mad by blowing up a balloon of mad. I let the balloon go away. Then, I can think about the next thing. That's how I do it without getting into a tantrum." We frame control issues based on rigidity as having a "sticky brain." The brain has a hard time shifting. Medication for ADHD often helps, as well as a structured but nurturing home.

I like children and adults to be able to predict when control issues are more likely to come up. That discussion is informed by children's and parents' increasing competencies in understanding when children feel vulnerable or overstimulated. Parents use a mixture of prevention and reassurance.

Helping Parents With Strategies to Reduce Controlling Behaviors

Many times we tell children to stop, but we do not help them to practice what we want them to do instead. We may tell children what we wish that they would do, but information from working memory is hard to access for impulsive children. I like to practice what we want children to do instead of controlling. We combine scripts and real-time practice, with positive rewards.

In session, I might have children practice describing what is causing their controlling behavior, signaling anxiety to a parent. It might sound like, "Mom, I am mad and scared when I get hungry. I am afraid that you will get busy on email. I start thinking that you do not care."

Mom may say, "I do care. I have an energy bar beside my computer. You can come to me, telling me that you are hungry. I won't be mad at you. If it is going to be a little while before dinner, I will rub your back for a minute and you can get the energy bar to hold you over." Then, we role-play that a couple of times in my office, which assists kids' memory systems. I respond with praise for both parent and child.

Some children like to announce what everyone in the family should be doing and when. Sometimes we move this into a more adaptive form, asking them to write up a family schedule, but not to be the one who enforces the schedule. In role-play, with me telling them what to do and how to do it, I ask how they feel. "Really annoyed!" they say.

"Yes," I say. "That is how people feel when you go past their boundaries. Boundaries are those invisible fences that tell us what's our business, or our bodies, or our stuff. So, stay back!"

We might make a short list of what a person's stuff is. Then I say, "I think that you are a great kid, and deserve lots of smiles and friends—at school and at home. I don't want you to be annoying, because it gets in the way of people feeling friendly toward you. So let's give you a different family job instead. You won't feel as important as an adult, but I think that you'll be happier."

I might have a reward system of 1 to 5 minutes of something good for every time parents notice children behaving in a friendly way, with boundaries. If they mess up, they can get a little job to make it up to the family, such as sweeping the walk, unloading the dishwasher, and so on. However, in the interim they would continue to earn rewards. They simply could not redeem their rewards until the job is done. Some parents give money instead of minutes of something. Those minutes can be TV or video time, time playing catch with a parent, time riding bikes at the park, or some such. This simple system is mostly used to help children and parents notice particular behaviors and patterns. Again, I talk to parents about rewards as "giving the brain a cookie." Children are more likely to remember something, storing it as meaningful, if they get frequent rewards accompanied by praise.

Anger Issues That Interfere With Secure Attachment

Anger is an essential issue in treatment. In the beginning of this chapter I described some characteristics of children who are likely to present with attachment issues, who tend to be maltreated, prenatally exposed to alcohol and drugs, or moved to different attachment figures due to foster care or custody changes. Excessive anger is an expected part of mood dysregulation after complex trauma. Anger is also connected to disorganized attachments. Some children see bullying and aggression modeled, which they incorporate into their own worldview. And children are prone to overload and respond with rage when their fragile sensory systems have been subjected to prenatal exposure to substances. Coming at the problem from more than one angle makes sense, since anger origins are multiple. A message to send in therapy is to feel one's angry feelings instead of dumping them on other people.

When working on modeled anger in the past, I push for dissonance in children. For example, when children remember someone raging, throwing things, I say, "Was what they did right?"

"No!" They exclaim.

"Then, you sure don't want to be like them, do you? When you are acting like them, it's like saying it was OK. Lucky for you, you have parents and a therapist who know that you have a good heart. They are going to help you so that you are on a different path than that guy."

We may have a few more back-and-forth comments about this, in which I bring up some of the injustices children have endured. I want children to separate from a desire to imitate the person who modeled use of anger for control and goal attainment. We may discuss that there were only two options in the past—be like the victim or the abuser. Now that there is safety, another option is available.

If children are expressing anger because of prenatal substance exposure, I go over daily schedules with families, making visuals since these children do best with visuals. We can pick out patterns of overstimulation, developing a ceiling on how many transitions or how much stimulation can occur in a day. I also teach children to say, "I think that might be too much for me." One young man, coming in alone as an adult, showed the internalization of these capacities. "I pay a little more rent so that I have my own space. I need time alone every day to do well. I need down time after work. I also need to hit the gym when I start to get angry. A roommate wouldn't be a good idea." I worked with him as a child and young teen. He had been a remarkably angry boy. He did beautifully with a combination of attachment trauma work and attention paid to issues from prenatal exposure. As an adult, he was self-monitoring. He was able to select activities to reduce anger and environments that reduced stressors.

Self-Skills for Anger

Every child working with me has a cool-down plan for anger. When little things cause anger during the day, adults can mentally put them into perspective and reduce anger. I ask parents to speak aloud about some of their ups and downs. We go over this in therapy sessions, helping parents to become aware of physical cues that alert them to begin using regulation capacities. They can cue their child, helping with self-skills and working them into daily life. I also elicit examples from the parents or children of when something happened that anyone would feel irked by. Children can give advice about how to handle anger and make a plan.

I capitalize on events that are causing children to be angry. We use parents as encouragers as we come up with three or four things that kids will choose as their calming strategies. First, we have them note their bodies. I want them to be aware of their physical changes. Sometimes we do a body map of anger to help them notice early anger signs in their bodies.

Kids with quick surges of anger might choose from the following: pushing their hands together very hard, lifting something heavy a couple of times, running in place for two minutes, doing a seat push-up five times, doing a whole body muscle tighten and release five times, or an all-over shaking of tense muscles like athletes do when preparing to compete. I describe that their bodies need a place to release their energy. We practice some of this in the session, all together. Rather than shaming them for anger, we reframe it as their body doing its job, but needing to be taught what is appropriate. I talk about this as emotional toilet training for kids who like toilet humor. "You don't put your poop just anywhere. It has to go in the toilet. Anger can't just go anywhere either or we stink up the world."

We also talk about the retreat and regroup remedies for quick surges of anger: splashing cool water on your face, taking a break in the bathroom or bedroom, putting ear buds in for a music break, or telling your parents that you need to go calm down before anything else.

With slower-escalating anger, we have kids take a bike ride, read a history book, listen to music, draw, or take a bath or shower with the chance to write nasty or angry words on the inside of the shower with water-soluble markers—rinsing those words away at the end of the shower.

For children who have been overwhelmingly frustrated due to neglect or trauma, frustrating life events are connected with a lack of a parent or adult to help them. By encouraging parents to use soothing ways, give suggestions for calming, teach de-escalation strategies, and accept a normalization of anger, we are giving children new experiences. Their attachment figures are present and caring. Many of the techniques are classic cognitive-behavioral therapy techniques but within a context of attachment, which provides an incubator for stress regulation skills.

Last, we make a plan. When children are angry, usually there is a problem to be solved. Using the attachment figure as a resource, we try to make a plan that will address the problem that may have caused the fierce anger. Children and their parents get very good at moving from saying, "I am feeling really frustrated" to asking, "What's the plan?" This is a difference from what they may have experienced before. No strategies may have worked in the past. So plans were useless. There was only rage or dissociation. Now there is an opportunity to make a plan when something frustrating occurs. We practice this in session, including the satisfaction of thinking about using the plan and how that will make the person feel.

Anger as a Signal for Attachment Needs: Trying New Ways

Constance Dalenberg (2000) describes anger as a signal for attachment: "Pay attention to me!" I talk to kids about our baby boss brains. As babies, we use our anger to get people to come close to us. After a certain age, people actually distance. Children have implicit memories of people ignoring them. I tell kids that we all have to teach our baby brains not to shout at people when we need help and attention—even though we still feel like it.

I also teach parents to say things like, "Remember that I am a listening parent. Are you able to look at my caring face and remember that I care about you?" Or the parent can simply inhale and exhale a couple of times and say in a soothing voice, "I'm here."

Some children have a hard time waiting. I give them a signal, a light squeezing of Dad or Mom's hand with the parent giving a countersqueeze, indicating that the message has been received. The parent will look for a break in conversation and give attention. We try these techniques in the office. The point of the exercise is to encourage successful circles of communication.

Asking for Help Without an Argument

Our attachment style informs how we ask for help. If people expect others to be unresponsive, ineffective, or shaming, then asking for help is pricey. Because of this, we script and practice direct, positive ways of asking for needs to be met. Parents need help in giving direct help with shaming children. These are examples of changes.

Child: "I need help on my math homework. I lost the assignment and do not know how to do the story problems." This replaced, "You are probably going to be mad at me and won't help anyway. You will say that it's my fault."

Parent: "Your assignment is posted on the school website. I will show you how to look. If we can't find it, we can call Michael in your class. Do you want help working the first two story problems together?" This replaced, "I have told you that you have to write your homework in your planner." Or "You give up before you try. At least try!"

Or children might start reaching toward parents when upset, then stop. I compliment them on their good idea. And I ask parents if they noticed the hand and whether they wanted to hold their child's hand or put an arm around the child. We do the interaction together, this time completing the action and commenting on how right it feels. I may take a photo.

Here is an example of handling fears and expressions of mistrust.

Child: "I am worried that you will forget to pick me up after day care." This replaced, "You never get there on time to pick me up. And you just don't care. You make excuses."

Parent: "You are worried that I might forget you, that you aren't important to me. You are actually on my mind all day. You are my most special person. Next time, look in the pickup line and you will see me smiling at you from the car." This is said with physical touch and gaze. This replaced, "I have been late three times in the last year. Just because I'm not first in line, you get mad. You are not being fair." The latter was said with a closed body posture and tense face.

Other times children's expressions of needs may be hard to understand. For example:

Child: I want to go with you to the store.
Parent: OK. Get your coat.
Child: Why do I have to wear my coat? It's not cold.
Parent: It's 48 degrees. You have to get your coat or you are not going.

Child: Why do you make everything hard? You aren't fun.
Parent: You are the one ruining things!

New dialogue:

Child: I want to go with you to the store.
Parent: I like spending time with you. We'll get our coats on together.
Child: I don't want to wear my coat.
Parent: I hear that. Our old way is to have a fight so that we don't have a good time. Can we try a new way? [Parent pauses for de-escalation, with a hand on child's back, and a smile.] I want to spend time with you. Take your allowance with you, if you want to spend your money. I don't want you to shiver. You choose, coat or hoody.
Child: I'll take it, but I won't put it on.
Parent: Fair enough. Take it in case. I want people to see us together and know that I care about you. Taking a coat lets people see that I pay attention to you.

Anger Reinforced by Parents, Correcting This Pattern

Some parents, due to their abuse issues, become so sensitized to children's anger that they start walking on eggshells around children. They often capitulate rather than having to endure a tantrum. This contributes to distance between parents and children. A child said, "I know that she is going to give in if I keep going. I know that it's wrong. I don't like myself, but it's her job to fix this, not mine."

Sometimes I ask parents to get some therapy for themselves in order to reduce their reactivity. I talk to parents about their plan for withstanding the anger that will emerge as kids test their resolve. I talk with kids and parents together about boundaries and the calm way that boundaries are going to be enforced with reasonable consequences. Often in the car, in spite of their acquiescence in my office, children will instruct parents, "That consequence is NOT going to happen."

Consequences do need to be enforced consistently and reasonably. Especially in single parent families, it can help to bring in a friend or relative to help with the reinforcement of a consequence. It helps children to realize that there is societal support for the parent's position. For example, the parent describes that chores need to be down by a certain time or else a consequence will occur. If the consequence is no video gaming if the child/teen does not have their family chores done by a certain time, the friend arrives just after that time and carries the video gaming system out to her car, driving it away. Or the parent and relative work together to remove the remote controllers and cords, taking them to an adult's work place until compliance has occurred for a reasonable length of time.

This boundary reinforcement is not done in a nasty "I won" manner. Instead, it is said in this fashion: "Everyone needs to learn to accept 'no,' and rules. It wouldn't be fair if other kids learned and you did not. It's part of growing up, so we don't look silly by having a meltdown." I might model a silly tantrum, which makes kids laugh. Then we go over body posture, for, example, a sigh paired with a giving-away gesture, hands extended with palms out, saying the word "whatever." This indicates that the disappointment is no big deal. We practice it in session. Parents model it at home so that they can use that gesture when disappointed.

I tell kids that it is part of parents' job to teach children to accept "no." Parents have to set limits, trusting that their children will still love them—after they calm down. Parents need to hear this information when they are avoiding children's anger by capitulating.

Sometimes children get furious, parents rage in return, children begin to cry, and then parents scoop up children to comfort them. This is a worrisome domestic violence pattern in the making. Children and parents learn to hurt and get hurt before they get close. I am serious about bringing this to parents' attention, coming up with a plan to stop it. It often takes months to fully arrest. Our strategy is to make certain that parents disengage before they rage. Having parents walk outside the house, rather than engaging, may be necessary. It does not mean that the parent is leaving the child, but is breaking the cycle. While typically I keep parents with children to help them to soothe, in these cases we temporarily separate until parents are able to stay calm enough to parent well. Often the mutual escalation cycles are due to stress that builds, with a major fight at intervals. It helps to do something to change the pattern of activity, perhaps going to the library or having friends over instead of staying home with the fight brewing. Families also find it helpful to have physical exertion to discharge tension.

Consequences When Anger Injures Relationships or Property

When children have injured people or property, it helps to think of repair and restitution. For example, a 10-year-old boy took a mentor teacher's tablet, hid it, and returned to find it gone. He could not understand the need to repay, since he had derived no benefit from the theft. As we talked, I found that he stole the tablet when his mentor teacher gave friendly attention to another child. We worked on the repercussions of his relationship with the mentor. Since the boy was a reading partner for a first grader, I created an example that included how he would feel if his reading partner stole his lunch and hid it. Even if another child ate the lunch, it would still make the boy feel bad.

Because so many of these children have poor reflective capacity and theory of mind, understanding the injury to relationship must include feelings preceding the mistake, in this case, jealousy. I want children to develop reflective capacity. In this case, we made a plan for a series of family jobs to pay the mentor. He kept half of the money that he earned, contributing half to the repayment project. When he repaid, it was done with dignity. He apologized for the injury to the relationship as well as with money to restore the stolen item.

I work on making it right as much as possible. Sometimes kids lose relationships with friends because of anger. With empathy, not

"I told you that this would happen if you didn't change," we talk about mistakes as important lessons. We are in agreement that they do not want to lose other friends by scaring or being mean to people. A critical piece of the conversation is evoking their belief that they can change.

It is important to apologize, even if the person does not want to proceed in a friendship. My messages are that we are all learning; we have all hurt people; we all need to calm our anger so that it doesn't hurt our friends; and we practice at home so that we have these skills and friendly habits. Since children are forming friendships and healthy habits during this stage of life, schools emphasize the same lessons. I make a point to mention that I will help them to become successful, providing hope.

Helping Children to Respond Verbally, or Nonverbally, to Effective Parenting Moments

Even when parents are nurturing, children may not respond in a gratifying manner. Children may have little experience with the positive cycles of expressing needs, getting needs met, and feeling regulated and enjoying connection. When parents' patterns become positive, children do not necessarily jump for joy. Even if they have sat in my office, complaining plaintively about what they want in attention and nurturance, when parents change, children may be rejecting, not accepting. Like the child who has been left too long at day care, who has missed her parent and watched the door for the last hour, they turn away when their parent arrives.

We make a plan to role-play what happens when someone responds positively to you, but you do not go on to answer, nod, or respond. In role-play, I take on the role of the nonresponsive child, with the parent doing something nice while I remain self-absorbed—avoiding eyes, body tilted away, and wordless.

I ask parents how they felt. "Sad and confused" is a common answer.

I ask children how I looked. "Like you don't care." "You think that you are better than her." "You are mad about something else." I nod in agreement.

Then we play out responding. We role-play having the parent doing something nice for me as I play the child. I have the child cue me to have positive responses like, "Thank you. You are nice."

I ask the parent how that felt. "Great. Expected. Like you like me." Finally, we might use two examples of nice things that parents want to say to their child. This time, the child responds contingently. I compliment the child and ask how the parent feels. The parent responds positively, with a smile, hug, or little laugh to reduce tension.

I like to put in a temporary reward system to encourage more of this positive responding. The children are more likely to remember to respond positively if there are consistent rewards in the beginning, with less consistent rewards over time, such as 2 minutes of a video, a dime, or some other reward that can be given about 20 times a day for 2 weeks. After that, we space out the reinforcement for this goal.

In session and at home, the emphasis is on the parent's emotional satisfaction in the child's response. I encourage parents to follow up, saying how much they enjoy parenting their child. Other responses that therapy targets include giving eye contact, allowing parents to finish a sentence before the child starts walking away (depending on the age), or hugging back.

Keeping Parents Healthy During Treatment

It sounds matter-of-fact when I give parents stock advice for parenting children with attachment or trauma problems: keep balanced moods, be nurturing and empathetic, and use consequences and redos instead of emotional parenting. In fact, it is extremely difficult to maintain this parenting approach when children are dysregulated and not so gratifying. Careful parents feel tremendous pressure to do it right. Even casual parents describe a sense of helplessness at times. It feels awful to share some of their children's moods. They want to escape, at least for a little while. Or parents describe getting tangled in their responses to children's emotional push and pull as they play the reciprocal to their children's avoidant and anxious patterns. Parents describe an urge to engage in control battles, acting like toddlers. Some do.

Because real change in children takes some time, I want to talk about parents' mood struggles, finding solutions that will give them regular little breaks. The break helps them to return to equilibrium. If parents' even moods never existed before they began to parent their child, no break is enough. They need work on their own moods. But breaks are still helpful with their extreme moods.

After describing trauma impacts to parents, some professionals think that having parents understand childhood trauma will transform parenting. It helps. But knowing the why and what of trauma in a learning setting is easy when compared to living out a connection to a child with such a background. Parents can feel dysregulation from an inner place. Some parents say, "It makes me feel crazy." "I never thought that I'd feel these feelings about a child. She is calling the shots in our home. I am doing what I should. But I resent what has happened to our family."

A key task for therapists is validation and empathy for parents' sensori-emotional turmoil, without making their children the problem. Beyond psychoeducation, therapists lend their regulation and emotional care to parents. This takes the form of processing some difficult interactions, or hearing about frayed places and working together on family routines. It is important that the load on parents is bearable, and that they know their breaking points.

I model nurturance with children (within the limits appropriate for a professional relationship), help parents to phrase nurturing comments, and work with them to script limit setting for children in a nurturing manner. But it is important to recognize and compliment parents' successes in therapy. I help them to develop a consistent nurturing approach that fits their overall style. We describe the issue as helping children to transform their way of relating to fit into a safe and loving family. The reality is that parents have the pressure to become safe and loving.

In sessions, we will go over the family schedule, looking for problematic times and making plans for those times. Parents typically give up activities for a year or two. We try to start with onerous obligations. Parents need validation that they are entitled to their sense of exhaustion. Specialized parenting for children with attachment and trauma issues is really as hard as they feel it is, even if friends do not understand. This theme of validation is especially true for foster and adoptive families. Support groups are necessary for families so that they do not feel so alone.

Preventing Parenting Burnout or Secondary Traumatic Stress

For more difficult children, I recommend respite care. Some parents have become so focused on their children's particular needs that they want to find the perfect respite situation. I suggest the goal of just getting a break. When there are other children in the family, it is important to be able to give quality time to all children, without the added parenting stress of keeping an eye on the more difficult child.

The stress of caring for a child with attachment problems can make marriages or partnerships start to feel like work, with all resources going into managing children. The romance evaporates. In a weekend conference for foster and adoptive parents, parents brought up a common problem, how to get time and energy for romance and sex. They talked about ways to have couple fun and good sex, not just quickies. (The conference sponsors seemed a bit nonplused, but the conference reviews were great.) Some of these ideas were scheduling sex certain evenings a week, saving back energy and time. People put fun, sex, and romance on the to-do list, near the top instead of the bottom.

A goal is for everyone in the family to have their needs met. Because of children's trauma and attachment problems, parents can feel that the everyday needs of others should be deferred in light of the suffering or behaviors of a family member. Parents may move into a crisis mode, deferring their own needs. But a prolonged crises mode cannot be sustained without burnout and damage to mental health or relationships.

Therapists have specialized training on trauma exposure. They can build in practice supports like consultation groups and days off, unlike parents. Parents may be in the danger zone before they quite realize what happened. I see parental depression regularly in my practice—along with its sidekick, anxiety. Depression makes it hard to be nurturing and sensitive, or to have the energy to set limits. Instead people feel numb, irritable, and unable to mobilize strategies to change their situations. When parents are arriving in therapy depressed, more directive help than is typical may be necessary from their therapist. The suffering parent is in trouble. That may mean beginning an antidepressant, regular therapy for the parent, getting in-home supports, and dumping energy-draining nonessentials.

Protecting parents' regulation and well-being are necessities in providing them as a secure base of regulation for their children. It helps to check in with parents on key areas like sleep, relationships with other family members, exercise, friends, spirituality, and time to prepare and eat good meals. All the people in the family should find their lives satisfying, even if they live with suffering. If the amount of emotional pain that they are experiencing is high, then I want to put in a commensurate amount of support, with joy-producing activities for family members. I recommend to parents that they do not wait for suffering to be over to start a satisfying life. Forge it within the present.

CHAPTER 5

Treatment for Parents

Parents may ask for therapy for attachment, stating clearly, "I know that I am the problem." Other adults may recognize during our intake narrative that they are not providing security for their children. For these families, the treatment plan begins with work with parents, and later incorporates children.

People with secure attachments in early childhood will tend to replicate this relationship pattern when forming new attachments. Having experienced a secure attachment relationship as children, they play the reciprocal role as adults. Of course, there are some individual variations dependent on personality. But absent mental illness or traumas, they tend to develop parent-child or romantic attachments with the ability to regulate strong emotions and enjoy the emotional safety of their adult attachments (Johnson, 2008).

Most individuals coming for treatment have had insecure attachments in their growing-up years or have losses and trauma. They want something better in their lives, but find their efforts complicated by defenses, anxiety, and anger. Many of the uncertainties that they bring into therapy are rooted in past experiences that they are reexperiencing in close relationships. This confusion can be seen in sensory expressions—wanting to run, push away, look away—and simultaneously get close and hug. Their confusion is also conveyed through a mixture of contradictory feelings—shame, love, loss, and hope.

The concepts of secure attachments are an easy sell. Who quibbles with the values of caring, empathy, respect, and coregulation within the safety of a relationship? But as mentioned in Chapter 3, as clients' internal working models of attachment are activated, shame, loss, and fear with visceral connections come into play. Attachment is governed by the limbic system, with sensori-emotional processing occurring both at this level and upward in the cortex. Attachment schemas, which are limbic system–mediated, also connect downward to the viscera, heart rate, and respiration. This means that the work, by nature, will include our clients' body-based sensations, with strong emotions associated with their attachment memories and current experiences. When attachment schemas are activated, our clients often have vivid body sensations.

As therapists stay present, we help our clients to integrate their previously disowned or dissociated feelings. The therapist's physical stance is an empathic leaning forward, maintaining a steady emotional keel. If clients exceed the threshold of tolerance, therapists help to bring them back into regulation.

Helping Adults to Transform Affect Into Empathy for Themselves

As our clients experience pain, abandonment, loneliness, fear, and visceral upset in the office, the therapist shows empathy, steady regulation, and compassion. Through this ongoing contact, clients are able to internalize these qualities, replacing shame and disgust with compassion and empathy for themselves. This compassion toward themselves becomes a source of empathy for others.

Some clients come in for a shorter time, asking for help when there are intersections between their attachment stressors and their current lives. For example, one woman had a secure attachment until the age of 9, when her parents began coping with a sibling's serious illness. As this client faced special needs in her own child, the intersecting issues caused her to seek help. She remembered disconnection from her mother. She processed these memories and proceeded to plan for her child without, as she said, "falling into an abyss."

Other people use therapy to rework their patterns of attachment, making significant shifts over a period of time. People are motivated by their desire to be a secure attachment figure to family members. They will brave exploring feelings and memories for the people they love.

Transference Issues and Expected Patterns of Countertransference

Adult clients typically will cast the therapist in the same role as their attachment figure. If the client had insecure dismissive parents, the therapist will be perceived as being ready to discount ideas and feelings, and miss important information. Therapists may feel that they have to do extra to show their sensitivity. They may get discouraged by the lack of progress, becoming weary of their clients and responding with impatience and distance. Therapists may want to terminate before they should.

Balanced work for these clients will include validating experiences, processing grief over the insensitivity shown to them during childhood, coming to an understanding of why parents did not respond to their needs sensitively, and giving them the experience of having their feelings heard without the therapist overfunctioning or doing less.

Clients who are anxiously ambivalent in their attachment backgrounds may want to take care of their therapist or bring gifts—beyond a societally normal gesture like holiday cookies. This is kindly discouraged, without embarrassing clients, but by bringing to their attention that the time in therapy is for them. They are worth their therapist's time. They do not need to take care of their therapist to reduce shame over getting therapy time or to fear that the therapist with be angry or withdrawing. Small therapist gestures such as adjusting position, checking time, or briefly looking away may be misinterpreted as disinterest. It is important to have a discussion of the therapist's imperfect availability. If I am distracted or have a cold, I tend to describe this to clients in the beginning of the session. It helps them to know that they are correct; I am slightly less available. I do not ask for nurturing but affirm the lesson that people can be available to you with some variations. It is not a cause for alarm. Over time, clients become more tolerant of variations.

As anxious clients improve, they may correct and restate their points of view. They make choices to meet their own needs outside of the sessions. These are gains as they become more confident. They say that their friends, spouses, or partners are seeing them as more stable. Their children are finding them to be more emotionally capable.

Avoidant clients have had childhoods in which they were criticized or treated harshly by parents. When these people come into therapy, they are often surprised at the degree of hurt that they are causing in the lives of the people they care about. If they are not able to use strategies of avoidance, they tend to become highly anxious when dealing with issues. Often these clients have a demeaning manner toward therapists. Certainly the therapist should not allow abusive behavior, but subtle, negative attributions about the therapist are expected in these sessions. Over a period of time, there is a gradual expectation from clients that I will both help and respect them. They will have made comments previously indicating that I have limitations in a number of essential personal and professional qualities.

I tend to see avoidant clients in family sessions for the first time, especially in custody situations, rather than have them enter therapy by themselves. They will also arrive, knowing that the situation is grave, when their children have been traumatized. Once in the sessions, they begin to ask for extra time for themselves. It is a palpable relief to them when I make certain that there is space and respect for their feelings and wishes. By the time they get to therapy, usually other family members feel alienated. Working with avoidant clients requires clarity about the therapist's position. I am showing them respect because of their worth, not because of the success of their harsh or critical attitude.

Strategies When Parents' Relatives Evoke Negative Affects

When working with parenting adults on attachment issues, often there is ongoing negative contact with the adults' parents, the children's grandparents. When parenting adults show disorientation and disorganization, safety issues need to be considered. Promoting security in attachment will entail processing previously discounted or dissociated feelings and events. Therapy includes practical steps to protect clients and help them to learn the skills to protect themselves. While this book's focus is not trauma treatment, it is imperative that reenactment of trauma is discussed and interrupted.

With the help of the therapist, adults can see themselves as being able to decide what type of behavior they will choose in their interactions with family members. As one woman said to me, "You told me that I should get my locks changed so my parents couldn't just walk into my house. I couldn't imagine the fallout from that. But after I got over the shock of it, I thought, 'What could be worse than what I have now?' Having my parents shout at me over the phone is much better than in my kitchen. I don't want to cower or shout back. And I don't want my kids to grow up seeing me flinching. I want my kids to respect me."

The example shows the effectiveness of helping a client to differentiate between previous helplessness in childhood attachment experiences and her agency in the present. It had a direct, positive influence on her attachment to her children.

Adult clients need reminding that they have options. Just because the attachment figure is dismissive does not mean that clients have to be anxious and pursuing. They can stay the course as confident people who deserve contingent responses to their needs. Those needs can be met through other adult relationships.

Sometimes a spouse or partner is a source of dysregulation, influencing parent-child attachment. One woman said, "My husband blames me for everything that goes wrong. I have made my peace with this. I think that this is the best he can muster, given his background. I considered divorcing him but decided not to. I don't accept his appraisals of me. I have friends and my brothers to rely on. My kids know that I am there for them. I do not stand there when he goes off on me. I tell him to come talk to me when he's calm—and leave."

In the situation above, the adult has processed the information about her husband. She maintains the best regulation possible, given the circumstances. She uses compassion for herself and for her husband, rather than demeaning either of them. While certainly not an ideal relationship, her approach reflects the work she did in counseling. Her sensitive attention to her children improved after she worked through her approach to her husband.

Some adults with insecure attachments come in for short-term assistance, asking for parenting strategies when they feel confused, angry, and threatened. As the therapist provides stable connection with warmth and acceptance, the therapist becomes an alternate reference point for clients. Working with adults for 3 to 6 sessions, as a prelude to parent-child work, helps to set the stage for a different attachment pattern in the dyadic work.

Adult Clients and Touch

Touch is a critical part of increasing connection. Adults find that a demonstration of appropriate touch is helpful. Touch that is rough, dominating, or overly clingy might be what adult clients experienced. Positive touch, with both connection and boundaries, can be taught by the therapist and then led by the parent, as described in Chapters 3 and 4.

Frequently, therapists are more disposed to discuss state of mind toward attachment, work on narratives, or address trauma and loss, leaving out body-based techniques. Attachment is a physically rich, early-developing brain-body system. Our minds are open to new attachments throughout the life cycle. Physical touch continues to stimulate these attachments. It is extremely important to include body work within attachment work.

Teaching Parents to Use Body-Based Techniques

As described in Chapter 3, the palms of our hands, when stroked or rubbed just a little while holding hands, provide a strong sense of connection. When palms are stroked, typically one person's thumb gently moves across the well of the palm of the other, producing a desire for eye contact. This type of palm stroking is used to alert a sleepy baby to start or finish nursing. Often parents will stroke the baby's palm, or the baby will slide his or her hands into the parent's palms while feeding. This touch is strongly associated with care and attachment.

I demonstrate hand-holding or palm stroking if clients do not seem to have such touch in their repertoire. Then I ask if an adult will reach over to hold hands with their child as we practiced. The soles of the feet are also very sensitive. Some people are open to foot rubbing, which entails placing a child's feet in a parents' lap and having the soles of the feet rubbed. This tends to be more appropriate for parents and younger children.

When stroking a person's palm, with me sitting opposite, I can mentally count, "1001, 1002, 1003," and then see their eyes move from their hands up to my face. I make certain that I am smiling in a reassuring manner. I demonstrate this to the parent, who is then able to use this touch and the timing of touch with a child. Sometimes I have to lend them my smile, reminding parents to smile.

In attachments, people seek proximity. Often I observe families who are sitting too far away from each other, expressing through their bodies their mistrust of safe proximity. Parents can be encouraged to sit within 3 feet of their children for increasing periods of time. As parents move closer, children may feel the need to fidget to discharge excess emotional intensity. Parents often say, "Stop wiggling," which is distancing. Instead, I hand kids fidgets to help them keep regulated. Fidgets are hand-sized textured balls or small bean-filled figures that provide stimulation and just enough defocus. They are tangible symbols of my acceptance of the need for a regulation device.

Parents and Hugs

Sometimes anxious or disorganized parents or children cling too tightly. Parents may want to merge with children, not allowing enough autonomy. I let parents know that when they have given a hug, they can lean back. I am also able to coach "one-two-three" hugs: "One, come into the hug with a smile. Two, hug. Three, smile and back up, holding onto the good feeling." These structured hugs help people feel more comfortable, with practice limits for the person who clings too long (Gray, 2012b).

Hugs and embraces typically result in downregulating of arousal or stress as part of a pattern of coregulation, as made safe within the therapy setting. Clients who had parents who were dysregulating may need positive encouragement to hug, just as their children did in Chapter 4. In sessions, parents sometimes give abrupt or unwelcome hugs, dysregulating their children rather than helping them. Parents in these cases are hugging to reduce their own dysregulation, rather than meeting their children's regulation needs. I tend to use a soothing voice but ask the parent to focus on me while we use a technique like breath control or tense-and-relax. That approach models adults taking responsibility for their own regulation.

Sometimes children avoid parents' hugs because the other shoe drops after the hug. The parent engages in shaming, saying something like, "This is a lot better than Friday, when you completely ignored me and rolled your eyes" or, "Don't squish me," instead of fluidly moving their body into a comfortable position.

Parents are maintaining distance and ambivalence and undoing the emotional connection that the hug was supposed to provide. Sometimes I help a parent to note the effect on the child. I will separate the parent at that point, gently inquiring about the interaction. For example, "It seems that when you are asking your teen to get close, you are already expecting that it will not go well." "You are sending a message, 'not too close,' or 'I am still not ready to trust you after Friday night.' Is that what you meant? Do you want your child to move back or be close?" That type of concerned but close questioning allows people to make a choice. It gives them power to actually behave in a manner that is cohesive, or else describe how they are conflicted. If conflicted, we can work on the issues that cause the conflicts rather than relating in a contradictory manner.

To decrease intensity, in the midst of the more body-based work above, I may ask attachment figures to breathe with me, giving them a moment to calm. Sometimes we move into schema consolidation instead of more body-based work. I ask them to notice how pleasantly their touch was received by their child. I ask them to see the expression on their child's face, noticing how effective they are in comforting and connecting through touch.

Cheek Stroking

Gentle stroking of the cheeks remains a cue for closeness and is a comforting touch throughout life. I show parents how to stroke a cheek. I can also demonstrate this to children by having them stand in front of me and reaching out to show them, with the parent watching next to me. I say, "It is going to feel a little strange because I'm not your parent. This is just to show it to your mom." If it feels too intimate, I may use a puppet to demonstrate, using playful language like, "Let the dolphin give you a little kiss on the cheek." When parents try the technique, they have the timing and affect model. Children feel more comfortable, because it is a parent doing the intimate gesture. Cheek stroking by parents can be comforting to children who have memories of trauma and loss.

Parents and Regulating Touches on Children's Backs, Shoulders, and Heads

Other touches that are particularly helpful in building connections include having parents squeeze shoulders (gently) with a little shake. This type of shoulder joint compression, with its warm, downward movement, simultaneously causes children to breathe out deeply when they have been holding their breath high in their chests. It can progress into some natural work on slowing the breathing, moving into regulating the breathing by using the diaphragm muscles.

Some kids like to have their heads gently scratched or their backs scratched or stroked with a gentle, circular motion. The attitude around these physical gestures is a light, "I see you and like you." Parents who have not experienced this type of touch in childhood generally learn the rhythm and affects around touch very quickly. They like the feeling of competence that these attachment skills give them.

Parents who have had harsher backgrounds tend to escalate as children get dysregulated. Instead, I demonstrate how parents can stand behind their children, enfolding them, and saying softly by their ears, "It's OK, there, there," or similar simple, soothing words. The voice tone is kind and rhythmic. There is a sing-song tonal quality that calms the person. The slower heart rate and breathing of the parent will also help to regulate the person who is having difficulty. I model this to parents, if it is appropriate for their situation. Parents then use it with their child, with the pressure and cadence demonstrated. Parents describe feeling much more competent. They will say, "I really like having things to do when my child is upset. It helps me to stay calm." Of course, they are reflecting on the calming technique that I used with them as much as what occurred with their child.

Gaze and Heightened Expressive Emotions: Lighting Up the Relationship

When adult clients are having trouble with attachment, they tend to look down and away far too long, or try to hold gaze too long and too intensely. There is a comfortable amount of gaze unique to the neurology of individuals and the degree of safety or closeness that they feel with each other. Some adult clients are so accustomed to angry, shaming, or disinterested looks that they avoid gaze. I might ask an adult to look at a child more, leading by expressing positive emotions, instead of conveying dread or worry.

There is a normal rhythm of gaze. If adults have lost their rhythm, the therapist can help them with a cadence. Humans do not gaze without interruptions. Instead, we look, break, look again, look away, and so forth. The therapist can help parents to come up with a cadence that works for them until they become more comfortable. First I have adults note their normal gaze-break pattern when in comfortable surroundings. Sometimes they can replicate that pattern to some degree with their children. Some adults can measure the tempo of gaze as we do with music and dance, for example: "Gaze 1, 2; look away, 1, 2; gaze 1, 2, 3; look longer 1; look away 1, 2." While adults practicing gaze with their therapist is helpful, it is discouraging for children or teens to see someone having to practice the skill of looking at them. I have parents work on this without children in the room. A lot of their difficulty in gaze has to do with adults' own early attachments, so it is best handled in individual therapy.

No one wants to look at people who look back at them showing anger or disgust. I suggest that adults ask for gaze in a 7:1 ratio of positives to negatives. I will pair food, shared interests, touch, playfulness, and laughter with gaze. I show adults to use a light tapping on the bridge of the nose to indicate, "Look at me." Some children understand this nonverbal without a description. If I do describe it, it sounds like this: "I want you to see my face to know how I feel about having you here today." I say this with a smile and tapping the bridge of my nose, which leads their eyes to my eyes. Seeing the approval on my face helps them to pair gaze with positive emotions. Then I request that parents use this light nose tap at home.

Adults who come in for therapy have latent playfulness that needs to flourish. I like parents to create little games that require facial clues. For example, parents say with a big smile, "I have hidden a Skylander card in this room. Where is it?" With exaggerated facial expressions and eye movements, the parents give facial clues to the location of the prize. Or parents invite kids to dance to oldies music, act silly, and use campy expressions in response to music. Playfulness is easy to pair with facial expressions. It is especially helpful for teens—even as they share dismay at the goofy behavior of parents.

At times eye contact means witnessing pain. Adult clients who have not had comforting parents may stare when their child is distressed, rather than lend supportive eye contact. They may look away and then try to distract or distance. If children are weeping in the room, I will say, "Do you know why they are crying?" Sometimes the parent does, sometimes not. I will speak for children who are not able to put their experience into words. Sometimes I speak for children when their words are too readily discounted. I will coach a response of reciprocity from parents, if it is possible. But I provide eye contact with the person expressing sorrow to help maintain regulation and connection between myself and clients. The eye contact that I am modeling for the parent is an expression of compassion.

Parents may become wary of gaze when their children are angry, and especially when their own angry parents expected a submissive and averted gaze. Parents may develop a pattern of gaze aversion. I can work on that issue in time alone with the parents, making that a target for change. I ask parents for 30 to 50 "eye, smile, touch" repetitions in a day—that is, eye contact followed by a smile and a touch. We use "eye, smile" repetitions, minus the touch if children have complications from sensory issues or if they find touch to be negative. I encourage parents to tap the bridge of their noses with younger children, asking for eye contact with a smile, prior to handing over a plate, a toy, responding to a request, and so forth. The parents can intermittently thank children for the eye contact with a simple phrase like, "Thanks for connecting with me." These inclusions take just a few seconds to create a positive pattern of connection. (After positive patterns are established, the nose tapping and eye, smile repetitions can be discontinued.)

Sometimes parents' anger, depression, or addiction have caused children or teens to be gaze avoidant. In therapy I ask parents to tell their children about the change in their lives. Parents apologize for being angry or unavailable, along with an explanation as to why that occurred. When I set the stage for this conversation, I approach the topic through children's or teens' self-interest. I say that they did not receive the positive attention that they deserved. I ask them if they would allow themselves to receive some of the positive looks and smiles that they missed. Often they say no. However, that often will change over the course of weeks in therapy sessions. Their earlier refusal is a mixture of self-protection and payback. Payback, a staple of childhood, is summarized as, "Now you know how a lack of response feels. How do you like it when it happens to you?" I coach parents to accept the message rather than withdrawing. Later, children tend to allow themselves to be wooed with the positive gazes that are their due. When resistance persists, I spend more time processing earlier pain, gradually creating dissonance around being stuck in the past.

Using more expressive facial expressions helps to heighten emotional content in therapy sessions. Therapist facial expressions and voice tones are brighter and more exaggerated, which can infuse the session with more energy. Parents with attachment issues may be using flat voice and expressions except when they are angry. This new relational model helps them relate in a more attractive way to their children. There is a consistent infusion of vitality into the session. This helps to support clients who are attempting to make changes in their relationship but who have gotten tired and negative. The sense of hope, compassion, and joy that brightens up the session helps parents to experience more of those states while still being authentic. It also models the honest joy of appreciating and enjoying each other.

Changing Narratives to Allow for Secure Attachments

Parents often are hopeless, showing a lack of agency as if they were still children in their first attachment. I like to spend time exploring the differences between the parent's childhood situations and their current options. This is not just a left-brain narrative discussion. It includes expressing feelings of grief, pain, and shame. After these emotional and visceral moments, parents feel an increase in their energy for change. Parents will choke out, often through tears, comments like, "I felt worthless. I was constantly on-guard. I had a knot in my stomach for years." As these feelings emerge, there is better connection from subcortical structures to thoughts. Parents will say things like, "I don't want my children to go through what I did." "I want to be a caring parent." Our discussion moves quickly from wishes to reality.

My response is, "I will help you to succeed. I'll support you and teach you."

A client related her narrative in her concluding session: "My mother was mentally ill, incompetent to care for herself. My dad left me with her when I turned 16, which meant that I began working full-time, finishing school at night, and paying our bills. I was on my own, caring for my mother. To keep any connection with my dad, I learned not to ask for much. I was doing the same thing in my marriage. I am great at taking care of wounded people, not myself. I just tried not to think about how much I missed out. I didn't think that I was worth care. When my husband started to drink and gamble, at first I was frozen. My boys saw me as weak. In therapy, I realized that I was passing on a sick pattern. I changed. My boys deserve a capable parent. I took over our family business and legally protected myself so our assets were not gambled away. I disciplined my son and got him back on track at school. We all went to Al-Anon. I deserve good friends and love. I've stopped making banana bread for everyone in the neighborhood. I make some for myself and my boys." This is an example of a changing narrative that allowed for better attachments and sense of self.

People can agree that their parents were intrusive or dismissive or scary. They no longer should have to live like that. But when in emotion-evoking situations, they can reexperience immobilization. When people have had neglect or trauma in the early years, the tendency to become immobilized is a risk. Helping people to identify what they are feeling in their bodies, and to describe when they felt this way before, helps them to integrate in the presence of a caring therapist. A client said, "I remember a scene from my childhood. It was a summer day and I wanted to play with the other kids. But I couldn't get past my mother. I would have to listen to her for as long as she needed to talk about her needs. She'd cry. I just wanted to get past her and into the sunshine."

As this woman described her body-based feelings, she felt anger and shame, as well as immobilization. After she identified the sensory feelings in her body, she was able to connect to her responses to her children when she felt similar feelings. Her clarity was enhanced by the way that we included her motor impulses. She had wanted to push her mother aside. In session, she gestured with a strong, sweeping motion. But she was also afraid of the motor impulse because she would be alone, shamed as a "selfish, selfish girl," in her mother's words.

Our work allowed this woman to have empathy for herself. She increased empathy toward her youngest son, who was emotionally needy. At intake she called him a "selfish, selfish boy who is ruining my life." We processed with clarity and empathy the sensory-based memories and the thoughts. She used the empathy for herself to empathize with her son's feelings.

Exploring Client Histories for Secure Attachments

Many adults who come in for therapy will not have had a secure attachment figure as a parent. But they may have had a special neighbor, aunt, uncle, or teacher who played the role of an attachment figure for a period of time.

During initial sessions with clients, clients may reference a positive bond or attachment in their lives. I like them to talk more about that, so I am able to reflect on the positive qualities of that person, and what it conveys about my client. If clients do not automatically reference someone, I ask if there ever was such a person in their lives. If issues of worthlessness come up, I can reference that relationship as evidence that they were worth caring about. Clients might describe their peace and connection when with these teachers or relatives. They are often tipping their hand, describing what they want from me or what they want to be to their children.

Adults who have complex trauma histories are prone to seeing things in an all-or-nothing manner. They tend to think of people as totally available or unavailable. It is useful to reference real relationships as examples of healthy limits; for example, "My aunt cared about me. But she also had other priorities. She worked and vacationed. She spent time with me, but had limits."

The therapist could say, "So, you enjoyed relationships with limits before."

It is easier for people to think about changes if they are able to reference past examples of success, including the feelings involved with these relationships. It increases the ability to think flexibly about relationships.

Clients' Shame and Therapists' Shame: Countertransference

Any therapist should maintain a consistent awareness of how their attachment patterns influence their reactions to clients. But this is particularly important in attachment-focused therapy with families. Shame is a consistent theme in attachment work. It is hard to capture since so many of us use defenses against shame that include placing shame outside of our conscious awareness. Tracking our feelings of shame in ourselves and clients is helpful. It is also helpful to understand what we tend to do if we feel shame. For example, if we notice excessive caregiving for clients, we should think about whether our shame is being masked (Wallin, 2016). Are we trying to prove to our clients and ourselves that we are really worthwhile?

When shamed, or reexperiencing our emotions around attachment figures, maintaining an internal conversation about what is happening and how we are responding is a necessary and humbling endeavor. When we tend toward being dismissing and avoidant, we externalize blame and tend to blame our clients when things go wrong. When we tend toward being preoccupied or anxious, we tend to internalize blame. We think that our clients do not like us, will quit, or think that the problems lie within us. When we have not resolved our attachment issues, we show heightened emotions:

provoke and get angry, act submissive and apologize, dissociate or act as rescuer (Wallin, 2007, 2016).

People traumatized in childhood tend to see two options: blame me or blame you. Therapists will be tempted to take paths led by shame or outrage, depending on their attachment histories. Knowing that clients' attachment issues will be influencing us, we do best when, in David Wallin's words, we are "keeping an eye on our clients and an eye on ourselves" throughout the sessions (2016, p. 28).

Therapists constantly bring their experiences and feelings into therapy. Sometimes we want to collude with our clients, not expecting as much because of worries about conflict. Other times we set boundaries too rigidly, avoiding the opportunity to give clients empathy and affirmation (Wallin, 2016). Attachment-focused therapy is an excellent path to humility for therapists who allow themselves to leave the false position of being all-knowing. For myself, when I'm feeling grandiose, a wiser internal voice intones, "The bigger you are, the harder you fall." The return to humility is not debasing. It clears the way for day-to-day work together with our clients as we explore, feel, analyze, and consider alternatives. If we have too much power, our client has too little—impeding collaboration. If we have too little power, then our clients have no counterpressure to change.

Including Family Members in Therapy Sessions

When an adult is coming in for therapy for attachment issues, the work may begin with the adult alone but often moves to include children. For example, the treatment might be for parent depression, which then frees up capacity to hear and attend to the needs of children. Countertransference issues will need a reassessment once children enter the sessions.

Therapists need to enter therapy knowing their family of origin and current attachment patterns, along with their strengths and weaknesses within those patterns. Sometimes it seems that our adult clients have worked through issues, only to find that there is a lot more work to do when children arrive in therapy. When working with parents who are harsh, for example, depending on attachment style and regulation abilities, therapists may feel immobilized, get anxious, or go into lecture mode. Some things are clearly harmful and illegal. It is also true that the person in the room is there for help. By bringing a family member into the room, clients have conceded that they want things to change. Many parents will try out their old ways first, rather than moving to change themselves. I point out that certain behaviors have not been working for them thus far. My reinforcing their efforts will not make them more successful. For example, parents may use long, shaming lectures and encourage me to join in.

When parents use harsh, authoritarian parenting, I may start by mentioning that that style seems logical to some people. Then I mention that it is more likely to result in aggressive kids. If parents were raised in such a way, I might ask them to remember what it felt like to be on the receiving end of harsh parenting. Did they feel the same confidence and love that many other children felt? Some people feel that it kept them from risk, so we may want to examine whether or not they can reduce risk in other ways. I may give an example of children whose families used authoritarian parenting and their teens' later struggles with confidence, anger, or standing up to dominating people. I react in a consulting role, rather than reacting as if the parent is a bully and the child is set upon. It does not help to polarize. I might ask about the feelings of onlookers when the parent is harsh with the child, exploring the reality of negative social reactions as evidence that the intergenerational method may not be socially sanctioned. Finally, I can move on to elicit contradictory feelings at using harsh parenting: believing that a hard hand is necessary, noticing that people want to rescue the child, and feeling ashamed. As a parent's contradictory feelings and thoughts emerge, dissonance smooths the way to change.

Prior to including children in the session, it is important to think through the way in which therapists are already supporting parents and how that support can continue in the next phase. I often arrange for some individual sessions. In that way I can keep their connection to me strong, allowing for repair after missteps.

As an example of my misstep, a woman asked at the beginning of a session whether a behavioral consequence that she used for her child was typical parenting. I told her, with a distracted eye on the clock, that it was quite restrictive. The mother had experienced a major loss the week before, so my bluntness hit her hard. I apologized to her later for the ill-timed remark. I should have delayed discussing the issue for a couple of weeks. She told me that she had been hurt, that I was not in tune with her vulnerable state, and that while I was correct in the answer, I was poor in timing. She was right. I apologized for making her path harder instead of easier. She accepted my apology and we continued to work well together. Had I stepped back to think about her support needs, I would have included more time for her rather than rushing on to the child-parent portion of work.

As parents become more confident, they sometimes want to include people who are important to their parenting success. Sometimes they want to use their therapist to keep themselves regulated in working on some family issues. Or they want to expand competencies that they have learned with a family member. This can include bringing a spouse or partner, friend, or relative into the session.

The inclusion of an adult might last for several sessions or just a single visit. For example, a man wanted his wife to hear his narrative. It included how his adoptive father belittled him for being "emotionally immature." He wanted his wife's empathy as he described how this had influenced his reactions to his daughter's developmental challenges. He said that his wife had wondered about his passivity and anger, instead of working together with her. He wanted my emotional support as he talked to wife. But after a brief period of empathy, his wife wanted to use the sessions to move into the long-delayed planning for their daughter.

In the next session, when I worked with this man alone, he described feeling that the significance of his situation was brushed aside. That gave us space to discuss his wife's motives to access services for their daughter. He said that he was especially attracted to

his wife because of her nurturing and competent parenting potential. He did not want her to change as a mother. But he needed
to ask more clearly—and sometimes more than once—for what he
wanted. After having been parented by one dismissing and one critical parent, he tended to convey his needs to his wife in a muted
manner, and then become discouraged. Including his wife in the
session was a great decision on his part. He invited her back intermittently. He was then able to do some work on attachment with
his daughter.

Before joint sessions, I explore with the client what might happen
if feelings of collusion, being betrayed, or jealousy might come up.
Plans include asking for a moment alone, scheduling the next session to make sense of what just happened, or asking for clarification
of thoughts and feelings right in the session. On rare occasions, a
grandparent asks to come in to provide support but moves into an
emotional attack. I will interrupt the session, thank the person for
coming in with information, have him or her wait in the waiting
room, and then proceed to make meaning of the preceding with my
client for the rest of the session.

I will agree to have a person come into the session who is confusing to my clients. For example, a woman asked me for a joint meeting with her mother. The mother detailed her loneliness and unmet
needs in the session, asking her daughter for more support—daily
calls and frequent visits since her daughter was at home during the
day. I described her daughter's attachment energies as appropriately
more devoted to children and spouse, and the daughter's time as
limited. She had an in-home tech job. While empathizing with the
woman's loneliness, I helped define boundaries that were realistic
about time. We discussed the mother and daughter's previous pattern of role reversals and their movement into a healthier pattern. We
updated that work as my client added children through adoption. I
encouraged a stronger grandparent role but underscored the reality
that the grandmother was going to receive less emotional energy.
This session reduced resentment and pressure. During the therapy
session there was a reluctant buy-in that things had changed.

I am regularly asked to include grandparents when a parent is in treatment with me and their children have special needs. Often grandparents are afraid of the parenting stress on the parents, and especially if the parent is a single parent. The grandparents are requesting information in order to enhance family support. The grandparents also want to know if I am doing everything possible to help. I am available for these sessions, settling with parents ahead of time what must be kept confidential.

There are situations in which I will not move from individual work to any type of family work if clients cannot tolerate the emotions of shifting to dyadic work. We discuss this openly as my best clinical judgment that the client should do the dyadic work with another therapist.

Depression and Stress

Depression commonly impedes attachment. Not only does it inhibit responsiveness to children, it decreases capacity with other adults. In intake, without shaming, an assessment of depression is standard good practice, whether by interview or through completing a scale like the Beck Depression Scale (Beck, 1996). I describe the physiological aspects of depression as stacking the deck against successful work on attachment. Specific work on depression is begun, as well as a referral for a medication consultation. Sometimes there are problems that were deferred due to depression, but now would cause hopelessness in anyone, such as a home construction project that has spilled into every room, or taxes not filed for years. As described in Chapter 1, stress also contributes to problems with attachment. Practical steps to solve problems are discussed.

When parents change in their connection capacity, asking children to trust them can be a hard sell. In order to reduce children's wariness, the children need to process the notion of a reason that makes sense to them. Using role-plays can be very helpful in expressing mixed feelings. The following example displays these features.

A parent who had been severely depressed was not emotionally available to her children. Her partner brought the children in, helping them to understand that no one had done anything wrong, but that their mother's brain was "running too slowly." She needed medicine and help. As their mother improved, the children needed help in reducing their avoidance. Even though they understood the logic of depression, they were angry. They expressed this anger through slow responses, brushing past her, and suggestions that their other mom should take over.

In going over the reasons, we validated the children's fear that they would begin to depend on her and then would lose connection again. We talked through the benefits of risking being open to a loving relationship even if another depression cycle occurred. Then we role-played the children ignoring their mom and treating her with avoidance. They helped me to script lines. "No, no. You won't hurt me again. You can live in the house, but I won't really share with you. I will ask my other mom for bedtime stories and food. You are shut out!" In role-play, I acted as the formerly depressed parent.

I asked the children how they felt in the role-play. "Not good," they said. "Like we were blaming her for something that wasn't her fault." As I inquired further as to whether part of them liked expressing their anger directly, the bolder boy said, "Yes. It felt like we got her back." After processing their anger and loneliness, I asked whether they had had enough of holding and expressing anger. They agreed to talk to their mother or me when some of these feelings came up. Then I asked their mother if she had something to say. This we did not script.

She said, "The worst thing about my depression is that I knew that I wasn't there for you. I felt guilty. It wasn't your fault that I wasn't giving you attention. I loved you but felt like I was in a deep well and could not reach out to anybody. I am better now. I am doing a good job as a parent. It would make our family happier if we could all move past my depression. I don't want depression to ruin our family's love for each other."

I asked the children if they wanted to hug their mother. They said that they did. Then I suggested that they move beside her on the sofa, each with one of their mother's arms around them. They were pleased with themselves that they did so. One child began to poke at

Mom. I told her that she did not seem ready to connect all the way. I told her that it might take a while, but that she had the choice to keep poking as if Mom needed the poke to pay attention, or just to say, "Mom, I need something from you but I don't even know what!" (After a few tries of scripting, that is what we came up with.)

At that point, the mother said with animation, "I think that you want someone to play with." Mom responded to her poking by tickling her a little. The family decided that they would take the dog and go the dog park after the session. (They had sneaked the dog in past the receptionist for attendance in the family session.) I followed up in later sessions with some scripting so that they could verbally express their anger when it came up, without fears of destroying their mother.

The above is an example of ways to construct a new pattern that bridges the risk children take in attaching to parents more securely. Since they do not have abstract ability until their middle school years, they need help in finding words and experiences that portray their fears and ambivalence.

Planning Scripts to Help to Process Anger Toward Parents

If children have fears that include trauma, significant trauma work may need to be completed prior to having a role-play like the one above. This is especially true in situations of domestic violence or long hospitalizations. Even after trauma, the chance that children will become overwhelmed and start to move into immobilization or dissociation is a concern. Writing out a social story first, with simple figures and thought bubbles over their heads, will help with regulation. Children can see that there is a conclusion in the role-play. In the thought bubbles, you can give them two choices. They can pick the rejecting one first if they like. Then, after they have expressed their negativity, they may say that they want the positive choice. Significantly, they feel more powerful in a situation that formerly made them feel helpless.

With parents in the room, children are encouraged to give voice to their feelings of pain and loneliness. In the office we express empathy for what they went through, and then talk up the courage that it takes to love and to try again. I also help them to identify their desire to have connection and care. If they have tried the rejecting choice, I encourage them to try the loving choice in order to see which feels best. Of course, the loving choice almost always wins out. If it does not, often we can approach a loving choice after building more stability into the parent's attachment cues, trying again in a month.

Helping Parents With Children's Ambivalence and Anger

Parents may invite role reversals or get angry or anxious when children behave with ambivalence. Spending time considering children's reactions, and the meanings behind the behaviors, helps parents to remain regulated in sessions with children. Parents whose own parents had personality disorders often overreact to the normal narcissism or strong emotional states of their children. Helping to provide clarity in these cases is best accomplished before children come into the room.

When children come in, I ask parents or children to choose an activity or discussion topic that will allow them to relate. I will certainly make suggestions. Parents know that their old response to children's pushback will feel predictable to their children. There will be conflicting desires on the part of both to change to something better—and to switch back to the old way.

When children show the mixture of responses, I ask them directly to try something new with the parent. We talk about how it feels to let go of defenses. Sometimes we bring out play shields that parents and children can use to describe how they are feeling. They use the shields to describe the need to protect themselves from an emotional or physical attack. Occasionally we bring out soft swords as well, so that they can show aggression. Kids will often say, putting the swords up, "I don't really want to hurt my mom or dad. This is play."

Parents may have taught their children to be sarcastic through example. Using sarcasm against the parent is a kid's sneak attack when parents move away from an authoritarian parenting style. Parents tend to get angry, reasserting themselves by getting loud or being sarcastic in return. If I can warn parents ahead of time not to fall back into that pattern, it helps them to script what they will do and say when this occurs. One parent's script was this: "I'm sorry that I brought sarcasm and yelling into our house. I am trying to do something better. Over the next two weeks, I will ignore some of your yelling or nasty comments, simply asking you to try again. After a couple of weeks, if you have not stopped, I will start giving you a job to make it up to me, or you will lose a privilege, or you might have an earlier bedtime. On days without snotty comments or yelling, we will have rewards. Let's think of some good rewards for both of us. The rewards will start today, the consequences in two weeks."

Sometimes children will ask why parents have previously parented so poorly. Without undue focus on the parents' issues, parents with or without the therapist's help can give simple explanations like these:

- It was the way I was raised, and I did not know another way.
- I was under a lot of stress and was always angry.
- I was told that a dog-training approach, with me as alpha dog, would be a good idea.
- I did not know that raising you with a mean voice and words would make you feel so bad.
- I was using drugs and alcohol. My brain did not work right. My brain is good now since I found out that I'm allergic to alcohol.

Parents describe how they have learned a better way and will be practicing it because the children are worth the better way.

Notice that the parents are describing their changed approach truthfully. They normalize that it will be a process. They are describing what will occur when children act out. This anger is not vague or airbrushed. Children's angry behaviors, like screaming and hitting, sometimes followed by anxious wails that parents will leave them, tend to bring families in for the dyadic part of the work. I ask children to bring some of their ambivalent feelings into sessions, challenging them: "feel your angry feelings, talk about your angry feelings" instead of "doing your angry feelings."

Giving Voice to Children's Needs so Parents Respond

It is common to find a discordance between what insecure parents think they are conveying to children and what they are actually doing with their bodies. If a parent is backing away from a child, in our dyadic work we can describe what it feels like to each party. I do a type of interview: "How does it feel when Mom is backing away?" I include a description of the facial expressions and body language of the person backing away: "What do you think is happening with her?"

Parents will say, "I didn't realize that I did that. When I get close, for some reason I feel like I should back up. I don't know why."

I often challenge them to drop defenses. "Do you have to continue to do it this way?" I use words that convey that they could try to get closer, allowing comfort, care, and resonance. Depending on the child's age and my relationship to the parent, and with permission, I suggest that people "skooch a little closer." We summarize what happened and how it feels. Then we repeat the interaction.

When parents do not want to get close, it may be because they are withholding affection due to an unresolved issue. For example, I had a mother who said, "You want me to be close, and I am having a hard time. He ate all of the leftovers that we were to have for dinner this evening. We have rules." That allowed for a conversation about what it felt like to have a parent distance when a preteen made a mistake. I inquired, "What was that like in your growing-up years when you did things like this?"

The mother responded, "I just didn't. I knew not to! My mother would've had a fit."

I continued, "So she used her anger and distance so you did not misbehave?"

"Yes."

"And you want that type of relationship with your son? You like the way that you felt, and still feel, about your mother?"

"No. Not at all. That really messed me up!"

I responded. "So you don't want to pass on your mother's parenting to your son? Or you do?"

Mother, "No. I don't. I can't stand it when I see myself acting like her!"

I continued, "So that's not really who you are, what you believe. Would you be able to use consequences instead of withholding?"

In this case, we spent about 5 minutes reflecting on the narrative, accessing empathy for Mom and her childhood, and then using that empathy as a touchstone to create empathy for the son. The food fight over nurture and control was telling. While we could have spent time working on that and its symbolism, my sense was that the mother would have been out the door.

I also said that it was possible that her son was setting this up as a love test. The mother had been emotionally abusive in the past. Would she hold her gains or swing into fighting?

The son said, "I'm sorry. I wanted to know if you had changed. I knew you'd be mad. But it wasn't just about testing. I get really hungry. I play soccer and feel like I'm starving when I get home. It is a long time before you get home from work. I couldn't wait."

The boy was appealing on many levels of attachment—feed me; be close to me; I'm annoyed at having to be without you after a long day; and so forth. We talked about how hard it is to want to be with a parent who is stuck in traffic and delayed. We discussed his loneliness, his hunger, and how he rather wanted to be nice to his mother and was simultaneously angry at her. When he came home after sports practice, he was afraid that a kidnapper would be hiding in the home. After an early, severe trauma, this was a hard time for him. I helped him to convey these thoughts.

In response, the mother wanted to explain the logistics of her work schedule. But at this point I intervened: "It's not about the details. We have needs for closeness, protection, and food that are not rational. He misses you and is afraid, lonely, and hungry. Just like in your childhood, you understood the details of the custody arrangement but were still quite lonely and sad when you had to be with your mother. How could we solve those problems?"

For the first time she looked fully in his face and leaned forward. "I didn't know that you felt like that. I could FaceTime you from work. Would that help you? We could make more food. I didn't know that you were really that hungry."

The mother and son made a plan and talked with video access when he got home. Mom was on the phone as he entered the empty house. They talked for a few minutes before she finished her work day and the commute home. They made more food, basically two entrees, for a growing preteen. (This was simple education that hunger wasn't to be discounted. He was in touch with his body needs.) And I helped her see how much she was wanted. She was not her mother, with whom she had a disorganized-avoidant style. Instead, she had done a good enough job, in spite of her son's trauma, that he wanted to spend time with her. We worked on giving limits, backed up by consequences, instead of using emotional parenting. The mother's own mother had been very controlling of food, which had caused her lifelong battles with entitlement, weight gain, and enjoyment of food. We discussed food and nurture in the session, conceptualizing how mom and son wanted meals. Both were talented cooks, so this created a shared activity for them a couple of times a week.

As I helped to give voice to the son's needs, and he more clearly conveyed his dependency needs, his mother could respond to his attachment needs in a contingent fashion. Her voice tones dropped, her cadence slowed, and her eyes changed from narrow to open and caring. She accepted that she was a caring, hard-working parent. She was a strong woman who needed reassurance that nurturance and sensitivity would be as successful as harshness and vitriol to control behavior. As the relationship showed clear improvement, she became better at listening to her son's needs while encouraging his areas of mastery.

Including Parents or New Partners

Adults in therapy for attachment issues may want to include coparents or partners who participate in parenting children. Including these people creates an opportunity to discuss attachment security and the strategies in place for enhancing connections. As a clinician who is accustomed to working in a certain manner with a child and parent, I have to spend time connecting with the coparent or partner, making certain that the newcomer feels welcome. I may feel a little dismay. "Just when the case was going so well, now I have to add someone new." I may be invested in our success. (I remind myself to take off my queen crown before it is knocked off.)

In the first session with the partner or coparent, I like to find out the new person's impression of the work so far. Even if the work is helpful, it produces a change in roles. Helping them to adjust their roles is part of what helps maintain progress and a forward direction for the family. One father said, "I know that our son has changed a lot in the last 6 months. I got used to having him either withdrawn or acting out. Now he's expecting normal attention. I need to figure out what to do with him. That's why I am here."

It is easy to fall into a triangulated position with parents who seem to threaten the therapeutic alliance. It helps to determine what is threatening these coparents or partners and how to deal with their fears. For example, when one parent is having attachment issues with children, the other parent may encourage couple dependence or distance. Parents who begin enjoying their children tend to shift into a position of being more assured or asking for more couple closeness. This transition can be explained in a positive way, with new positive goals for the family.

Sometimes a child or teen has been the problem focus of the family. As the family does better, the adult relationship conflicts are more apparent. There can be rifts in couple relationships. I will refer to couples therapy for necessary long-term work. But meeting with adults to discuss patterns of scapegoating can be preventative. Normalizing the tendency to focus on children as the problem allows parents to see this as a typical but undesirable pattern.

Some parents describe feeling that once a problem is fixed with one child, another child moves into the crosshairs as the problem child. Making plans for ways that adults can have everyone in the family doing well is an important task. I tend to frame it this way: "Once you have made these satisfying changes in one relationship, it makes it easier to use skills in another." "Now that you have made strong progress in one area, it allows you to focus on another."

This chapter has focused on ways to help parents improve their attachment to their children. It includes many family-oriented activities, most of which are parent-led. This approach allows me to focus on parents' attachment patterns, in the same ways that I focus on children's patterns in Chapter 4. The chapters on treatment for adults versus children give us two lens, providing a clearer view of their processes.

As a rule, parents tend to give rewards and positives less frequently than I request. I do not handle this punitively, but use positive praise with parents when they are positive. I commiserate with parents; it is hard to remember new ways, which is why I expect to remind and encourage parents as they make changes.

In sessions, there is always an interplay between parents and child. Attachment is dyadic. The separation of these chapters allows for special consideration of parents who have difficult attachment histories.

CHAPTER 6

Treatment for Adolescents

Secure attachments in teen-parent relationships are marked by trust, collaboration, encouragement of exploration, and a sense of being understood or seen by the parent. These qualities in parents will smooth the maturational path for teens. Teens push at limits, get better at decision making through practice (failures and successes), increase competence in interest areas, make and maintain friendships, determine how they are the same as and different from their parents (and their foster or natal parents), and learn to handle emotions and social situations, hopefully with the support of their families.

When teens come in for treatment, it is often due to mood or behavioral issues. I am interested in what is behind the behavior. It is easiest to begin treatment by attending to a teen's pain. I begin by inquiring about when teens have felt wounded or let down by their families. This is similar to the evidence-based approach used by Dr. Guy Diamond and colleagues (2013), in *Attachment-Based Family Therapy*. The early sessions with teens do not include the parents. Instead of behavior as a focus, the teen's pain and isolation are topics. I ask to hear why teens gave up on parents as providers of engagement, resources, limits, regulation, and other aspects of emotional or physical care. The teens' wounding will need some empathy and processing before they open themselves up for repair and problem solving with parents.

For example, Alex said, "I used to come home to an empty house in middle school. I was 11 years old. I was scared. I tried to tell my parents, but they said that this was my chance to show responsibility. They said that I could go to after-school activities. Those activities are canceled a lot, like, 'Sorry, we're taking December off.' I'd hang around school sometimes and the teachers would say, 'Don't you have somewhere you need to be?' It was embarrassing. I took the hint. So by the next year, I had friends. We'd go to each other's houses after school. Yeah, we did some things we shouldn't have done [drinking beer at each other's homes, smoking pot, and shoplifting]. But what did they think that I'd do? Sit in that empty house and be that scared little kid?"

Helping teens to review what led them to give up on their family is a critical piece of the therapy. Therapists can help with coregulation and compassion as teens describe what led to their avoidance. If parents are introduced too soon, with the strategy of avoidance being impossible, teens often become increasingly anxious and escalated. For that reason, it is important to process some anger and to help with regulation prior to meeting in family sessions. Unlike the work mentioned earlier with younger children, the therapist will provide more regulation than the parent for a while in most cases.

Avoidant teens have decided that their parents are not available for emotional support. They reject the parents' worth as helpers. Their worldview is that their families are inadequate or unreliable ("f'd up," as they put it). They shut down opportunities for emotional support, saying, quite sadly at times, that they have no choice but to become self-reliant or peer-reliant. They may or may not stay within behavioral boundaries. Some do not because they do not buy into family conventions. They are making a point with their behaviors.

I find it helpful to talk to parents about the approach of first going through the teens' hurts, before having some sessions on repair. Then they can move into better connection and behavioral change. If parents are not aware of the process, they do not understand why the therapist is not dealing with behavior first. In the example above, an avoidant teen's painful memories were reviewed in session. His mother knew that this was part of the process of therapy. She apologized and described her mistake in taking bad advice on building independence. She asked Alex to start spending some time with her. Alex agreed, brushing tears from his eyes with his fists. His mom said, "I've really missed being with you." Alex's mom initially had agreed to come in to hear Alex's feelings, because I told her that it was the next step. While in the session she became caring and open to better shared experiences.

Future sessions included a combination of individual and family sessions, eventually with requests for better behavior as Alex was better connected to his mother. When Alex skipped school, she got the call from the school, left work, and arrived at home. Without drama, she took Alex and his video game–playing friend to school for a late arrival. Alex accepted a consequence, a job that took the amount of time that it took his mom to leave work and collect him. She stayed empathetic during his initial protest at the task, but enforced both the limit and consequence.

Key in both the individual and family work is allowing teens to move toward individuation and autonomy, but with family support. The goal of attachment security is to keep attachment figures available, but not intrusive. Parents are empathic, but encourage coping. They enjoy closeness but also enhance opportunities for friendships. They are curious and supportive as they see the type of person their teen is becoming.

When teens are depressed or anxious, parents may miss these mental health problems. They see irritability and avoidance of responsibilities instead. Depression and anxiety are regular concomitants of attachment issues in the teen years. I like to have teens complete the Beck Depression Inventory II or Screen for Child Anxiety Related Disorders (SCARED), child version, when there is a question about mood (Beck, 1996; Birmaher et al., 1999). When anxiety may be connected to complex trauma, the Body Awareness Questionnaire, which captures autonomic nervous system symptoms, is also informative (Porges, 2015). These tools are a helpful way to discuss how much anxiety, depression, and pain teens may be experiencing.

Teens usually feel a sense of relief once their distress is quantified. Even though they may say lightly, "It's nothing—I'm just a little depressed," they worry that something else, inchoate and mysteriously bad, is separating them from others. They do not have a fund of information such that they know about positive outcomes of treatment for anxiety or depression. Using scales can open a discussion on the severity of depression or anxiety and what plan fits their needs. I want to give them options for relief. I discuss from the beginning the possible use of medication to help them so that they do not have to use alcohol, drugs, or self-harm for relief. Even if we do not use medication, it helps teens to know that they have options.

In individual session with parents, I share the parenting characteristics that promote secure attachments in teens. I ask that they begin transforming their parenting with suggestions such as these:

- enhance dreams and encourage areas of mastery;
- help teens develop insight into their thoughts and feelings as well as insight into the thoughts and feelings of others;
- enjoy their teens;
- set and enforce limits with consequences, not emotions;
- behave in an authoritative manner, not an authoritarian manner;
- find new areas of engagement so parents find ways to have fun with their teens;
- monitor vulnerabilities and strengths in social arenas: bullying and social rejection versus friendships, academic or sports stress versus coping, or resolution of trauma and loss versus dysregulation of thoughts and feelings;
- help teens to envision and take steps toward a maturity that includes an income and support network;
- create resources and accommodations for teens with slower executive functioning development or disabilities; and
- maintain hope when there are problems, which teaches teens how to recover from mistakes or get help for any mental health issues that arise during this stage.

They do not:

- lecture and talk excessively;
- mandate instead of giving information;

- refuse to compromise, which stalls movement toward teen autonomy;
- act harshly, leading teens to believe that their parent does not care;
- diminish teens or other family members in order to gain dominance;
- behave violently either psychologically or physically, causing teens to fear, love, and hate their parents;
- reduce time when parents are available to teens, because the teens have reached puberty;
- criticize teens' dreams and hopes through critiquing their thinking, reducing their confidence in their thinking;
- request that teens stay centered on the parent's life and needs, meeting the parent's needs at the expense of the teen's own progress toward identity and independence; and
- use tough-love approaches when teens do not have the resources to cope with mental health issues or mistakes.

After making progress with teens and parents separately, we begin some family sessions. Parents initially hear their teen's feelings about lack of support, connection, or respect that led to the breakdown in communication. Then, with the therapist's support, the parents are encouraged to be sensitive and engage with the teen. Parents can express empathy and sadness for their teen's pain, as well as a request for a better relationship. On the basis of the better relationship, teens are asked to step up. Parents give limits and use consequences to enforce the limits, valuing their connection with their teen and increasing their positive statements, facial expressions, and time spent with their teen.

I am clear with parents that teens are growing up in a different time. Parents cannot raise the teen to live in the world that they lived in, since things are changing so rapidly. Parents need information from their teens as much as teens need information from parents to understand and find their places in the changing world. Teen brains are biased toward change and exploration, necessary for their adaptations to a changing world. The point is to keep them safe in the process of exploration.

One of the most significant things that I have said to teens is that they are important members of their families. Most teens, when struggling with attachment, do not feel like they are. Some say, "It seems like my family would be better off without me." That is an ominous statement, often accompanied by an admission that teens have thought that it would be better if they ended their lives. They need encouragement to reinvest in the family. The good news is that teens want to be connected and accepted in almost every case.

How teens are regarded by their parents is one of the issues teens most talk about to each other. They want relationships through which they feel valued and connected to parents, even if escalations occur at times and they stomp off.

Parents in therapy are surprised at how seriously their off-the-cuff comments are perceived by their teens. And since teens are going through active brain remodeling, they tend to be slightly tilted toward paranoia in their perceptions of others' faces and comments. Parents need to be careful with words when responding to teens. Teens have a keen memory for devaluing comments. In sessions, parents frequently need to repair these slipups, with sincere apologies. Interestingly, after those repairs, teens will often begin to apologize, in turn.

When teens are sarcastic, yell, make negative comments, or want to engage in emotional wrestling, sometimes parents return the favor. But parents are not peers. Parents are to lead out with the secure attachment S factors: "be *seen,* be *safe,* be *soothed,* and feel *secure*" (Siegel, 2015, p. 34). Their words are to increase all of the S factors.

Therapists who are parenting or have parented teens, and who are reading the paragraphs above, may be stricken with performance guilt. If their adult children still like them and if they are functioning well, parents, myself included, may feel a humble sense of gratitude that our weak areas did not derail development. (I also enjoy some memory editing of those years, skipping over the rough spots.)

Working on attachment with teens accents therapists' transference issues. Professionals may want to be the friend that they needed as a teen, rather than including parents in attachment work. Therapists may recognize the need for more or less autonomy, depending on their own teen relationships with their parents. A chaotic therapeutic approach on the part of therapists may not stem from teens' issues, but instead may reveal therapists' lack of resolution around shame, autonomy, and support during their teen years.

Teens and Society

Our society struggles with the teen years. We move from a childhood model of spending ample time with our children, to dramatically decreasing time in middle school and into the high school years. Teens blame parents as being too busy, and vice versa. Teens may beg to be on a select team or spend many hours a week with friends, without understanding how this will make them feel later. Because long-term thinking has not yet developed in teens, they tend to be blindsided by the negative aspects of their decisions. They blame parents when feeling overwhelmed or less supported. Teens routinely tell me that they are stressed. The use of smartphones has further challenged relationships. Often parents and teens alike are on phones when they are together. Teens and parents are not practicing emotional attunement or engaging when they are on their phones.

As a society, we have not responded as quickly as the advertising industry to the early-maturing bodies of teens. The onset of puberty for girls is much earlier than a few decades ago. We are not providing teens with the degree of emotional support necessary to cope with these changes. We expect self-reliance and responsibilities for social behaviors that match teens' bodies but not their brains. For example, African American girls are routinely held to high standards of responsibility because of social expectations linked to their earlier puberty. These young girls still need ample time with nurturing adults and parents who will coregulate and guide them. They need downtime in the family nest, both as individuals and in the company of their friends. Teens are often grateful when parents turn away competitors for their teen's time. Welcome words are,

"Let's have some family downtime." In fact, parents are acting as a recharging station for teens, as well as some of their friends.

Safety and Defenses

In some cases, family members are engaging in violent or unsafe behaviors. It is important to develop a safety plan that is specific as to when to call 911, contact a crisis team, hospitalize, walk out the door, or call in a relative or friend for help. This is a concrete and specific plan, often written down, so that people stay safe. Safety trumps everything.

One woman said, "I let my 13-year-old daughter hit me. I said, 'Go ahead. I'm tough. And I will still love you. I will never abandon you.'" This type of approach is a distortion of attachment understanding. I asked this mother to immediately act to protect herself. We worked on de-escalation techniques with her teen daughter as a first activity.

My script to replace the one above was this: "Your parents love you, but they need to be safe in their own home . . . just like you do. I hear that you are testing to see if they are going to dump you. That's not a way that I can let you figure that out. I know that you love your parents, at least some of the time, and would feel awful later if you hurt them. I will help you with skills. If you don't use those skills, the crisis team will come to your house to help you with skills. If the crisis team is not available, we will call 911 to send police over." At this point the teen said, "What will the police do?"

My response was, "I'm not sure. You might go to juvenile detention, or you might head to the hospital, or they might just tell you to calm down. It is hard to say. That's why I'd like you to work with me now. If you go to the hospital, or detention, you will end up having to work on those same calming-down skills, and then come home. How about just skipping the leave home part?"

Over a series of weeks, this teen calmed remarkably. "I don't want to see the police. I think that I could beat them up." She said with an evil grin, "But I don't feel like it." Obviously, we still had a long way to go, but the first step of safety was in place.

If there is violence in the home, with a family member unwilling to embark on a change process, I will not work to take away a teen's defenses. In fact, teens need to maintain those defenses. I describe this to parents. A man whose nose-to-nose verbal tirades had distanced his son came in asking how to make his son seek him out. "Stop yelling at him. It is emotional abuse," was the unwelcome answer. In spite of a year of court-ordered anger management treatment, family members were targets for his anger. In this case, the young, high school–age boy and I spent time problem solving on ways to get emotional safety. His mother did not protect him. So he spent an increasing amount of time with his aunt and grandfather. Fortunately, they lived a short bus ride away. He wanted to stay home to protect his sister, but could not do so. I made CPS reports. His father agreed that his son should leave to be with relatives when things escalated. Instead of following his son and yelling, "Get back here!" the father agreed to stand down as his son went to Grandpa's home until things cooled down.,

There are limits to what people are willing to do. Certainly my wish was that the father would work harder on anger management. This teen and I spent some time working on his desire to be with his father in spite of his limited ability to control his father. He also acknowledged needing to find alternate models. "I don't want to be that kind of guy, hurting my family. I need to be around some respectful people." With that wisdom, he found an attachment figure in his grandfather. Not surprisingly, his academics picked up when he spent time with his grandfather. Sometimes good therapy is finding alternate attachment figures who can coregulate teens and give them models for the future.

It is not fair to people to open them up to more hurt that includes a lie—that the attachment figure is safe. You can always work on teens' state of mind toward attachment, helping them to see that they are deserving of all the S words. As in the example above, we were fortunate to have an alternate attachment.

Using the therapist as a model for secure attachment is the way to go when no other figure is available. In those cases, I do not collude against the parent, making them "other." I do help young people develop a rudimentary working model of why their parents' attachment patterns formed, any adaptive value this style had in the parents' lives, and ways to maintain a healthy sense of self when connecting with their parents. That work helps young people to protect their self-worth and develop a secure state of mind toward attachment, while differentiating from parents.

Increasing Attachment Security in Teens Who Are Pushing Away Too Far and Fast

Some teens are separating from parents too quickly. Of course, individuation and autonomy are positive processes during the teen years. But teens need to maintain some connection. One man said, aggrieved, "My parents didn't notice for 2 weeks that I had moved out! I dropped out of school at 16 and started working. What could I be today if they'd paid a little more attention? When I bring it up to my parents today, they just don't have much of an explanation. They sigh and say, 'OK. OK. We weren't perfect. Now get over it.'"

When parents have allowed teens to make life-changing decisions, or teens push away too fast, sometimes it is because parents have found other things to do with their time and attention. Therapy can be a wake-up call to finish the parenting job. Parents still need to be nurturing while setting limits and opening opportunities for their teens.

Often dismissive parents lacked careful parenting themselves. A review with the parents of some of the negative repercussions of that dismissive pattern may help them to examine their intergenerational pattern, as in the example above of the man who quit school. Often parents will try to reframe this as a positive at first. Staying on a curious and empathic tack, therapists can question this defense. In therapy it is fruitful to ask about how casual parenting made the parents' own teen and young adult lives difficult. We ask for descriptions of some of the feelings around those years. As those feelings emerge, therapists have an entrance into the negative impacts, with motivation to choose an attentive, sensitive option.

Sometimes in the therapy session there is a blunt discussion of the need to redistribute time. Parents may debate the importance of work or social plans that supplant adequate parenting time. I acknowledge that career tasks are important. But I also point out that I cannot reframe the clear message that their decisions are sending—their teen is not a top priority.

A father and I discussed a career opportunity. It meant seeing his teens about two days a month for over a year. "This is a once-in-a-lifetime opportunity," he said.

"So is parenting your teen," I replied.

Sometimes realistic discussions cause enough dissonance that parents decide to recalibrate. Other times I will discuss with teens ways that they can process parents' priority list without damage to their self-worth.

Avoidance After Losses in the Early Years

Because this life stage means eventual movement away from home and parents, some teens revisit earlier losses. Children who remember losing their parents through foster care moves are particularly vulnerable. As they have reminders of losing their first attachments, and maybe more if they have several foster care placements, they feel anxiety and pain. In order to have control over the loss, they may leave home too early or leave through chaos. In fact, many of these young people will need more time at home because emotional functioning and skills are not as developed as in peers who had more fortunate beginnings.

Therapy includes some psychoeducation about this trend. I also suggest talking with young people about early loss and normal feelings that might emerge as they think of leaving home. As a high school boy said in session, "A job. Leave home. I just don't feel ready! I'm just a kid!" He had previously masked leaving with a flippant approach, saying, "I can hardly wait to leave. I'll get a job. No problem."

Defining the continuing contact that young adults will have with parents is necessary in these cases. It seems obvious that teens would know that they would be with families at holidays or for visits or vacations into the future. But their earlier, often abrupt moves seem to have primed teens to think that parents will become shadow figures, like their first parents. Therapy helps parents and teens to develop a concrete course for moving out. Since many teens will not be leaving home as their parents did, this requires some forethought. If teens are not heading to college or a full-time job in their late teen years, as the parents did, there needs to be a defined course to independence. Attachment security is enhanced when parents describe themselves as being available for emergencies, moving help, holidays, and so forth. This "into the future noodling" imagines how often young adults will stop in to see their parents, whether parents will hug them, and whether they will be fed when they do stop by. Note that the attachment information is sensory based and practical—proximity, eating together, and meeting of some dependency needs. (I admit that I am compelled to feed my adult children who stop by. Surely intergenerational transmission is at play.)

Attachment-Enhancing Activities With Teens

Connecting with teens does not have to be complex. Sometimes simple ideas for connection are the best. I recommend these to parents through psychoeducation, listed below.

Eating Together

Teens tend to be hungry. Attachment, eating, and food are all connected. I suggest that parents have a teen's friends in for pizza or to hang out with food around. Parents who bond with their teen's friends will help the teen to have the advantage of time with friends with automatic, pleasant supervision. Of course, parents will come in and out of the spaces where the teens are together. When teens are struggling or there are situations that are concerning, friends may turn to parents, letting them know that there is a problem. Friends support parents as the nice parents who like them and who feed them, which helps when teens are having difficulty.

Feeding people feeds trust when the eating together is done with smiles and nurturing. Cooking together is a good connecting activity if teens are inclined. Food prep is a natural time for conversation as teens gather in the kitchen, sampling the food. I suggest that parents put out appetizers so that teens come into the kitchen and talk during meal prep. Even if parents like takeout, everyone eating together and enjoying the time serves the same connecting purpose.

Teens and Touch

Teens tend to touch or hug their friends a lot. Teen boys regularly bump, block, and jump on each other. Teen girls hug a lot and play with each other's hair. Some teens do not want to be hugged by parents during teen years. I do not suggest forcing it. Instead, I ask parents to stay friendly and try again in a few months. In a gentle and playful manner, some parents will ask for a hug on their birthdays when teens are in a push-away mode. This sounds like, "I know that you are very mature now, but I would like a hug for my birthday if you could somehow manage that." Over time, the pushing-away teen tends to come back into range unless there are sensory issues or trauma related to hugging. The parent mode is inviting, not intrusive. No one wants to be hugged against their will.

For teens who are not open to hugs, other choices are available. Parents can lay a reassuring hand on their teen's shoulder, help with nails or hair care, or give a casual pat on the back. Parents whose hugs are met by a "no" should accept this limit as an expression of the teen's individuation and boundary setting. It is not usually a long-term limit. Parents who have attachment insecurity tend to be confused about whether to keeping hugging or touching their teens after a "no." Therapists can help parents to process some teen rejection as part of the normal course of teen development.

Interests and Emerging Identities

As teens develop, they want parents to notice that they have identities separate from their parents'. A helpful message from parents is, "You are a very interesting person. I am enjoy getting to know the person that you are becoming. I know that we are different and I accept you." The idea is that they are distinct in their identities, and are seen and able to connect to others in their families and friendships. Since teens morph a lot during these years and want a strong role in their own self-discovery, it helps to be general about the specific ways that parents see them. However, parents can discuss strengths, talents, and hope for the future.

Play Activities for Parents and Teens

Teens have a lot of energy. When parents want to connect, parents may need to move off the sofa and into activities that combine high excitement, movement, and interest. Whether it is chasing Pokémon, jumping on a trampoline, paintballing, kayaking, or playing basketball, parents who are connecting through enjoyable play activities will continue to develop their attachments through play. This can include the teen's friends at least part of the time.

Neutral or Positive Zones

Parents who use their time together to check on teens' progress on school or chores, providing consequences or prompts, may give their teens the impression that they are only concerned about performance. I suggest having some times together that are free of advice or prompts. These are set aside for enjoying each other—mealtimes, car rides to sports or lessons, and so forth. When parents have time that is spent only on relationship, teens can relax with their parents. They associate parents with support and enjoyment, not criticism.

Teens who are having difficulties need more enjoyment and support, not more emphasis on their weak areas. It helps teens to feel valued when they are enjoyed for a little while every day. Therapists and child development experts describe delighting in the child as an attribute of attachment in early life. This delighting in your teen is just as critical. In a personal example, I saw my husband holding our teen daughter's red track shoe. "Look at this little shoe," he said with a tender look on his face. "Can you believe how she runs?" At a track meet, his expression showed the attachment balance of delighting in her while expecting her to run hard.

Teen Worldviews

Teens teach their parents about life in their generation. I find that it is helpful to parent-teen relationships to hear about the realities that teens are facing. Listening more, being curious and empathic, allows for the development of a shared perspective. Parents become more attuned, which increases their sensitivity in the relationship.

Consulting Role

Sometimes parents, or therapists, want to guide. But they take over. It can help to ask whether teens would like some information. Sometimes I model this in session. I can say, "Would you like some information about this?" For example, it might be online classes. Sometimes teens will say, "Ahhh. I'll let you know." They will come back, saying, "I am interested in what you mentioned yesterday." Effective parents set themselves up to be consultants for teens and then young adults. They are authoritative, not authoritarian. Lectures simply dump information on teens. This does not mean that parents cannot set limits. Certainly they need to set limits and consequences. But teens need to learn to reach out for help without feeling shamed, stupid, or overtaken. The earliest autonomy lessons are recast in the teen years. Within secure attachments, teens explore their world within limits, take their places with confidence, get overwhelmed and yell or sulk, and know that they have parents who support them.

Parents Provide and Enforce Limits, Without High Emotion

Emotional parenting does not create a secure base for attachment. Instead, enforcing limits will help teens to believe that parents are reasonable and sane, even when teens do not agree with their parents. Parents may need to calm themselves before interactions. (All parents have missteps in this area.)

When parents use emotional parenting, they escalate their teens. Teens may become even more escalated. They can easily move into a pattern of mutual escalation. Some teens have to cut parents off in order to calm down. I find it helpful to talk alone to parents about staying regulated in order to help their teens to maintain regulation. It is fine for parents to say, "I need to calm myself and think about this. Let's talk in about an hour." This models a good problem-solving approach when emotions are high. (This does not include ignoring teens for many hours, giving sidelong, furious looks at them in the meantime.)

When parents misread the situation, accuse, yell, and otherwise mess up, a good repair is necessary. Parents do this well by offering a sincere apology, with some restitution if appropriate. Parents can explain their error to the extent that it informs understanding of the situation. But too often the explanation becomes a rationalization. A therapist can guide, saying, "But your explanation does not excuse the behavior, does it?"

The parent is able to get back on track, saying "no." Some parents turn the explanation into a role reversal, expecting their teens to regulate parental emotions and self-worth after the apology. When parents have disorganized patterns of attachment, they may use role reversals when highly stressed or shamed, even if they do not regularly show role reversals. Therapists can work on this pattern in family sessions in therapy.

The list above describes careful, attachment-oriented parenting. Many families get by with some fairly sloppy interactions in the teen years and make it through. The more challenging the teen, the more emphasis parents will need to place on careful, attachment-oriented parenting. Rather than making parents feel judged, I like to frame it as a way that parents can get the most positive change in their relationship. It is strategically wise. It holds the most potential for family happiness.

Assisting the Development of a Resilient Sense of Self After Losses

Teens may be signaling great distress with their behavior. When parents of teens come in saying, "Can you believe what he did!?" I reflect at times, "Can you believe what he had to do to get someone to pay attention to his misery?"

Sylvia, 13 years old, had a week of getting louder and more daring, telling sexual jokes to middle school boys. Finally the school staff called home. Her mom said, "I decided that instead of reacting, I'd ask a few questions." Sylvia was ready for criticism. Instead, her mother said, "I think that something is going on at school. Could you share what seems to be upsetting you?" It turned out that all the girls in her class were invited to a party—except her.

The mother said, "I called up the birthday girl's mother, who said, 'We decided on the number because of the seating in the cars. It wasn't personal to Sylvia.'"

Sylvia had been the scapegoat in a previous family. Being a bad girl was how she signaled her needs for attention to previous parents. She was repeating a pattern. In therapy, Sylvia's mother was supportive of her daughter, providing empathy and some outrage over the party. In the session, Sylvia cried, with her mom hugging and comforting her. Sylvia asked for a transfer the following year to a school with more options for friends. Sylvia brought up her core wounding from earlier losses from a series of foster homes. She said that she needed more help with cliques at school. Her mother, like most adult women, was well aware of the power of cliques during her own teen years. Sylvia and her mother went to the mountains on the party day, inviting a friend from her sports team.

Upon reflection, Sylvia observed that showing power by getting boys sexually wound up was not her best choice—although entertaining. In therapy, we used the opportunity to discuss Sylvia's self-perception of being bad. When rejected, she believed that she was bad and acted it out or used self-harming. It gave us opportunities to process her earlier life losses and difficulties asking for help. In two former homes, there simply was no help to be had. She could numb herself or act out. She was repeating the pattern. Sylvia and I discussed reviewing sexual abuse issues as well.

Sylvia and I talked frankly about avoiding more rejections, since she really did not need more pain in her life. This was a practical discussion, with pros and cons of picking stable friends as a core group, with an addition of one flamboyant, emotional friend. She laughed when I said that her flamboyant friend limit did not include her friendship with herself. She chose to volunteer in an animal rescue shelter as her outside activity, rather than drama. She began to cook for herself and the family, which stimulated more eating together—an attachment activity. We worked on self-skills, as well as yoga and horseback riding. But Sylvia was somewhat annoyed at the result of our discussions. "Now I hear your voice in my head, Deborah," she said. "No offense, but sometimes it kind of ruins the moment. I'm not cutting now, which everyone is soooo glad about. But it was fun to be edgy." I did brainstorm to increase the positive, exciting, and safe elements in her life, which she accepted as my lame, best effort. Such is teen work.

Developing an Accurate Theory of Mind After Maltreatment

The development of theory of mind is an essential task of therapy for teens and parents. By understanding the emotions and motivations of others, family members behave in a more attuned, sensitive manner. For example, a father was describing how lazy and complaining his son was. "He says that he wants to play basketball, but we have moved just two blocks from a public basketball court and he won't even walk up there. He wants us to drive him to his old high school." I asked this dad to accompany his teen to shoot some baskets, just under the supposition that his son might be feeling shy or awkward, not lazy. The dad came in and said, "He was trembling when he got to the court. His eyes and head were down. Later, after we played a while, some guys started passing him the ball. On the way home he was so grateful. He kept thanking me. He puts up such a defense that I forget how anxious he is about this move. His abuse background is something that I keep forgetting. I'll do a better job now that I realize what's going on."

Teens who are coming in for attachment-focused therapy tend to be vulnerable youth. Abuse may be occurring in their homes currently, or it may have occurred within previous families. Some teens insult and control their parents, only to ask to sleep in their room that night. Or teens may be obnoxiously directive to parents, only to be clingy, anxious, and using baby talk at other times. It is common to see these variations when teens cannot seem to find a strategy to tolerate stress or to connect with parents. We work hard in therapy to build scripts and methods of signaling parents when teens have needs, with parents responding to the needs, as described in earlier chapters.

In the teen years, therapeutic emphasis on developing theory of mind can include watching movies, hearing parents' stories of mistakes and successes, and analysis of other teen or family member problems. Therapists can help teens to note and make sense of their feelings. After abuse, many teens have learned to shut off feelings automatically. In sessions, we can talk about noting body sensations and then determining what these feelings mean. The goal is to increase teens' awareness of their thoughts, feelings, and interests as they are aware of others'. In sessions, parents, teens, and I construct situations of choice. Teens are given options. These might be vacation plans, choices of two schools, dinner, or a weekend event. Teens note their parents' thought and feelings, their own, and then make a choice that considers both.

After abuse, this is hard for teens. They tend to want to please others too much, when aware of the other's thoughts and feelings. Or they shut off the other, pleasing themselves. We can use real-time examples so that teens get practice with balancing their wants with others' wants and feelings. Their anxiety and depression are reduced with this type of self-agency accompanied by theory of mind towards others. I point out to them that being a major player in their own lives is critical, and that they are stepping up.

Developing an Accurate Theory of Mind After Loss

Grief, specially delayed or complicated grieving, often appears as depression in teen years with deleterious impacts on attachment. Teen brains become increasingly abstract over these years. Any prior losses are revisited during these years, with narratives reworked with abstraction, rather than literal meanings.

There is a sharp reduction in buffering from themes of loss and trauma, simply because these topics are part of school and friend discussions. While some parents attempt to insulate their teens, it is rarely very effective. When a 13-year-old boy came in for therapy, his father said, "Don't bring up anything having to do with the death of his mother. He will obsess over it." In fact, his school reading list included a series of books on parental death. He started looking at his mother's photos every night before he went to bed, and was wondering if he should join her. Almost all teens do best if parents put effort into enhancing coping instead of assisting avoidance. When asked about her death at intake, he said, "I think of her constantly. Not bringing her up makes it worse. My dad can't handle it and can't help me. We are in the same house but don't connect."

If parents are not attuned to the loss issues of their teens, it further stresses attachments. And if teens remain in grief states, it impacts their abilities to respond to attachment cues. Support for grief work is the best way to work on both attachment and functioning under these circumstances. If grief work has been done in the past, an update is undertaken for the abstracting teen who is forming an identity. This work often starts at about age 11. As sexual hormones are shaping the body, the brain is also being shaped for abstraction, making this an ideal time for integrative work.

I like to encourage parents to use their attachment relationships to help teens with grief. I include parents in the therapy, depending on the teen. Often these youths will say that they do not want parents in the room. I accept that. Then I come back asking if they want me to talk to their parents about some of what we worked on. Often teens will say "yes." They might ask me not to share some content, which is fine. When teens cry, I will ask, in some cases, if they want the parent, who is in the waiting room, to come in for comfort. Often teens will agree. As we walk from the waiting room, I tell parents that their teen is very sad and needs them. Walking into the room, most parents immediately size up the situation and hug the teen, who weeps. Since many teens experienced their losses without comfort or connection, especially in situations of traumatic losses or emergency foster care placements, teens tend to project this isolation into their loss experiences. As they cry and are comforted by parents, they experience care that they did not expect to receive. Parents find it deeply fulfilling to meet this need, naturally assisting movement toward secure attachment.

When teens grieve, I want parents to be aware of normal reminders of grief, like anniversary dates or circumstances. A minor loss may evoke feelings of a major loss. Helping parents to be aware of these issues will allow them to move toward comfort and away from the insensitive attitude "What's the big deal? What got into him?"

The concept of emotional resources is an important one for parents and teens to understand. When working through grief, teens tend to need more sleep, a quieter home, a more relaxed schedule, and time with parents in the family nest. The teen will be more irritable. Rather than a quick consequence, it is more helpful to say, "It seems that something is going on with you. How can I help?" It is fine to say that parents don't want others to be treated poorly through irritable comments or behavior, but their concern should be more focused on helping to restore the grieving teen's well-being. For example, a teen made nasty comments about relatives who were planning to visit and stay with the family. After an empathic investigation, the teen said, "I just don't feel up to it. They will be there exactly on the anniversary of my mother's death. They *forgot* my mom. Why do they think that I'd like to go shopping and to the water slides *that* day?"

In fact, the relatives had thought to distract and cheer up the teen by their visit. When their well-intentioned efforts were explained, the teen felt better supported. Then she responded to her dad, "Will you tell them that I appreciate their care, but I'd have to fake it? I want to be quiet, maybe listen to music, and look at videos of Mom."

When at all possible, I include parents in the comforting and processing during teen grieving. I enhance the emotional looping of parents—seeing the teen's pain, responding with care, with the teen feeling comfort. This looping builds a pattern of reaching out for care to the right people. It helps the right people to get better at seeing and meeting needs.

Therapy Tasks for Teens After Loss of an Attachment Figure

Work on grief includes these necessary components:

- helping teens to process information about the loss,
- helping teens to process identity information related to loss,
- correcting distortions of meaning by presenting accurate and factual information,
- reducing trauma-contaminated identity perceptions,
- desensitization to trauma-related reminders,
- ability to hold onto the positive aspects of the person lost to them,
- recognition of reenactment patterns,
- practice reaching out to positive friends and attachment figures,
- mastery and competence areas that equip teens with confidence in the future,
- compassion for self, and
- a future plan for when to reach out or signal to people that they need help.

Any therapist working on attachment losses and reconnection will work on the essentials listed above. To the degree possible, attachment figures will be included in plans to comfort and assist in grief work. A helpful book with an assortment of practical ideas for teens is *The Grieving Teen* (Fitzgerald, 2000).

As I write this, an image comes to mind. I was in a session in which a teenage boy was weeping and discouraged. He could barely speak. I said, "Are you feeling like giving up?" He nodded.

He said, "Why try? She screwed me over and then overdosed! She's wrecked my life! What's the use? Can you say that I'll ever get over this?"

I said, "Yes. This is horribly sad, but I think that you can have a decent life." I said to his aunt, "Do you?"

She said, "Yes. It's hard, but I think that you are going to make it. I'll be there for you every step of the way."

He did make it.

Over and over again, research and experience show that resiliency is entwined with secure attachment. Throughout the teen years, therapists have the opportunity to enhance the security of attachments through this period of rapid brain change, using support and coregulation. These opportunities come into our office as problems. I shape therapy to meet attachment relationship goals, including real-time experiences during which parents and therapists provide sensitivity, comfort, and regulation for teens.

CHAPTER 7

Modifications When Working With Highly Stressed Families

When families are highly stressed, therapists may encounter their own stress limits. Key to progress is forming a supportive connection with families, giving them a sense that someone cares about them. But clients' lack of regulation often overtaxes the regulatory capacities of therapists. There can be some self-protective distancing through a cool and impersonal approach. Since it is clear that people need to borrow from the emotional resources of the therapist, this is a conundrum. A tendency to treat people as "other" increases the shame people experience as part of stress. They have to endure being treated as contagious in order to get help.

Therapists can start in a reassuring way with families by saying, "You are in the right place. It is great that you have made it here." One family member said to me, "In our first visit, I felt like I was carrying the weight of the world on my shoulders. I felt some of the burden shift to you by the end of the first visit." This is both the good and bad news. That is precisely why therapists need to stay supported. We need to have the resources to take on some of the weight, caring while maintaining boundaries and without owning the problems.

As described earlier, I like to come up with therapy plans and strategies during intake sessions. However, with highly stressed families, sometimes the first visit is not strategic. We act to alleviate the most extreme distress or avoid the worst consequences. A woman who came for help with attachment issues with her child revealed that she was being beaten. During intake, she called her brother, who arrived that evening, helping her to move to a relative's home. She used domestic violence resources to start the process for a no-contact order. After safety was in place, we turned to work on attachment.

When families are highly stressed, services are commonly delivered either in their homes or in an easily accessible location, with connections to other service providers. Prioritizing short-term safety issues and providing a safe nest is a first-order task. Some people respond, "That sounds like social work casework more than therapy." I concur. Safety is always primary. I like to find out what the most immediate threat is to the family. Whether it is a violent child or teen, a frightening neighbor, medication that has run out, or lack of rent money, we prioritize that first. That means that we turn to community partners or family members to help with immediate needs. That may mean giving people the emotional support to make calls with me there beside them. Sometimes they hold out the phone, saying, "Help me to say this!" When people have never learned how to reach out for help, or are so immobilized by their circumstances that they avoid the stress of the first steps of solving a problem, these active and practical steps are necessary. Yet if the work stays at that level, people may continue to reenact traumatic material or form trauma bonds with people who are harmful to them or their children. Part of the intake consists of getting buy-in to begin therapy, even if the intake goals are delayed as in the case above.

When parents are highly stressed, it is hard for them to be attentive and sensitive to their children. In the domestic violence case above, after getting out of the abusive situation, ongoing therapy looked very similar to the processes detailed in Chapter 4. An ongoing issue was psychoeducation around trauma and prevention of further trauma. The woman and her son both benefited from attachment and trauma work. She had one failed reunion, with another abuse incident, but managed to get out quickly with an awareness that it was her job to be protective and strong. Dyadic work included sensitivity to her son's trauma and support as he processed trauma.

Accommodations for Clients Under Extreme Stress

People who have high stress over a period of time are more likely to have changes in their executive functioning (Anda & Brown, 2010; Healthy Generations Think Tank on ACES, October 2014). Children who have had chronic stress or complex trauma often show deficits in their executive functioning (Dozier, Peloso, Lewis, Laurenceau, & Levine, 2008). Their brains will have been shaped for a high-stress environment that prioritizes short-term survival. When working with highly stressed families, therapists do best if they accommodate their approaches so that they are tailored for this group.

Accommodations for People With Executive Dysfunction

Executive functioning influences:

- processing loads—how much the brain can handle before it gets full;
- working memory—the brain's short-term chalkboard;
- verbal memory—retaining information given verbally;
- generalizing ability—applying information from one situation to another;
- initiating—getting going, or knowing when and how to start;
- organizing and planning;
- big-picture understanding that helps the details make sense;
- self-monitoring, or making adjustments to fit in socially;
- inhibition, being able to stop oneself; and
- effortful attention, being able to maintain or change attention when it takes an effort (Gray, 2012b).

The following is a list of suggestions for families who need accommodations.

1. Use this format when giving information, which helps the brain to organize incoming information in a meaningful way:
   A. Overview—what is the issue, or big picture?
   B. Show how details fit in the big picture.
   C. Summarize.
2. Ask what parts people get. What parts don't they get? Wait until they respond. (Do not start from the beginning, explaining information all over again.)
3. Ask people to tell you when their brains are full. People have processing loads that need respect. Take a stretch break when brains are full.
4. Use visuals, especially when people need to make choices. Do not expect people to hold a verbally described idea in memory while comparing to another verbally described choice. Use visuals so they do not have to rely on auditory memory or processing. Have them take the visuals with them, if possible. Our visual cortex is better at handling multiple streams of information (Siegel, 2010). Visuals help people to hold an idea while comparing to another choice.
5. Limit words. Seven-word sentences are ideal.
6. Speak more slowly.
7. Use ample white space on printed pages.
8. Mark starting and finishing points on pages. Consider color coding. (Put rules and regulations on the back of pages so forms are not so complex.)
9. Work on a sample with clients, for example, math problems, medical forms, or applications. Show an example of completed forms.
10. Remember the body. Allow for drinks and stretches. Keep your body relaxed when you are working with stressed people. Stress regulation is always improved when clients are working with a person with good stress regulation (Gray, 2014).

Communicating With Highly Stressed People

Stress is a necessary part of life. Our bodies respond by producing a burst of specific hormones. These hormones give us the energy and urge to mobilize, to solve problems, and to respond physically to stressors in situations such as these:

- studying hard for exams,
- providing first aid to people in emergencies, or
- fixing homes and property after a bad storm (van der Kolk, 2013).

Nonstop stress actually damages us. It impacts our memory, our ability to understand complicated information, our ability to organize, and our ability to find words for what we need. Because of the brain's processing impact from stress, therapists notice that it is difficult for stressed family members to track.

The following is a guide to communication with stressed people. It is applicable for both children and adults, to use in social service settings, or within families.

1. Challenge: Brain changes occur, making it difficult to remember things or to organize life. Brain changes may include impulsivity, seeing details and missing the big picture, problems organizing, difficulty with complexity, inability to screen out noise, and limits on how much information the brain is able to process.

    Suggested responses: Number events. For example, in speaking to children we might say, "There are three things that we do to finish:

    #1 is _____,
    #2 is _____, and
    #3 is _____.

    "What is number one?" Child responds. The parents say, "Great. Let's start."

    In speaking to an adult, we could say, "We leave in 15 minutes. We must do three things before we leave. First, I want you to get the yellow meeting folder. Second, both of us will get coats and keys. Third, I will bring the dog in. Will you please get the meeting folder now?"

- Initiating is part of executive functioning. When to start becomes a moving target—and a tremendous source of frustration for everyone. Set a time for starting. "What will be the time to do X?" Let the person set the time if at all possible.

- Use raised fingers to help with counting. For example, say, "There are four things that we need to do in the morning before school." Put up four fingers. Name the items. Then put up the first finger, saying, "Start." The visual cues help.

- List daily schedules. Use visuals for small children. Include free time or choice.

- Put in time on the daily schedule for talking or problem solving. Teach the brain to defer worry and to schedule problem solving.

- Speak simply. Use shorter sentences. Speak more slowly. Put the subject and verb in that order. Shared stress often causes people to talk too much. Do not become the background noise for an overwhelmed person.

- Maintain predictability. Reduce variables such as overnight guests, transitions, traveling, or changing daily schedules.

- Give breaks during the day for exercise or goofing off. The stressed person has more need to run off or work off high stress. Some need naps. Provide time for these breaks.

2. Challenge: The person ignores or forgets requests that are given in a normal tone of voice with a normal amount of emotion. Suggested responses:
   - Set and enforce limits, but do it calmly. Resist adding your emotion to their organizational problems. Big emotional displays may work in the short term to get the attention of the anxious person but over time create even more anxiety in work, home, and relationships.

- Create written memos as reminders. Computer-based or cell phone reminders work well.
- Normalize their experience. An important message is: "Right now you seem stressed. It is normal for any of us under stress to forget or tune out. I do not want to nag you. If there is something important, how should we handle reminders?" See if the person has ideas. If not, suggest two. Let the person choose one. For example, a teen asked if he could create a checklist. Another teen put a reminder on her cell phone calendar.
- Notice and comment on times when clients remember. Help them to see their increasing mastery of daily demands.

3. Challenge: Stress makes the person harder to connect with. Suggested response:
   - Create times for connection. Meals are an excellent time to connect. Talk about favorite foods, recipes, and tastes. It helps the person to enjoy life.
   - In a family situation, consider getting or sitting a dog if you struggle to find things in common. You can always talk about the dog. Also, dogs are a good antidote for low mood.
   - Increase positive looping: back-and-forth conversations that are completely positive.
   - Make zones of time that are completely positive. For example, homework, jobs, or chores are off-limits during mealtimes or in the car.
   - Touch a person positively if it is permitted.
   - Value the person's friends, making them welcome.
   - Lie down with the person when talking, if this is appropriate for the age, sex, and relationship. It is more relaxing to speak when both are stretched out on the bed or on the couch and an easy chair.
   - Have times when you are sitting and easily available (not tensely avoiding others). The TV, computer, or cell phone texting does not signal that you are available.
   - Look for topics that are common to you and the stressed

person such as singers, sports, paintball, the pyramids, ancient peoples, and so on.

- Include a mix of ideas for family projects. Elicit the stressed person's ideas and be sure to incorporate them. (Often stressed people have a sour first reaction followed by positive involvement.)
- Elicit the person's worldview. Do not argue with it, but show curiosity and interest in how the person came to that point of view. Talking aloud will help people examine their own thinking.
- When the stressed person withdraws, do not withdraw in turn. You can conclude, "It seems that you are done talking right now. I hope that we can talk again sometime."
- Do not pretend to connect when you are not able to connect with the person. Work at connecting, but avoid being artificially happy acting. It feels false and awkward.

4. Challenge: Person loses a sense of hope or perspective. Suggested response:
    - Maintain hope. If you are not on a positive course, hold fast to the notion that you will find resources that will give you hope.
    - Qualify negativity while extending empathy. "It seems that you have kind of given up right now. I have not. However, I can accept that things seem bleak right now. I am so sorry."
    - Do not exaggerate the differences between yourself and the stressed person by saying, "I do X and therefore [do so much better than you]." The person is already feeling hopeless. It is easier to say, "It seems that you feel that nothing will help right now. Most of us go through times like that." Later, you can ask if the person wants some ideas about how things could change. Or "Let me know if you want to talk about this further."
    - Help people generate their own ideas and perspectives when in relationship dilemmas. Do not tell them what to do. Do allow them the chance to discuss pros and cons.

5. Challenge: Person lacks or has difficulty with self-skills. Self-skills include putting things into perspective, being flexible, calming, generating strategies or plans, and looking at things through another's perspective without losing one's own point of view or interest. Suggested response:
   - Model self-skills (see above).
   - Teach self-skills to younger children and teens or adults who are open to them.
   - Enroll children, teens, and adults in skills groups.
   - Help clients calm with you, using your well-regulated brain to teach them the pattern of calming.
   - Give stressed people the chance to use their perspective taking with you or others.
   - Help them to generate ideas for others.
   - Make plans and develop strategies for difficult or stressful situations.

6. Challenge: Feelings are not stable. Suggested responses:
   - Keep yourself centered and stable. You need to stay healthy in attitude and body.
   - Do not limit your commitment, but do limit your exposure to the amount of time or stress that you are able to handle. The message is, "I am not always available; I am always committed."
   - Share the wealth. Include other stable adults in supporting the stressed person. (Watch out for jealous reactions if the person says something like, "Ms. X helped me so much in just an afternoon.")
   - Maintain self-interest. Have interests and activities beyond the sphere of highly stressed family members or clients. Their stress does not define your ability to enjoy your life.
   - Help to provide perspective. For older children, teens, and adults, help to explore alternatives. This sounds like, "I wonder if we could explore, just for a moment, a possible compromise or alternative." This works better than, "I think that you are overreacting."

- Show compassion for their wounding, their pain, when they get stuck in an all-or-nothing position. Acknowledge the pain. But see if they are able to move into more helpful ways of thinking.

- Give ample attention when things are going relatively well. Share the pleasure of spending time with them when things are stable. This encourages more stability, since they get attention when steady.

- Give the stressed person the sense that you are holding them in your heart and mind. Stress includes the distortion that there is no one to count on who really understands or cares. Counteract this with comments like, "I noticed you. I was thinking about you. I am here for you."

- Model and practice calming techniques like deep breathing, meditating, praying, singing, listening to music, walking, exercising, and so on.

Reflecting on Successes to Build a Sense of Mastery

When people have high stress, they often have to admit to a temporary lack of agency in order to obtain necessary help. This can contribute to a loss of a sense of mastery or agency over time. For example, to obtain insurance coverage, people must be diagnosed and accept the diagnosis. To get household help, a disabled person has to admit an inability to handle household tasks. This makes it particularly important to emphasize capabilities. Without being falsely cheery, it is important to note and capitalize on strengths.

I worked with a client who had been removed from her foster care guardian and placed back with her birth mother at age 14. She was sexually abused by her mother's boyfriend and ended up homeless at 18. After a serious medical problem and hospitalizations, she incurred medical expenses for which she could not pay. She received Social Security Disability but had no idea what to do with the hospital bills prior to receiving disability. She declared bankruptcy at

22. Her church pastor let her live with their family since she had no housing. I provided counseling, built on her strengths, and worked on ways to reduce risks. We worked on her attachment and trauma issues that interfered with life goals of employment, housing, and finding a safe and loving romantic relationship.

We worked on her pattern of issue avoidance, helping her to spot self-destructive patterns. For example, when she moved out into housing, she saved stray cats, which would have caused her to lose her lease and security deposit. She recognized the danger in counseling and took the cats to a shelter. A couple years later, she asked me to meet with her potential husband to give some general advice on stable living. That advice was based on their individual trauma histories. However, I was also able to highlight the ways in which she was coping. Eight years later I casually ran into them. They were happily married and had maintained a steady income and lifestyle. "We beat the odds," she said. "Nobody thought that we could do it. But we made it. You were right about me. You knew that I could figure things out."

Success in this case hinged on the way this woman saw herself through the eyes of her foster mother, who passed away when the client was 16 years old, and after she was returned to her birth mother. She remembered many things that that woman had pointed out as strengths. Remembering that her foster mother always said that she was good with numbers, and after accessing this memory in therapy, she got a part-time job that involved bookkeeping. With highly stressed families, we look carefully not only at the difficulties that are destabilizing them but at the ways that strengths can lift them. Her attachment to me was a continuation of her attachment to her foster mother. In many of the early sessions she was inconsistent. She missed buses, and once she met with me at a restaurant when her transportation plan fell through. After she stabilized, she made regular office visits. Allowing for this type of growth curve is necessary in high-stress therapy.

Changing Support Levels as Clients Improve

When clients are at risk, suggestions need to be quite concrete, and sometimes more directive than is comfortable for me. For example, I have asked people to text from our session, reaching out for help when they know that they should but cannot initiate. This should be uncomfortable to therapists so that they are not overreaching into another's life decisions. Or I may temporarily need to show patience with missed appointments when their lives are in disarray.

Over time, part of the attachment connection with the therapist ripples out into developing a support system. For example, one of my clients claimed that other women did not like her due to sexual competition. She gradually changed her position on friendship. Her friends included female confidants who helped her to establish sexual boundaries. She enjoyed her relationship with me and felt that she could replicate that with other women—without having to pay for therapy.

Relationship building with a therapist includes skills that can be used in the future: coregulation, maintaining proximity to safe people, and recognition of core self attributes of self-agency and personal value. These skills help people to either move out of high stress or develop skills that help them to cope more successfully when chronic high stress cannot be avoided.

CHAPTER 8

Spirituality, Faith, and Attachment in Clinical Work

With wide variations in people's worldviews about spirituality, faith, and God, my approach in this chapter is limited to practicalities. This chapter looks at clients' attachments to God as influenced by their attachment figures and life events. The chapter assists therapists whose clients want to include this spiritual aspect in their attachment work.

God as an Attachment Figure

For some clients and therapists, their attachment to God is like that to a primary attachment figure. Their life narrative includes their creator's attributes—either a distant God who started things up and is now preoccupied, or a God who is personal in both love and care. Some clients' beliefs give them joy, energy, and a sense of being seen in the universe. Other people describe feeling outside of God's love and care. Notions of joy and unity are for others. They believe that their God does not answer their prayers and does not intervene in any meaningful way when they are hurting.

Clearly, for many people attachment styles are applied to beliefs about God. Major religions including Judaism, Christianity, and Islam all use attachment-related imagery and descriptions.

I am not of the opinion that therapists should take on the position of spiritual advisors. Certainly they may refer people to them. I am aware of the ethical position of not imposing a therapist's beliefs on others due to the power imbalance of the therapeutic relationship. Yet attending to this attachment perspective is extremely important to people who are spiritually oriented. A therapist's cliché answer will be extremely dissatisfying for people who are thinkers.

When talking to people about attachments to God, I can frame the dialogue with some questions:

1. "How do you think and feel about God, or about your spirituality?" Some people find that their faith in God, and the quality of their faith, is paramount. Others have no belief in a God, but feel themselves to be spiritually aware in other ways. This type of question helps people to identify themselves as either participating in an attachment relationship with God or not. It does not exclude them from spirituality but includes people who have a connection to Nature, humanity, or a cosmic force for good and regeneration.
2. "If you do believe in God, what emotions arise when you think about your relationship with God?" People may describe a sense of shame or distance, joy and care, or a passive belief accompanied by few emotions.
3. "Do you think of God as intimately caring about you and your life, or not?" At this point, many people will go on to discuss the way in which they depend on God in everyday life, giving more detail by themselves. If not, I can ask the next question.
4. "Do you reach out to God in times of pain and confusion? If so, does this help you? Has your relationship with God changed? Can you tell me more?"

Attachment issues tend to have impacts on spiritual relationships, in positive and negative ways. Many times therapists are unwilling to help clients process the information related to a loss of their spiritual relationship with God. Or therapists who do not have a belief in God downplay the importance of this relationship for clients.

Therapists may compartmentalize clients' faith issues as separate from the rest of emotion and belief. The lack of integration leaves clients hanging.

Therapists who avoid the issue of belief may signal that it is not important to the therapist, which is distancing. Clients have more difficulty working through their attachment narrative if they do not have help with the loss of connection to God. After trauma or attachment losses, it is common for clients to question God's care or to describe that they can no longer feel God's presence.

God's Attributes, Religious Training, and Attachment Patterns

For parents who have a loving, personal relationship with God, their parenting goals include giving their children a template to understand a loving God. Parents who have secure attachments tend to describe God to their children in secure attachment terms. Their ideal for attachment to God is intimate, resembling an adult-child secure attachment.

Parents who raise children in an authoritarian and rule-bound manner will preset children to experience God with ambivalence. These parents feel a need for connection but feel that they can experience God's love only when they are playing by the rules. Because we are human, the rules are broken, creating ambivalence in our relationships with God. Shame causes people to avoid God's presumed displeasure, but lack of contact with God causes them to want to come close. They try to follow rules in order to avoid more shame, but their relationship with God lacks much joy or comfort. These parents may be harsh and rigid with their children.

Dr. Karyn Purvis countered this view of God, describing shaming, harsh, and authoritarian parenting as contrary to healthy parent-child attachment relationships or a loving God (Personal communication, 2015). The following progression shows the parallels between parenting with a secure state of mind toward attachment and parenting as preparation to understanding a loving God.

1. Child experience: You keep me close to you. You are reliable. I will not be abandoned.

    Parent-child attachment belief: I can trust the character of my parents.

    Spiritual belief: I can trust the character of God.

2. Child experience: You value me. You are responsive to my needs for food, soothing, comfort, and companionship with you.

    Parent-child attachment belief: I am worth your attention. My needs are important.

    Spiritual belief: God loves me and cares intimately about my needs.

3. Child experience: You teach me about my world without shaming me. You include teachers who do the same.

    Parent child attachment belief: I can reach out to authoritative helpers without being shamed.

    Spiritual belief: I can look to God for guidance.

4. Child experience: You recognize my feelings, name them, and respond to them. I can learn and understand about my feelings and others' feelings.

    Parent-child attachment belief: I have a foundation for empathy and sharing and will use it to help others.

    Spiritual belief: God cares about my feelings and those of others. My life can please God, who is compassionate and cares for others.

5. Child experience: I want to please you because I am so connected to you that I am aware of your pleasure and disappointment. Your thinking and feelings influence me.

    Parent-child attachment belief: I will be a sensitive and caring family member.

    Spiritual belief: God wants us to love each other. We are interconnected.

6. Child experience: You notice my competence, talents, and curiosity.

    Parent-child attachment belief: I have unique talents and abilities that are to be developed and enjoyed.

    Spiritual belief: God made me with special qualities to enjoy and use for the greater good.

7. Child experience: I can get help with psychologically overwhelming events and feelings.
    Parent-child attachment belief: Reach out for help to trusted others when overwhelmed or needing advice.
    Spiritual belief: I am dependent on God and made for interdependence with God's family—other people.

8. Child experience: You teach me how to cope with problems and how to solve them, even if I caused the problems.
    Parent-child attachment belief: I can be accepted authentically. I do not have to lie or defend.
    Spiritual belief: Approach God for help in times of trouble. God will not abandon us during duress.

9. Child experience: Intimacy is enjoyable.
    Parent-child attachment belief: Love others deeply.
    Spiritual belief: God wants a close, enjoyable relationship.

10. Child experience: Problems in the relationship will be worked out sensitively and promptly.
    Parent-child attachment belief: Good relationships require emotional maintenance.
    Spiritual belief: Say "sorry" and fix relationships. Love each other. Tell God you are sorry when you mess up and accept forgiveness.

In fact, there are spiritual rules that must be observed in every religion, but these rules often break down to simply this: love God and love each other.

The attitude toward offenses and shame is dealt with in a straightforward manner. When you offend each other, go to the other person and make it right and then come to worship God. There is a spiritual standard for what therapists call repair in relationship ruptures.

Sense of Closeness to God

Jewish, Christian, and Islamic scriptures include descriptions of God's love as intimate and caring. These scriptures lend an understanding of the interconnectedness of faith and security in attachment. People request love and comfort from God, as well as help and guidance in the here and now. The outward ripple is an understanding that God cares for other people. Requesting emotional care from God awakens people to the notion that they might be the answer to the prayers of others. People are motivated to love others and forgive others in order to please God. It is reminiscent of families in which siblings try to get along to please their parents—albeit reluctantly.

There are clear parallels between secure attachments and the reciprocity in people's relationships with God. When most vulnerable, people seek proximity in attachment relationships, including those with God. An interesting study describes how children reach out to God when lonely or in times of stress (Granqvist & Kirkpatrick, 2016). Their attachment relationship to parents tends to predict whether they think that God will be closer to them in times of need or stay distant. In intriguing studies, children with secure attachments moved a figure that denoted God to a position closer to them when they needed help. This included children of nonreligious families. Children who had insecure attachments kept the God figure the same distance away when there was duress.

Kirkpatrick and Shaver noted not only a correspondence relationship, as noted above, but a compensatory relationship between attachment and God. Some individuals find in God a surrogate attachment figure (1990). Granqvist and Kirkpatrick (2016) list this surrogacy as helping people to regulate distress. I have frequently seen this in clients in my practice.

Practical problems in applying this material may arise quickly. For example, when people believe that they are to live in unity, a therapist who suggests cutting off contact with abusive family members will cause dissonance until people can work on the connections between distance, forgiveness, and concepts of loving themselves and others. As people struggle to find ways to forgive others or deal with feelings of hatred, clients feel concern about their own connection to God. But when people have a relationship with God that most resembles secure attachment in people, they can be encouraged to ask God to help them to forgive. Or they can be encouraged to allow God to guide them as they protect themselves from further harm, since God loves and values them. They can be safe while maintaining a compassionate attitude toward the other person. They can be encouraged to let God be God, doing the judging and changing in the other person's life. This is the type of restorative process that includes a client's value of staying close to God and working within the attachment system that they have with God.

Some clients of faith are worried about the degree of anger that they feel. It helps to frame anger as God given, helpful to prevent injustices to themselves, their families, or greater society. But once stock is taken of the harm, with boundaries clearly established, the process of letting go of the anger is healing. It does not mean saying the injury did not happen, but it does mean letting go of anger once clients are safe and have processed the meaning of the injury.

Of course, some situations call for ongoing anger since the need for action is continuing—racism and human trafficking are clear examples. In practical terms, clients can look up examples in their scriptures of who God gets angry at and why, and God's love, judgment, and forgiveness. Using a spiritual context can help people to move to a better acceptance of their own emotional states as God given.

Contribution of Faith to Sense of Safety, Coherence in Life Narrative, and Connection to God and Others

Clients who have a close connection to God feel that they are cared for, loved, and seen, even during hard times. They tend to have a sense of optimism that comes from a belief that God will be with them in times of trouble. God will intervene in their day-to-day troubles at least some of the time. There is peace and love that comes from spending time talking to God (praying and meditating) or reading in scriptures about God's love. Plus, as African human rights activist Bishop Tutu observes, there is optimism that believes that right does win out in the end, even though life can be tragic at times (2011).

For many people, their experience with God is marked with a sense of joy and personal commitment. They describe a desire to please God, because God cares deeply for them. In Christian belief, Jesus, a Jewish rabbi and God's son, sacrificed for the human race, allowing for restoration between God and people—the ultimate repair in attachment. For people of Christian faith, this belief provides a context for their life narrative and a basis for relief from shame. It also compels them to relieve others from guilt, forgiving others as they are forgiven.

Therapists who are aware of these beliefs can help their clients utilize faith strengths in life narrative work. When individuals profess the faith position above, they can be helped with their day-to-day issues within the context of forgiveness of themselves and others, restoring a sense of proximity to God and connection to themselves and others. It can lead to discussions of unconditional love from God to them, and how it is expressed to the people to whom they are attached.

God and Trauma or Loss: God's Love and Care When No Divine Intervention Occurs

People want to feel that life is safe and predictable. Because life is not this way, clients ask God for help in the form of deliverance from the circumstance. At times the cry to God is for relief from pain.

Attachment experiences that people have had will tinge their perception of whether or not God cares or hears, or whether or not they feel worthy of God's caring. A stance of "miracles are available if you just have faith" can be problematic. It can undermine faith when people feel that God is performing miracles in abundance—but not for them.

Clients who have fixed their sights on automatic deliverance can stop believing that God listens or exists. For some, this loss of belief in a loving God is a crushing blow, the final insult from trauma and loss. Trauma and loss are alienating. Loss of belief in a loving God completes the estrangement (Herman, 1994).

When helping clients who feel disconnected from God but want a restored relationship, therapists can bring up the parallels in adult-child attachment. When in pain, children may not feel the presence of care. But the care is still there. When clients are experiencing trauma, the numbing effects of trauma make it hard to feel care. As this applies to other attachment relationships, it is a possibility with God.

I spoke to a friend, not my client, whose child had died of cancer. A year later his son was raped. He said, "I know that God is good. But I cannot feel much of anything right now. I think that God was weeping as my son was raped. But I am pretty numb. People think that you will feel the closeness of God when you are in trouble. I have in the past, but not now. It is one foot in front of the other. People ask me what lesson I learned from this. God doesn't arrange things like this so that I learn a lesson! God's help for me has been in friends that walk alongside my wife and me—and in a therapist who is helping my son."

This man was in a grieving process with attachment-oriented grief work that included God. He saw God as good but did not expect God to protect him from pain. But his faith in the goodness of God was still an anchor for him as he coped day-to-day. He experienced God primarily through people who prayed for him and cared for him when he felt in too much pain to pray.

Pehr Granqvist and Lee A. Kirkpatrick write, "Religion may promote mental resolution of loss by offering the bereaved both (1) the prospect of reunion with the deceased in the hereafter and (2) the perfect surrogate AF (i.e. God) for dealing with the grief" (2016, p. 932).

To the extent that the therapist can facilitate attachment-oriented conversations about God, it helps people with loss or trauma to understand the impact on all relationships. A friend described the following:

When I got multiple sclerosis, everyone prayed for me to get better. But I went from walking to a scooter in a year. I felt guilty. I was evidence of whatever flawed concept of God that they had. People in my church Bible study were bothered that I wasn't getting better. I was mad at God for giving me unstable supporters. I stayed mad for years and thought that if they were right, then God was mean. My dad took off when I was a kid. He left and my mom and I were on welfare. That was God to me. Now I realize that my Bible study group was spiritually immature, self-reinforcing in their naiveté. God is more like my husband and mother, kind and consistent. I have joined another church. These people accept that I have MS, and that God loves me in the same way that he loves everybody. I have a chronic illness and have to cope with it. God gives me strength to cope with it. I think that God loves me and helps me to see what I can do and enjoy in life. It was healing to reestablish my faith.

For clients who have faith in God, or want to have faith again, encouraging discussions of their insecure attachment figures and how they think that God operates the same or differently may allow them to move back into a more resolved relationship. Granqvist and Kirkpatrick write that "aspects of religions that are most consistently linked to mental health are partially those that express attachment components, including belief in a personal, loving God with whom one experiences a close and secure relationship" (2016, p. 932).

Belief in a loving God increases coping capacity, helps with regulation, and enhances joy. Joy is a common by-product of a personal relationship with God. By moving discussions into the attachment arena, therapists can use words and concepts that are easiest for people to grasp.

I have written this section proposing that a secure relationship with God is a positive goal for people of faith. Support for this position is based on research on the positive connections between mental health and belief in God. But I am certain that my personal belief in a loving God, and my faith as a practicing Christian, influence my interest in addressing these issues when writing on the topic of attachment. For people of faith, integration between all aspects of their lives is an ongoing process. Therapists can assist their clients in processing attachment-related thoughts and feelings about God. Having a template of God as an attachment figure will help clients to examine parallels between parental attachment figures and God, and whether they feel that they are within the scope of God's love and care.

Disorganization, Dissociation, Omens, and God

When trauma occurs, people may feel that there were supernatural omens that they missed. They hope to note these omens in the future, increasing safety. This type of thinking allows for some sense of predictability in the future. The issue of omens is a target of trauma work for clients. Temporarily, they make people feel a sense of control. But, as trauma work progresses, with clients feeling more resolved, therapists want to make certain that clients are not hemmed in by the rigidity of omens.

Some of these omens may include aspects of God. For example, a boy told me that he heard God speak to him. He was told to move inside a particular building during a time of danger. "Everyone likes that story," he said. "But I'm like, what about the really bad event in my life? Did I miss His voice when I got beaten up by a drunk person? What's with that? Sometimes I think that I need to listen, listen, and listen so that I don't get beaten within an inch of my life, caught outside in a natural disaster, or who knows what?"

This is an example of a belief influenced by trauma-related dissociation, which has acted to distort and disorganize this boy's strong faith. Because I kept him regulated as we worked, we could talk about his beliefs about God. He came in, concluding, "In the Bible God says that he is loving. Either I believe that or I don't. I believe it. I can feel God's love."

While this boy relinquished a system of cause and effect, he concluded that God would not be tricky, or rain pain down on him because he did not pray enough. He used his relationship with his father to come to understand it. "I have lived with my father since I was 5 years old. In all of that time he has done his best to be a good father. He nags me about my room, homework, and grades, but I know that he is absolutely watching out for me. God has to be even better than Dad. God isn't looking to get back at me for something. God doesn't forget about me. I wish that I could understand God and hear from God better, but I just don't think that I can understand everything this side of heaven."

This type of resolution allowed him integration at many levels. He could integrate the disparate—hearing God at one time and being surprised by a severe beating at another time. He did nothing right or wrong to cause either. He concluded, "Everyone wants to know the lesson after something horrible. Like, 'So, what lesson did you learn from that?' The lesson is that kids shouldn't live around drunks. I wish I had a deep answer, but that's all that I can come up with." His conclusion was reality based and still allowed for him to feel treasured by God.

Many people, under duress, ask God to intervene. Or they feel that they are outside of the range of God's love because of something that they did. To the extent that they feel that God is not there, or does not hear or care for them, they feel a similar type of insecurity in attachment that we observe in parent-child attachment systems. Treatment helps clients to integrate their spiritual connection to God into an organized pattern, even when they do not understand God. The outcome is better coping, sense of well-being, and a decrease in internal dissonance.

CHAPTER 9

Play and Attachment

This chapter is at the end because it is a fun way to end the book. Of all the ways that we attach to others, play is one of the most enjoyable but overlooked ways to strengthen attachment. Attachment is brain based. And our brains love play. We produce oxytocin during play. As Baylin and Hughes pointed out, "play triggers the release of opioids and dopamine, chemicals that combine to make play pleasurable and memorable. The opioid response makes the play feel good, and the dopamine response helps the players learn what makes the play fun, what causes the play to break down, and how to use this learning in future playful encounters" (2016, p. 194).

Play experts describe the value of physical play that requires us to move, make eye contact, think of another's point of view, stay with a play theme, keep a play partner satisfied, and improvise. This causes a growth in both executive functioning and theory of mind (Diamond, 2012). In Chapter 3 and 4 we reviewed toxic stress and neglect as weakening the functioning of our brains in sending information from the brain stem and diencephalon up to the limbic system and cortex. Bruce Perry (2015) writes compellingly about the need to strengthen these lower levels. An effective way to increase those connections is through play that includes physical activity—with just enough structure to keep it from chaos, or to reel it back in if it does move into chaos. Board games are low on the list. Freeze tag, charades, or capture the flag have greater integrative value by helping the brain to grow and speed up connections (Panksepp, 2009).

Play is not a frill. Play moves us out of our to-do lists, or worries, and into a free-flowing time that is full of the possibility of connection, imagination, and joy (Gray & Clarke, 2015). A boy who had extreme anxiety played in my office. He wanted to make a fort out of my quilts. Initially it was to shut me out. But when I suggested overturning my rolling chair and using the space underneath, he looked at me anew—a source of imaginative assistance. The inverted chair solved roof problems for the fort. He crawled into the fort, draping the door shut. Then he asked if I would like to visit him on his back porch. I lay on the floor, at his face level. I brought raisins, dropping them through the raised door into his hand one at a time. I handed him a silk pillow for his head. He thanked me and then asked if I had a nice pillow for my head, in a surprising glimpse of reciprocity. His father watched us and laughed, face relaxed. The boy peeped out and grinned. "Your dad thinks that you are a great builder—and cute," I observed. The boy dipped his head shyly, took in the positive, and said, "Let's keep playing!"

At the end of our time, the boy jumped toward his father, who caught the mood, upended his son, and rolled him around on the exercise ball in the room. "Catch me!" the boy said, including me. I grabbed his legs, his father his arms, and we rolled the boy back and forth on the ball. This type of play can help on so many levels. The boy had enough control that he felt comfortable. It was fun. It was physical. We were all connecting in a state of high activation, with attunement. This boy was learning how to trust adults and relax. The dad left worries behind for a period of time, just enjoying his son. The concept of delighting in your child was embodied. I did sprinkle a few comments about what I was seeing and feeling. When I went on too long, the boy cued me in a patient, adult-like voice, "Deborah, let's not waste our time together." He was correct in directing me to help him attach and relate socially through play.

I certainly did mention to him that his parents were safe and made sure that only safe people were allowed around him now, his major worry. But that information was integrated best through experiences. His anxiety was reduced at day care and church. He began to ask his dad to play with him.

Attachment not only includes connections to parents, but ripples out to connections to other adults. Children with attachment issues will have problems relating to parents and others in social situations. Play experiences with therapists or parents can help children to learn the social language of connection. Play is dynamic and most closely resembles the speed of real-life social interactions. It helps brains to find the information again when the contexts are similar. In comparison to feeling words on a page, play experiences are much more likely to be incorporated into new social patterns.

When working with children in therapy, we often do role-plays for the same reason—their brains are more likely to find the relevant info if it resembles real life. For example, a boy whose sister competed with him for attention reacted in such a way that his mother would give them both negative attention. This was a pattern that the brother and sister carried into their kinship family after severe neglect. His mother and I took turns role-playing his sister, while the boy stayed himself. Both the mother and I shamelessly overacted. Because it was playful, he was laughing and no longer seeing the situation as so serious. We role-played him taking different actions, including the motor movements. He thought that it was delicious. Adding a playful approach reduces the seriousness of the problem, making the solutions more fun and flexible. Play tells our brain's defensive systems to stand down.

The above does not mean that I use a nondirective play therapy approach. But, within a loosely regulated context, I want to use play and be playful myself. This approach reduces the alarm bells going off in children's brains. Also, the children are much more likely to want to come back to see me. They are more likely to seek their parents out for positive play experiences instead of staging battles for attention.

Play and Increasing the Desire for Connection

When I am having fun with children in sessions, parents look on, thinking that they are missing out. I suggest to children that we invite them in. Over time, children will swing to their parents, saying, "You, too! Come on!" We create activities that are fun for kids and parents. (For games and activity ideas, see Gray & Clarke, 2015).

I will assign parents time to play 5 or 6 days out of the week. The outdoors is preferable. (Parents are asked to please turn off their phones.) This enjoyment of each other tends to be self-reinforcing. Parents and children who are having fun together tend to find each other more gratifying. As a result, they build better connections. Parents enjoy parenting their children more. Play helps parents to move off the high alert of noting what wrong thing their child is doing next. Instead, they carry positive feelings out of the play experience. Jonathan Baylin and Daniel Hughes (2016) describe that eyes, voice, and touch stimulate a release of oxytocin in children and parents, enhancing oxytocin and dopamine releases during play.

Play is what parents and children deserve and need. For parents who are keenly interested in academics, I can point to literature that supports the positive influence of play on developing executive functioning, which is key to academic achievement (Diamond, 2012).

I encourage parents to be imaginative, introducing novelty. And I use novelty in my office approaches. Any time novelty is included in our daily lives, our brains pass the information upward to higher thinking centers to make sense out of the information (Perry, 2014). When children are expecting something that conforms to a negative view of the parent and other, and instead they get a novel response with disconfirming evidence, they reevaluate. For example, I worked with parents who came in after a month telling me that their son had never done better in attachment and adjustment. Then they found that money had been taken from their wallets, an old problem that was a signal of movement back into the negative patterns of the past. Instead of the drama, reverting to the old pattern, the parents and I decided to hit the reset button. The boy simply had to restore the money by a certain time, and then they would head out to their planned, fun vacation. Earlier in session with me, he first said that he did not take the money. Then he spit out the words, "I know them. They will ground me. Tell me that I'll never change. I know my dad. He's just waiting for a chance to ground me!" Instead, the parents behaved in a novel way and moved on to enjoy the best summer that they ever had. They enjoyed time playing with cousins, and no more theft. I made some comments to make meaning of this, but the parents made the greatest contribution by acting in a novel manner and then having their family vacation that included lots of playtime as a family.

Play and Stressed Families

Some families are so stressed that they want to spend all of their attention on family problems. This is dreary. It helps to talk to families about the concept of children's limited resources for problem solving. There is only so much energy children have to solve problems. They have limits on the amount of time spent on to-do lists or problems. But without a direct problem-solving approach, we can build more resource and reach goals through play:

- Play helps children with theory of mind—reflective ability on their part and theory of mind toward others.
- Play assists in attachment.
- Play makes life more enjoyable.

When talking to parents about the attributes of play, I find that they may go on to talk about how wearisome it is to try to play with children who do not seem to know how to play. Or parents themselves mention the lack of play experiences that they had as children. They may not have had any parents who played with them. Their parents said, "Go outside and play so that I can get something done."

I tell them that I will coach them to play with their children. Children often do resist the parents, act warily, or push limits with me at first. I model avoiding control battles by moving on to something fun instead of engaging over some knotty issue. I include cool down times with a cold drink or a big stretch. There are control battles at times that need spry redirection. For example, a child was drawn to the fire alarm outside my office. Turning this into a mock issue eventually worked well. "Chased!" I said. "Are you letting me know that you need to be chased?" The child paused, and I proceeded to walk him outside for a quick tag game. "Next time, just tell me or your mom that you want exciting attention, like a chase game. We will skip the trouble part with the fire alarm and go straight to chasing." I realize that this is suggestive. But a little guile is the privilege of being an adult.

As I play with children, I model enjoyment to parents, increasing their desire to play. I also model scripts for playfulness and closeness. After parents get a release of oxytocin, it is easier to sell them on play. And after experiencing joy in the session, they want to continue playing. Their children become better at cuing them.

As things begin to improve at home, parents may decrease playtimes again, unless they grew up with models of playfulness and family closeness. It takes some gentle reminders about the type of family that they want to be versus what they grew up with to encourage them to continue being playful and fun.

Play and Theory of Mind

Theory of mind is important to all of us in our day-to-day relationships. It helps us to move in unity with others—without losing our individuality. We spend less time apologizing for insensitive actions. We typically negotiate life with an awareness of how others are likely to think or feel in work or home situations. This decreases conflict and anxiety.

Often we are learning about sensitivity through the negative side. People point out to us when we err. For children who have a background filled with shame, this is a bruising teaching method. An easier way to expand a person's abilities in this area is through play. As children learn to negotiate play experiences, they are learning through a fun-filled, creative, or high-excitement experience. All it takes is a few sentences within the playtime to mention how parents are feeling during the game, and what their thoughts and motivations are. For example, in the airplane ride game, during which a strong parent zooms a child around like an airplane, the parent can say, "I love holding you close like this. It makes me happy. I wonder which is more fun for us—to swing you out fast like this," as the parent demonstrates the fast swinging, "or to go two times in a circle slowly?" The parent demonstrates slowly.

Parents can accompany the emotional information with actions. When present, I can say, "Ask your child to look at your face and guess whether your favorite is the fast or slow ride." The parent has to zoom the airplane a little more for this. After children guess, I have children ask parents why they like the game. Great answers are that parents like playing with their child, laughing, or having fun.

The balance in incorporating theory of mind activities is in keeping the game's spontaneity, while including a few insight-developing elements. The activity does not turn into a teaching exercise but does include some teaching moments.

Laughter as a Means to Reduce Defenses and Introduce New Concepts

When we laugh, it temporarily causes our defenses to drop. We can move behind defenses in the gap after the laughter. When I use jokes or laughter in the sessions, I can introduce material with less stress to clients.

Laughing about the human condition also reduces shame. Sometimes I will have a kid who ends up raging or throwing the F-bomb in a family that never expected to hear that word directed at them. The last thing that they want to talk about in my session is the big meltdown. So I might tell them about my friend who really had to use the bathroom after a long church service. She decided to drive home since it was close by. But when she got cut off in the church parking lot, she gave the other driver the finger. I ask kids, "Should she change churches? Should she call up the people she cut off, apologize, and tell them how much she had to pee?" They laugh at my poor friend's blooper. Then I say, "Should I laugh when she asks me about this?"

"No. Don't laugh, Deborah Gray," they say. "At least not in front of her."

I say, "Do you think that I did laugh when she called?"

They look at my face, read clues, and know that I did. Then we all laugh.

"So," I might conclude, "at least you didn't use the F-bomb in church, or give the finger in the parking lot! You are ahead of my friend. And everyone forgave her. But maybe we better stop that that F-bomb so it doesn't keep flying around the house."

This type of approach makes it funny and then easier when talking about anger and embarrassing expressions of anger. When we are laughing about the human condition, it is natural to discuss how we wish we had acted. Our mistakes do not exclude us from being loveable.

A teen I worked with did not want to be in a social skills class. She found it mortifying, but her school insisted on a once-weekly class if she were to get needed organizational help. As a last-resort protest, she fell to the floor in class, pretending to be in a coma. The teacher reacted to this episode quite personally, suspending her from school. In our next therapy session, the parents and I looked at each other and started to laugh. In session with the girl, the girl slumped in shame, ready for my critical comments. Instead, I threw three pieces of double bubble gum toward her. A softball athlete, she caught them in midair and popped two in her mouth. I said, "Well! You finally got our attention! But now we have to figure out how to make what you did look like it didn't work so the teacher doesn't feel disrespected. But it . . . actually . . . did . . . work." She grinned. And then we laughed together when her bubble broke on her face. We made plans to repair with the teacher and figure out an alternative for social skills.

When laughing together, the mistakes and foibles of the day seem to be put into perspective. We humans are all in the water together.

We are not minimizing trauma. But we are minimizing everyday shame and stress. We are also recognizing that there is a lot more to life than problems or therapeutic targets. Life is to be enjoyed when possible and should be punctuated by laughter. In therapy, our laughter is contagious. Attachment-focused therapy is designed to make children and families happier. My advice to therapists is to lead out with play, with exuberance and joy.

Epilogue

We hold hands with generations before us and to come. Writing this book has been a way to hand off lessons from my practice to the next generation. I am not done practicing, and I'm still learning, but the tide's turning; time to pass on what I know.

When writing this book, I took instruction from the therapists whom I taught in post-graduate certificate programs. They would ask me questions, "What do you do when the parents have their own issues?" or, "How did you phrase that so a 9-year old can understand it?" I realized that the attachment approaches needed to be explicit, providing both scripts and physical movements within therapeutic practice. I have written out what seems to have worked well for me and my clients. I hope that it is a starting point for others.

As I wrote, I realized that I was drumming up support. I am hoping that more readers will develop an attachment focus in their therapy practices. There is such an unmet need in this area. My waiting list has been full, and then full and closed, most of the last 25 years. Within a short time after training attachment-trauma focused practitioners, those with private therapy practices come to our consultation groups telling me that their practices are full and that we need more clinicians. While an attachment-trauma focused therapy practice has its rigors, the payoffs are immense. What could be better then seeing parents who, after therapy, are able to connect with their children, replacing disconnection and confusion with joy and resonance.

I am so appreciative of the community of therapists who join with children and families to help create secure attachments. The researchers and theorists are brilliant, and so generous with their wisdom. Where would the field be without them? But the therapists are the ones who open their minds and senses, joining with dysregulated children and parents, propelling families forward toward emotional security. It's such hard work! It has helped all of us who are working with attachment and trauma to have consultation groups, consult partners, and helpful professional organizations, including ATTACh (Association for Training for Attachment and Trauma in Children). We have a sense of camaraderie as we learn together and help each other. It is great to know that we are not alone in the work. To readers, in the same spirit, I hope that this book will help you and accompany you in your work.

I do not know a more precious gift to offer families than our help with loving connections. During intake, I often tell children the basics of attachment and trauma therapy: that I will help them get closer to parents, help them to feel more love in their hearts, or help them to feel less scared. I never lose respect for the poignancy of those phrases or the importance of those issues to each child and family. After we conclude our work some families might send me a holiday card. Others lose touch. It is as it should be. It is their family who enjoys the closest connections. They leave me with the privilege of having worked alongside them to the best of my ability.

Looking back over 30 years of work, I know that I gave to children and families, but I received from them the desire of my heart— to have a meaningful life.

Acknowledgments

I am knit into a caring community of therapists. I am so grateful to be part of a consultation group that values the growth of professional expertise as well as personal well-being. A special thanks to some long-term members, Megan Clarke, Mary-Carter Creech, Jill Dziko, Susan Flick, Sandra Gorman-Brown, Cindi Mack-Ernsdorff, Bill Soderberg, Laura Stone, and Sandy Swan.

Everyone at W. W. Norton has been lovely to work with. My thanks to Deborah Malmud, W. W. Norton Vice President, who piqued my interest in writing the book. Drawing on her familiarity with the attachment literature, she was able to help me to develop a coherent outline for the book. Thank you, Mariah Eppes, Karen Fisher, and Kate Prince for your dedication in correcting the manuscripts meanderings, rough edges, and hide-and-seek figures.

My friends and colleagues at ReFresh have elevated an entire community. Thank you for including me! Thanks for affirming the material in this book and encouraging me to finish it. My respect and love especially to Michele Schneidler, Dan and Kathleen Hamer, and Jyoti Jacobs.

My family, Joe, Summerlea, Gerald, and Tricia are my dearest people. I am so grateful to have such a family. I am particularly thankful to you as I finish this book. You are all tired of hearing progress reports by book's end, but provide support anyway.

My friend, Brian Andersen, Cascadia Training, has sponsored post-graduate certificate programs in Attachment-Trauma Focused Therapy. Thank you, Brian, for the cohorts over the last 10 years.

The classes allowed the material in this book to be taught, refined, and finally written in this book. It is an honor to work with you.

The Child Welfare Partnership/Portland State University have included me as a core presenter in the Foster Care and Adoption Therapy Post-Graduate Certificate Program over the last 15 years. Each class gave me exposure to particular attachment perspectives, which shaped the information in this book. Your dedication to train clinicians to serve the spectrum of needs in child welfare has been a plumb line for excellence.

Mary McGowan, Executive Director of ATTACh (Association for Training on Trauma and Attachment in Children), is zealous in promoting training. Mary, thank you for your encouragement to write out this book, making the material available to other therapists.

Thank you, Mom (Patricia Gray), for valuing attachment. My interest in child development and attachment started with watching you and Daddy. My thanks to Will and Sherri Gray, true friends, who are constant in valuing my writing and therapy, without taking me too seriously.

I work with children's pain and trauma, well-connected to their suffering. Writing this book's stories caused me to review children's histories. It can hollow me out. In contrast, the glory of God is fairly dripping from nature here in the Pacific Northwest. That beauty restores me. God's presence lightens me. Several times during the writing of the book I was able to retreat to the shore or forest, and then go on. I am so grateful for the enlivening presence of God in my life.

Special thanks to Dr. Colleen Gray, to whom I dedicated this book. You see to the core of things, including my life's work. This summer, book completed, we'll lie on the hammock and look at the stars. You'll sing, and our hearts will soar.

References

Ainsworth, M., Salter, M., Blehar, M., Waters, E., & Wall, S. (2015). *Patterns of attachment: A psychological study of the Strange Situation.* New York: Psychology Press. (Original work published 1978)

American Psychiatric Association. (2013). *Diagnostic and statistical manual of mental disorders* (5th ed.). Arlington, VA: Author.

Anda, R., & Brown, D. (2010). *Adverse childhood experiences and population heath in Washington: The face of a chronic public health disaster: Executive summary and selected policy excerpts.* Olympia, WA: Washington State Family Policy Council.

Baylin, J., & Hughes, D. (2016). *The neurobiology of attachment-focused therapy.* New York: Norton.

Beck, A. (1996). *Beck Depression Inventory-II.* San Antonio, TX: Pearson.

Belsky, J. (2015, September/October). The upside of vulnerability. *Scientific American Mind,* 41–45.

Berlin, L., Zeanah, C., & Lieberman, A. (2016). Prevention and intervention programs to support early attachment security: A move to the level of the community. In J. Cassidy & P. Shaver (Eds.), *Handbook of attachment* (pp. 739–759). New York: Guilford.

Bernard, K., Hostinar, C., & Dozier, M. (2015). Intervention effects on diurnal cortisol rhythms of CPS-referred infants in early childhood: Preschool follow-up results of a randomized clinical trial. *JAMA Pediatrics,* 169(2), 112–119.

Bernard, K., Lee, A. H., & Dozier, M. (2017, May 22). Effects of the ABC intervention on foster children's receptive vocabulary:

Follow-up results from a randomized clinical trial. *Child Maltreatment*, 2, 174–179.

Birmaher, B., Brent, D., Chiappetta, L., Bridge, J., Monga, S., & Baughter, M. (1999). Screen for Child Anxiety Related Emotional Disorders (SCARED). Retrieved from University of Pittsburgh, Child and Adolescent Bipolar Spectrum Services, http://pediatricbipolar.pitt.edu/resources/instruments

Blaustein, M., & Kinniburgh, K. (2007, February). Providing the family as a secure base for therapy with children and adolescents. *Attachment Theory Into Practice*. Briefing Paper no. 26, 48–53. Leicester, UK: British Psychological Society.

Blaustein, M., & Kinniburgh, K. (2010). *Treating traumatic stress in children and adolescents*. New York: Guilford.

Bledsoe, J. (2015, April 24). *Executive functioning*. Workshop presentation at SOS Conference, Spokane, WA.

Bowlby, J. (1988). *A secure base*. New York: Basic Books.

Briere, J. (2002, May). The revised self-trauma model. Paper presented at International Society for Traumatic Stress Studies conference, Vancouver, BC.

Buczynski, R., & Porges, S. (2015, April 8). Body, brain, behavior: How polyvagal theory expands our healing paradigm. National Institute for the Clinical Application of Behavioral Medicine. Webinar retrieved from http://stephenporges.com/images/nicabm_2013.pdf

Cohen, J., Mannarino, A., & Deblinger, E. (2017). *Treating trauma and traumatic grief in children and adolescents* (2nd ed.). New York: Guilford.

Cook, A., Blaustein, M., Spinazzola, J., & van der Kolk, B. (2005). Complex trauma in children and adolescents. Retrieved from https://www.researchgate.net/publication/264230700_Complex_Trauma_in_Children_and_Adolescents

Cox, A. (2008). *No mind left behind: Understanding and fostering executive control*. New York: Perigee..

Cozolino, L. (2006). *The neuroscience of human relationships*. New York: Norton.

Cyr, D., Euser, E., Bakermans-Kranenburg, M., & van Ijzendoorn, M. (2010). Attachment security and disorganization in maltreating and high-risk families: A series of meta-analyses. *Development and Psychopathology, 22*, 87–108.

Dalenberg, C. (2000). Countertransference and the management of anger in trauma therapy. *National Center for Post-Traumatic Stress Disorder Clinical Quarterly, 9*(3), 39.

DeKlyen, M., & Greenberg, M. (2016). Attachment and psychopathology in childhood. In J. Cassidy & P. Shaver (Eds.), *Handbook of attachment* (3rd ed., pp. 639–666). New York: Guilford.

Diamond, A. (2012). Understanding Executive Functions. Presentation retrieved from Development Cognitive Neuroscience Lab of Adele Diamond website, retrieved April 9, 2018 from www.dvcobneuro.com/videos.html.

Diamond, G., Diamond, G., Levy, S. (2013). Attachment based family therapy for depressed teens. Arlington, VA: APA.

Dozier, M., Dozier, D., & Manni, M. (2002, May). Attachment and biobehavioral catch-up: The ABC's of helping infants in foster care cope with early adversity. *Zero to Three*, 7–13.

Dozier, M., Lindhiem, O., Lewis, O., Bick, J., Bernard, K., & Peloso, E. (2009). Attachment and biobehavioral catch-up: Effects of a foster parent training program on young children's attachment behaviors: Preliminary evidence from a randomized clinical trial. *Child and Adolescent Social Work Journal, 26*, 321–332.

Dozier, M., Peloso, E., Lewis, E., Laurenceau, J., & Levine, S. (2008). Effects of an attachment-based intervention on the cortisol production of infants and toddlers in foster care. *Development and Psychopathology, 20*, 845–859.

Dozier, M., & Rutter, M. (2016). Challenges to the development of attachment relationships faced by young children in foster and adoptive care. In J. Cassidy & P. Shaver (Eds.), *Handbook of attachment* (3rd ed., pp. 667–695). New York: Guilford.

Dozier, M., Stovall, C., Albus, K., & Bates, B. (2001). Attachment for infants in foster care: The role of caregiver state of mind. *Child Development, 72*, 1467–1477.

Fearon, Pasco R. M., Belsky, J. (2016). Precursors of attachment security. In J. Cassidy & P. Shaver (Eds.), *Handbook of attachment* (pp. 291–313). New York: Guilford.

Feeney, B., & Woodhouse, S. (2016). Caregiving. In J. Cassidy & P. Shaver (Eds.), *Handbook of attachment* (pp. 827–851). New York: Guilford.

Fisher, P., & Chamberlain, P. (2000). Multidimensional treatment foster care: A program for intensive parenting, family support, and skill building. *Journal of Emotional and Behavioral Disorders, 8*(3), 155–164.

Fisher, P., & Gilliam, K. (2012). Multidimensional treatment foster care: An alternative to residential treatment for high-risk children and families. *Psychosocial Intervention, 21*(2), 195–203.

Fisher, P., & Kim, H. (2007). Intervention effects on foster preschoolers' attachment-related behaviors from a randomized trial. *Prevention Science, 8*(2), 161–170.

Fisher, P., & Stoolmiller, M. (2008). Intervention effects on foster parent stress: Association with children's cortisol levels. *Development and Psychopathology, 20*(3), 1003–1021.

Fisher, P., Van Ryzin, M., & Gunnar, M. (2011). Mitigating HPA axis dysregulation associated with placement changes in foster care. *Psychoneuroendocrinology, 36*(4), 531–539.

Fitzgerald, H. (2000). *The grieving teen: A guide for teenagers and their friends.* New York: Simon and Schuster.

Fonagy, P. (2002, March). *Practical preventative interventions with individuals.* Workshop presentation at conference: Attachment from early childhood through the lifespan. Lifespan Learning, UCLA, CA. Recording available through https://lifespanlearn.org/store

Fosha, D. (2004, February). Attachment through the lens of affect: Implications for clinical practice. Sponsored by R. Cassidy Seminars, Seattle, WA.

Fosha, D., Siegel, D., & Solomon, M. (Eds.). (2009). *The healing power of emotion.* New York: Norton.

Granqvist, P., & Kirkpatrick, L. (2016). Attachment and religious representations and behavior. In J. Cassidy & P. Shaver (Eds.),

Handbook of attachment (3rd ed., pp. 906–933). New York: Guilford.

Granqvist, P., Sroufe, L. A., Dozier, M., Hesse, E., Steele, M., van Ijzendoorn, M., et al. (2017). Disorganized attachment in infancy: A review of the phenomenon and its applications for clinicians and policy-makers. *Attachment and Human Development, 19*(6), 534–558.

Gray, D. (2012a). *Attaching in adoption.* London: Jessica Kingsley.

Gray, D. (2012b). *Nurturing adoptions.* London: Jessica Kingsley.

Gray, D. (2014). *Attaching through love, hugs, and play.* London: Jessica Kingsley.

Gray, D., & Clarke, M. (2015). *Games and activities for attaching with your child.* London: Jessica Kingsley.

Herman, J. (1994). *Trauma and Recovery.* New York: Basic Books.

Hesse, E., & Main, M. (2006). Frightened, threatening, and dissociative parental behavior in low-risk sample: Description, discussion, and interpretations. *Development and Psychopathology, 18,* 309-343.

Hesse, E. (2008). The Adult Attachment Interview. In J. Cassidy & P. Shaver (Eds.), *Handbook of attachment* (3rd ed., pp. 552-598). New York: Guilford.

Hesse, E. (2016). The Adult Attachment Interview. In J. Cassidy & P. Shaver (Eds.), *Handbook of attachment* (3rd ed., pp. 553–597). New York: Guilford.

Hesse, E., Main, M., Abrams, K. Y., & Rifkin, A. (2003). Unresolved state regarding loss or abuse can have "second generation" effects: Disorganization, role inversion, and frightening ideation in the offspring of traumatized, non-maltreating parents. In M. Solomon & D. Siegel (Eds.), *Healing trauma.* New York: Norton.

Hoffman, K., Marvin, R., Cooper, G., & Powell, B. (2006). Changing toddlers' and preschoolers' attachment classifications: The Circle of Security intervention. *Journal of Consulting and Clinical Psychology, 74*(6), 1017–1026.

Hughes, D. (2009). *Attachment-focused parenting: Effective strategies to care for children.* New York: Norton.

Hughes, D., & Golding, K. (2012). *Creating Loving Attachments.* London: Jessica Kingsley.

Johnson, S. (2008). *Hold me tight.* New York: Little, Brown.

Kerns, K. & Brumariu, L. (2016). Attachment in Middle Childhood. In J. Cassidy & P. Shaver (Eds.), *Handbook of attachment* (3rd ed., pp. 349–365). New York: Guilford.

Kinniburgh, K., Blaustein, M., & Spinnazola, J. (2005). Attachment, self-regulation and competency. *Psychiatric Annals, 35*(5), 424–430.

Levine, P. (2015). *Trauma and Memory.* Berkeley, CA: North Atlantic Books.

Lewis-Morrarty, E., Dozier, M., Bernard, K., Terracciano, S., & Moore, S. (2012). Cognitive flexibility and theory of mind outcomes among foster children: Preschool follow-up results of a randomized clinical trial. *Journal of Adolescent Health, 51*(2 suppl.), S17–S22.

Lieberman, A., Ghosh Ippen, C., & Van Horn, P. (2015). *Don't hit my mommy! A manual for child-parent psychotherapy with young children exposed to violence and other trauma* (2nd ed.). Washington, DC: Zero to Three.

Lozier, C. (2012). *The adoptive and foster parent's guide.* Louisville, KY: Carol Lozier.

Lyons-Ruth, K., & Jacobvitz, D. (2008). Attachment disorganization. In J. Cassidy & P. Shaver (Eds.), *Handbook of attachment* (2nd ed., pp. 666–697). New York: Guilford.

Lyons-Ruth, K., & Jacobvitz, D. (2016). Attachment disorganization from infancy to adulthood: Neurobiological correlates, parenting contexts, and pathways to disorder. In J. Cassidy & P. Shaver (Eds.), *Handbook of attachment* (3rd ed., pp. 667–695). New York: Guilford.

Main, M., Hesse, E., & Kaplan, N. (2005). Predictability of attachment behavior and representational processes at 1, 6, and 19 years of age: The Berkeley Longitudinal Study. In K. Grossman, K. Grossman, & E. Waters (Eds.), *Attachment from infancy to adulthood* (pp. 245–304). New York: Guilford.

NCTSN. (n.d.). National Child Traumatic Stress Network empirically supported treatments and promising practices. Retrieved

December 15, 2017, from http://www.nctsn.org/resources/topics/treatments-that-work/promising-practices

Nikulina, V., Widom, C., & Spatz, C. (2013, July). Child maltreatment and executive functioning in middle adulthood: A prospective examination. *Neuropsychology, 27*(4), 417–427.

Panksepp, J. (2009). Brain emotional systems and qualities of mental life. In D. Fosha, D. Siegel, & M. Solomon (Eds.), *The healing power of emotion* (pp. 1–26). New York: Norton.

Perry, B. (2015). The Neurosequential Model of Therapeutics as Evidence-based Practice. https://www.comtrea.org/files/users/mela niecole/ApplicationoftheNeurosequentialModelofTherapeutics inMaltreatedChildrenbyBruceD.PerryandChristineL.Dobson .pdf Retrieved April 2, 2018 from http://www.ChildTrauma.org

Perry, B. (2006). Applying principles of neurodevelopment to clinical work with maltreated and traumatized children. In N. Webb (Ed.), *Working with traumatized youth in child welfare* (pp. 27–52). New York: Guilford.

Perry, B. (2016, September). Neurosequential model of therapeutics. Presented at Quality Improvement Center for Adoption and Guardianship Support and Preservation, Tyson's Corner, VA.

Perry, B., & Szalavitz, M. (2006). *The boy who was raised as a dog.* New York: Basic Books.

Porges, S. (2009). Reciprocal influences between body and brain in the perception and expression of affect: A polyvagal perspective. In D. Fosha, D. Siegel, & M. Solomon (Eds.), *The healing power of emotion* (pp. 27–54). New York: Norton.

Porges, S. (2015, May 8). How the brain works with the vagus. Webinar retrieved from www.nicabm.com, https://www.youtube .com/watch?v=kntgKn54jX4

Porges, S. (2016). Body perception questionnaires. Retrieved from http://stephenporges.com/index.php/publicationss/21-body -perception-questionnaires

Porter, L. (2010). How to improve communication with people with cognitive/executive dysfunction in case work, social work, education, medicine. ACES Retreat, Seattle, WA.

Pynoos, R. (1997, August). Conference presentation, Traumatic bereavement in children and adolescents. Conference: *Victims of Traumatic Loss*. Whitefish, MT.

Rutter, M., & Rutter, M. (1993). *Developing minds*. New York: Basic Books.

Schore, A. (2002). *Regulation of the right brain*, Presentation at conference: Attachment from early childhood through the lifespan. Lifespan Learning, UCLA, CA. Recording available through https://lifespanlearn.org/store

Schore, A. (2003a). *Affection regulation and disorders of the self.* New York: Norton.

Schore, A. (2003b). *Affection regulation and the repair of the self.* New York: Norton.

Schore, A. (2003c). Early relational trauma, disorganized attachment, and the development of a predisposition to violence. In M. Solomon D. Siegel (Eds.), *Healing trauma* (pp. 107–167). New York: Norton.

Schore, A. (2012). The science of the art of psychotherapy. New York: Norton.

Shiller, V. (2017). *The attachment bond: Affectional ties across the lifespan*. Lanham, MD: Lexington.

Siegel, D. (1999). *The developing mind: Toward a neurobiology of interpersonal experience*. New York: Guilford.

Siegel, D. (2010). The mindful therapist: A New approach to cultivating your own neural integration from the inside out. Conference, Seattle, WA. www.online.pesi.com

Siegel, D. (2015). *Brainstorm: The power and purpose of the teenage brain*. New York: Tarcher/Penguin.

Siegel, D., & Hartzell, M. (2003). *Parenting from the inside out*. New York: Tarcher/Putnam.

Solomon, J., & George, C. (1999). The place of disorganization in attachment theory: Linking classic observations with contemporary findings. In J. Solomon & C. George (Eds.), *Attachment disorganization* (pp. 3–32). New York: Guilford.

Solomon, J. & George, C. (2016). The measure of attachment security and related construct in infancy and early childhood. In J.

Cassidy & P. Shaver (Eds.), *Handbook of attachment* (3rd ed., pp. 366–398). New York: Guilford.

Sroufe, L. A. (1995). *Emotional development.* Cambridge: Cambridge University Press.

Sroufe, L. A. (2002, March). *Infant Attachment to Adolescent.* Presentation at conference: Attachment from early childhood through the lifespan. Lifespan Learning, UCLA, CA. Recording available through https://lifespanlearn.org/store

Sroufe, L. A., Egeland, B., Carlson, E., & Collins, W. A. (2005a). *The development of the person.* New York: Guilford.

Sroufe, L. A., Egeland, B., Carlson, E., & Collins, W. A. (2005b). Placing early attachment experiences in developmental context: The Minnesota Longitudinal Study. In K. E. Grossman, K. Grossman, & E. Waters (Eds.), *Attachment from infancy to adulthood* (pp. 48–70). New York: Guilford.

Stern, D. N. (1995). *The motherhood constellation: A unified view of parent-infant psychotherapy.* New York: Basic Books.

Stern, D. N. (2004). *The present moment in psychotherapy and everyday life.* New York: Norton.

Tinienko, J., Fisher, P., Bruce, J., & Pears, K. (2010). Sleep disruption in young foster children. *Child Psychiatry and Human Development, 42*(4), 409–424.

Tutu, D. & Tutu, M. (2011). *Made for Goodness.* New York: Harperone.

van der Kolk, B. (2013, March). Trauma, attachment, and neuroscience. Presentation sponsored by PESI, Seattle, WA.

van Ijzendoorn, M., & Bakermans-Kranenburg, M. (1997). Intergenerational transmission of attachment: A move to the contextual level. In L. Atkinson & K. Zucker (Eds.), *Attachment and psychopathology* (pp. 135–170). New York: Guilford.

van Ijzendoorn, M., Schuengel, C., & Bakermans-Kranenburg, M (1999). Disorganized attachment in early childhood: Metanalysis of precursors, concomitants, and sequalae. *Development and Psychopathology, 11*, pp. 225-249.

Wallin, D. (2007). *Attachment in psychotherapy.* New York: Guilford.

Wallin, D. (2016, May). We are the tools of our trade: How the therapist's own attachment patterns shape therapy. Workshop sponsored by R. Cassidy Seminars, Seattle, WA.

Weinfield, N. S., Sroufe, L. A., & Egeland, B. (2000). Attachments from infancy to adulthood in a high-risk sample: Continuity, discontinuity and their correlates. *Child Development, 71,* 695–702.

Zeanah, C. (1996). Beyond insecurity: A reconceptualization of attachment disorders in infancy. *Journal of Consulting and Clinical Psychology, 64*(1), 42–52.

Zeanah, C., Scheeringa, M., Boris, N., Heller, S., Smyke, A & Trapani, J. (2004). Reactive attachment disorder in maltreated toddlers. *Child Abuse and Neglect, 28,* 877-888.

Index

picture(s)
  in life narrative work, 60
  in narrative work, 60
play
  attributes of, 272–80
  building more resources and reaching
    goals through, 276–77
  desire for connection associated with,
    274–76
  dopamine response and, 272
  novelty in, 275–76
  opioid response and, 272
  oxytocin produced during, 272
  physical, 272–73
  in reducing defenses and introducing
    new concepts, 278–80
  in strengthening attachment, 272–80
  stressed families and, 276–77
  theory of mind and, 277–78
  value of, 272–73
play activities
  for adolescents, 238
  for parents, 238
Porges, S., 145, 146f
"port of entry"
  in approaching changes with clients, 41
positive identity, attachment, and grief
    visual treatment plan, 123, 123f
positive zones
  in attachment-enhancing activities for
    adolescents, 238–39
PPP. see Preschool Parent Psychotherapy
    (PPP)
preoccupied parent
  insecure attachment indicators of, 48
Preschool Parent Psychotherapy (PPP), 35,
    31–33
problem(s)
  tiers of, 113–15
property
  consequences when anger injures,
    189–90
prosocial protectors
  role-play that allows parents to be,
    158–60
Purvis, K., 262

reactive attachment disorder 313.89
  diagnostic criteria for, 25–26
realistic expectations
  in presence of trauma and loss, 96–98
ReFresh conferences, 109
regulation
  in life narrative work, 60
relational misses
  in therapy, 44–46
relational trauma
  attachment-focused therapy for, 62–63
relationship(s)
  attachment (see attachment relation-
    ships)
  attachments as closest, 3
  consequences when anger injures,
    189–90

family, 43
  gratifying, 17–18
  healthy family, 43
  lighting up, 204–7
  secure, 5
  security developed by, 30–31
  teen-parent, 225
relationship problems or absences
  connection repair after, 151–53
relative(s)
  negative affects evoked by, 199–200
religious training
  attachment patterns related to, 262–64
repair
  connection, 151–53
  direct therapy's emphasis on, 54–55
  in secure attachments, 17–18
resilience
  disorganized category and, 23–24
resistant pattern
  of children, 12
respect
  theme of, 43
response(s)
  to effective parenting moments, 190–91
reward(s)
  for accomplishments, 95
rocking together
  comfort from, 70
role(s)
  as attachment-enhancing activity for
    adolescents, 239
role-play
  in expressing mixed feelings, 215
  within family sessions, 76–78
  that allows parents to be prosocial pro-
    tectors, 158–60
role reversals
  in attachment work, 177–78
Rose, R., 134
routine(s)
  enhancing attachment in children,
    145–49, 146f
rubbing upper back
  comfort from, 70
Rutter, Marjorie, x
Rutter, Michael, x

safety
  attachment figures as source of, 3
  faith in sense of, 266–67
safety issues
  for adolescents, 232–34
  for highly stressed families, 249
SCARED. see Screen for Child Anxiety
    Related Disorders (SCARED)
Schneidler, M., 109
Schore, A., 60, x
Screen for Child Anxiety Related Disorders
    (SCARED), 227
script(s)
  to help process anger, 217–18
secondary traumatic stress
  prevention of, 193–94

About the Author

Deborah Gray, MPA, LICSW specializes in the attachment, grief, and trauma issues of children in her practice, Nurturing Attachments. Her passion is to help families develop close, satisfying relationships.

In 2015, Deborah received a lifetime achievement award from the International ATTACh organization for her contributions to the attachment field. She has been the Henry Meier Practitioner in Residence at the University of Washington. Deborah is core faculty for two post-graduate certificate programs: Attachment/Trauma-Focused Therapy (ATFT) and Portland State University Foster and Adoption Therapy Program.

She continues to work in a clinical practice with parents and children, who help to teach her new approaches and techniques every day.

Deborah is the author of the books: *Attaching in Adoption: Practical Tools for Today's Parents, Nurturing Adoptions: Creating Resilience after Neglect and Trauma, Attaching with Love, Hugs, and Joy,* and co-author of *Games and Activities for Attaching with Your Child.*

Promoting Healthy Attachments: Hands-On Techniques to Use with Your Clients, the latest book, provides a wealth of techniques and scripts for clinicians. The approaches are practical, positive, and empathic.